Advanced iOS App Architecture

By René Cacheaux & Josh Berlin

Advanced iOS App Architecture

By René Cacheaux & Josh Berlin

Copyright ©2022 Razeware LLC.

Notice of Rights

All rights reserved. No part of this book or corresponding materials (such as text, images, or source code) may be reproduced or distributed by any means without prior written permission of the copyright owner.

Notice of Liability

This book and all corresponding materials (such as source code) are provided on an "as is" basis, without warranty of any kind, express of implied, including but not limited to the warranties of merchantability, fitness for a particular purpose, and noninfringement. In no event shall the authors or copyright holders be liable for any claim, damages or other liability, whether in action of contract, tort or otherwise, arising from, out of or in connection with the software or the use of other dealing in the software.

Trademarks

All trademarks and registered trademarks appearing in this book are the property of their own respective owners.

ISBN: 978-1-950325-61-0

Table of Contents

Book License 7
Before You Begin 9
What You Need 11
Book Source Code & Forums 13
    About the Authors 16
    About the Editor 16
Section I 17
Chapter 1: Welcome 19
    What lies ahead 20
    Who this book is for 20
    Where to go from here? 21
Chapter 2: Which Architecture Is Right for Me? 23
    Identifying problems to solve 24
    Boosting team velocity and strengthening code quality 24
    Examining the problems 27
    Increasing code agility 35
    Surveying architecture patterns 37
    Selecting a pattern 39
    Putting patterns into practice 41
    Key points 42
Chapter 3: Example App: Koober 43
    Koober 43
    Why Koober? 51
    Getting started with the source 52
    Key points 57
Chapter 4: Objects & Their Dependencies 59

    Establishing the goals 60
    Learning the lingo 61
    Creating dependencies 63
    The fundamental considerations 64
    Why is this architecture? 66
    Dependency patterns 66
    Dependency Injection 67
    On-demand approach 73
    Factories approach 75
    Single-container approach 81
    Designing container hierarchies 84
    Applying DI theory to iOS apps 89
    Applying the on-demand approach 97
    Applying the factories approach 103
    Applying the single-container approach 116
    Applying the container hierarchy approach 124
    Key points 131
    Where to go from here? 132

Chapter 5: Architecture: MVVM 133
    What is it? 134
    Container views 140
    Communicating amongst view models 142
    Navigating 143
    Applying theory to iOS apps 147
    Composing views 158
    Navigating 169
    Managing state 182
    Pros and cons of MVVM 188
    Key points 189
    Where to go from here? 190

Chapter 6: Architecture: Redux 191

What is Redux?.. 192
Applying theory to iOS apps.......................... 204
Pros and cons of Redux................................. 242
Key points 244
Where to go from here?................................ 244

Chapter 7: Architecture: Elements, Part 1 245
Introducing Elements 247
Underlying concepts of Elements 248
User interface 252
Interaction responder 260
Key points 267

Chapter 8: Architecture: Elements, Part 2 269
Observer 269
Use case 306
Pros and cons of Elements 339
Key points 340

Conclusion.. 341

Book License

By purchasing *Advanced iOS App Architecture*, you have the following license:

- You are allowed to use and/or modify the source code in *Advanced iOS App Architecture* in as many apps as you want, with no attribution required.

- You are allowed to use and/or modify all art, images and designs that are included in *Advanced iOS App Architecture* in as many apps as you want, but must include this attribution line somewhere inside your app: "Artwork/images/designs: from *Advanced iOS App Architecture*, available at www.raywenderlich.com".

- The source code included in *Advanced iOS App Architecture* is for your personal use only. You are NOT allowed to distribute or sell the source code in *Advanced iOS App Architecture* without prior authorization.

- This book is for your personal use only. You are NOT allowed to sell this book without prior authorization, or distribute it to friends, coworkers or students; they would need to purchase their own copies.

All materials provided with this book are provided on an "as is" basis, without warranty of any kind, express or implied, including but not limited to the warranties of merchantability, fitness for a particular purpose and noninfringement. In no event shall the authors or copyright holders be liable for any claim, damages or other liability, whether in an action of contract, tort or otherwise, arising from, out of or in connection with the software or the use or other dealings in the software.

All trademarks and registered trademarks appearing in this guide are the properties of their respective owners.

Before You Begin

This section tells you a few things you need to know before you get started, such as what you'll need for hardware and software, where to find the project files for this book, and more.

What You Need

To follow along with this book, you'll need the following:

- A Mac running **macOS Big Sur** or later.
- **Swift 5.5.2**: all projects have been written to work with Swift 5.5.2 in Xcode.
- **Xcode 13.2.1 or later.** You'll need Xcode 13.2.1 or later to open and run the example apps included in this book.

If you haven't installed the latest version of macOS or Xcode, be sure to do that before continuing with the book. The code covered in this book depends on Swift 5.5.2 and Xcode 13.2.1.

This book provides the building blocks for developers who wish to broaden their horizons and learn how architectures can help them build robust and maintainable applications and SDKs.

The prerequisites for this book include an intermediate understanding of Swift and iOS development. If you've worked through our classic beginner books — Swift Apprentice (https://www.raywenderlich.com/books/swift-apprentice) and UIKit Apprentice (https://www.raywenderlich.com/books/uikit-apprentice) — or have similar development experience, you're ready to read this book.

To get the most out of this book an understanding of Apple's new **Combine** framework would also be helpful. If you've worked through our - Combine Asynchronous Programming With Swift (https://www.raywenderlich.com/books/combine-asynchronous-programming-with-swift) book you'll understand more regarding the reactive programming used within this book.

As you work through the book, you'll be taken through a deep dive into different architectures for a fictional app named **Koober**. Each chapter will explain the theory behind each of the architectures first. The second half of the chapters will guide you through how the **Koober** application utilized the architecture and show you how the architecture was used within the application.

Book Source Code & Forums

Where to download the materials for this book

The materials for this book can be cloned or downloaded from the GitHub book materials repository:

- https://github.com/raywenderlich/arch-materials/tree/editions/4.0

Forums

We've also set up an official forum for the book at https://forums.raywenderlich.com/c/books/advanced-ios-architecture. This is a great place to ask questions about the book or to submit any errors you may find.

"To my beautiful wife Lauren, to my fun-loving angel Zara, to my son René Jr., to my parents who have given me everything, and, last but not least, to my furry pals Paco and Charlie. I love you all."

— *René Cacheaux*

"Thanks to my parents for buying me my first, second, and third computers, and making me put them together myself. Thanks for allowing me to take any path I wanted in life, even when it's a little crazy. Love y'all."

— *Josh Berlin*

About the Authors

Josh Berlin is an author of this book. He loves building thoughtful user experiences on mobile. He's currently an iOS engineer atHatch building products to help people sleep better. He's built apps for the iPhone and iPad since 2008. Josh recently finished culinaryschool in Austin, TX. When he's not coding, he's probably cooking or dreaming of food.

René Cacheaux is an author of this book. He loves to architect and build software. He currently is a Mobile Architect at Atlassian where his mission is to design Atlassian's mobile platform. He especially loves all things mobile and currently architects for both Android and Apple platforms. René has been engineering iOS apps since 2009 and has experience in mobile client and server engineering, mobile user experience design and product management. René has worked on a wide range of apps spanning from industrial sales enablement to world-wide social networking. René enjoys starting his days in true Austin-Texas fashion with a a breakfast taco alongside a freshly brewed cappuccino. In addition to building mobile apps, he loves to travel, snow ski, ocean kayak and root for his alma mater, the Texas Longhorns.

About the Editor

Darren Ferguson is doubling as the tech editor and the final pass editor for this book. He's an experienced software developer and works for M.C. Dean, Inc, a systems integration provider from North Virginia. When he's not coding, you'll find him enjoying EPL Football, traveling as much as possible and spending time with his wife and daughter. Find Darren on Twitter at @darren102 (https://twitter.com/darren102).

Section I

Chapter 1: Welcome

Welcome to *Advanced iOS App Architecture*. The main goal of this book is to thoroughly explain and show how to apply popular iOS app architectures, one by one. We can't wait for you to explore the architectures covered in the following chapters.

We absolutely love this topic. We are super passionate about architecture because architecture unlocks the ability for teams to grow and go quickly. Now, more than ever, it's very important to understand and apply good software architecture practices in our projects as apps are getting more complex and as development teams are pressured to deliver faster results despite constantly changing requirements.

What lies ahead

Chapter 1 through Chapter 4 introduce you to different aspects of the material covered in the book. We recommend reading these chapters before diving into any of the architecture chapters.

Chapter 5 through Chapter 8 are architecture chapters; in other words, they explore one architecture at a time. Each architecture chapter begins with a little history followed by a detailed theory walkthrough. The second half of each architecture chapter focuses on applying the theory to iOS app development. Each architecture chapter ends by covering the pros and cons of that architecture. Feel free to read these latter chapters in any order.

There are many architectures not covered in this book because we wanted to go deep instead of broad.

Who this book is for

This book is for iOS developers who build apps using Swift. The material in this book assumes familiarity with design patterns and with basic architectures — such as MVC — and basic architecture concepts, such as inversion of control. This book also assumes familiarity with Apple frameworks such as `Combine`.

If you're new to Swift, check out the raywenderlich.com Swift Apprentice (https://www.raywenderlich.com/books/swift-apprentice) book; for a refresher on design patterns, check out the raywenderlich.com Design Patterns by Tutorials (https://www.raywenderlich.com/books/design-patterns-by-tutorials); for an introduction to `Combine`, check out the raywenderlich.com Combine: Asynchronous Programming With Swift (https://www.raywenderlich.com/books/combine-asynchronous-programming-with-swift)

Where to go from here?

The next three chapters are designed to be introductions, so give them a read. Then, find the chapters for the architectures you are most interested in learning and go for a deep dive into each.

If you aren't sure which architectures you'd like to explore, we recommend reading the theory section of all the architecture chapters first in order to identify which architectures fit your needs the most. Then you can take a deep dive by reading the iOS app portion of the chapters you found most compelling.

Our hope is that, after reading this book, you will be able to apply different app architectures to different projects in a way that will unleash your team's ability to build quickly and soundly. Happy architecting!

Chapter 2: Which Architecture Is Right for Me?

By René Cacheaux

You might be wondering: Which architecture pattern is right for me? Honestly, there's no perfect universal app architecture. An architecture that works best for one project might not work best for your project. There are many different aspects to consider when establishing an architecture for you and your team to follow. This chapter guides you through the process of finding the best architecture for your project.

There's a lot that goes into shaping your app's codebase into a cohesive and effective architecture. Knowing where to start can especially be overwhelming. Every single file in your app's codebase plays a part in your app's architecture. There's no shortage of architecture patterns. Unfortunately, most patterns only scratch the surface and leave you to figure out the fine details. In addition, many patterns are similar to one another and have only minor differences here and there.

All of this makes architecture hard to put into practice. Fortunately, there are pragmatic steps you can take to ensure your architecture is effective:

1. Understand the current state of your codebase.
2. Identify problems you'd like to solve or code you'd like to improve.
3. Evaluate different architecture patterns.
4. Try a couple patterns on for size before committing to one.

5. Draw a line in the sand and define your app's baseline architecture.

6. Look back and determine if your architecture is effectively addressing the problems you want to solve.

7. Iterate and evolve your app's architecture over time.

Notice how selecting an architecture pattern isn't the first item on the list. The reality is that selecting an architecture pattern is less important than understanding the *the problems you're trying to solve* using architectural patterns. Taking the time to understand the problems you want to solve allows you to focus on the few aspects of architecture that really make a difference. While many problems will be specific to your project, there are several general problems you can solve through good architecture. The next several sections cover these general problems in detail.

Identifying problems to solve

Before embarking on any architecture project, you should first identify and understand the problems you'd like to solve. This will allow you to evaluate whether you're getting the most out of your app's architecture. A good architecture enables you and your team to easily and safely change code without a ton of risk. Making changes to code in a codebase that's not architected well is expensive and risky. The two primary problems that good architecture practices solve are **slow team velocity** and **fragile code quality**. Additionally, good architecture practices can help you prevent **rigid software**. The next sections cover these two primary problems followed by a section that covers rigid software.

Boosting team velocity and strengthening code quality

A good app architecture enables you to deliver features and bug fixes faster without compromising on quality. On the other hand, a less-than-ideal architecture slows your team down and makes your codebase very difficult to change without breaking existing functionality. Knowing this, what problems should you be looking for? Which problems can architecture solve?

Here are several problems that, when present, lead to slow velocity and fragile code quality:

- My app's codebase is hard to understand.
- Changing my app's codebase sometimes causes regressions.
- My app exhibits fragile behavior when running.
- My code is hard to re-use.
- Changes require large code refactors.
- My teammates step on each other's toes.
- My app's codebase is hard to unit test.
- My team has a hard time breaking user stories into tasks.
- My app takes a long time to compile.

You can solve these problems by applying architecture concepts. All of these problems have common root causes. Walking through some of the root causes will help set the stage for studying each of these problems in detail.

Understanding root causes

Each of these problems can be caused by two fundamental root causes: **highly interdependent code** and **large types**.

Understanding these root causes is important when creating a plan for boosting team velocity and strengthening code quality. So what exactly are these root causes, and how do you know if they've made it into your codebase? That's next.

Highly interdependent code

A typical codebase has a ton of interdependencies and connections amongst variables, objects and types. Code becomes highly interdependent when code in one type reaches out to other concrete, i.e., non-protocol, types. Types usually reach out to other types in order to read-write state or in order to call methods. Making one part of your code depend on another is extremely easy. This is especially true when a codebase has a lot of visible global objects.

Without properly encapsulating your code, your interdependencies can run rampant! The more you tightly couple parts of your codebase, the more likely something unexpectedly breaks when making code changes. This is further complicated by large teams with multiple developers because *everyone* needs to fully understand the interdependencies, which on very large teams may be an impossible task.

Large types

Large types are classes, structs, protocols and enums that have long public interfaces due to having many public methods and/or properties. They also have very long implementations, often hundreds or even thousands of lines of code.

Adding code to an existing type is much easier than coming up with a new type. When creating a new type, you have to think about so many things: What should the type be responsible for? How long should instances of this type live for? Should any existing code be moved to this type? What if this new type needs access to state held by another type?

Designing object-oriented systems takes time. When you're under pressure to deliver a feature making this tradeoff can be difficult. The opportunity cost is hard to see. The thing is, many problems are caused by large types – problems that will slow you down and problems that will affect your code's quality. You'll read about examples of these consequences in the following sections. For now, just know that breaking large types into smaller types is a great way to improve your codebase's architecture.

Now that you're familiar with the root causes, you're ready to dig into the problems that can cause slow team velocity and fragile code quality.

Examining the problems

If you're looking to boost your team's velocity and to strengthen your code's quality, addressing the root causes is a good start. But you might be wondering *how* the root causes affect team velocity and code quality.

> **Note**: As you read the upcoming sections, keep in mind that highly interdependent code and large types are just the *common* root causes. You'll see these common root causes in almost all the problem sections below. However, you'll also read about other, problem-specific, root causes.

With that in mind, it's time to examine the problems associated with team velocity and code quality.

My app's codebase is hard to understand

Have you ever spent hours trying to figure out how a view controller works? Code is inherently difficult to understand because code is textual. The connections between files and types are hard to see. Having a solid understanding of how parts in your codebase are connected really helps you reason about how your code works. Therefore, the way an app is architected plays a huge role in the ease of code readability.

There are several ways in which architecture can impact readability:

How long are your class implementations?

600 line view controllers are very difficult to understand. If all you need to know is how a button functions, fishing through 600 lines of view controller code will take a lot of valuable time. A good architecture breaks large chunks of code into small, modular pieces that are easy to read and understand. The more an architecture encourages locally encapsulated behavior and state, the easier the code will be to read. Think about the current app you're working on. If a new team member joins your team tomorrow and needs to understand a single view controller, what percentage of the app's overall codebase will that developer need to understand? This is a good gauge to use when evaluating how much your architecture is helping improve your code's readability. Unfortunately, most architecture patterns don't emphasize this point enough. The good news is that this practice can be applied to pretty much any architecture pattern. So this is more of a universal aspect of architecture.

How many global variables does your codebase have, and how many objects are instantiated directly in another object?

The more your objects directly depend on each other and the more your objects depend on global state, the less information a developer will have when reading a single file. This makes it incredibly difficult to know how a change in a file might affect code living in another file. This forces developers to **Command**-click into tons of files in order to piece together the control flow. This takes a lot of time. Similar to class size, carefully managing dependencies is unfortunately not emphasized enough by popular architecture patterns. Carefully managing dependencies is a universal aspect that can be applied to any architecture pattern. In fact, we apply this aspect to every architecture code example that ships with this book. We also dedicated a whole chapter to this. You can read more about managing dependencies in Chapter 4.

How differently are your view controllers implemented across your app's codebase?

Developers, including your future self, will spend a lot of time figuring things out if different features are implemented using different architecture patterns. Human brains are amazing at identifying patterns. You can take advantage of this ability by ensuring your codebase follows similar architecture patterns throughout. Having a consistent structure drastically reduces the cognitive overhead required to understand code. In turn, developers will feel more comfortable changing and improving older parts of an app's codebase because they'll understand the common patterns.

In addition, using consistent architecture patterns allows you to establish a common vocabulary. Speaking the same vocabulary helps everyone easily discuss and understand each other's code.

Those are just a few ways in which architecture impacts code readability. Improving your code's readability by applying architecture patterns and concepts will help you and your team boost productivity and prevent accidental bugs from creeping into your app.

Changing my app's codebase sometimes causes regressions

Have you ever seen a small, innocent-looking code change unexpectedly break some unrelated part of your app? The probability of this happening grows as code grows and as changes are made over time. If this problem is left unchecked, you're likely to recommend a complete project rewrite. In today's agile world, developers are constantly changing code. Therefore, architecting code that's resilient to change is more important than ever.

The main architectural cause for this problem is highly interdependent code. Say that you're fixing a bug in a content view controller. This view controller manages the display and animation of an activity indicator. The activity indicator should stop animating when the view controller finishes loading. However, the indicator keeps animating forever. To fix this, you toggle the indicator off by stopping the animation. You do so by adding code to the content view controller that turns the animation off. The fix then gets shipped to users. Before long, you discover a new bug. The indicator stops animating, but it starts animating again soon thereafter. As it turns out, the indicator is a public property that is also being managed by a container view controller. On completion of some work, the container view controller was incorrectly turning the indicator's animation on, when it should have been turning it off...! Ultimately, the problem here is that the control of the indicator is not encapsulated within the content view controller. There's an interdependency between the container view controller, the content view controller and the activity indicator.

You can't see the effects of code changes easily when you're working in a codebase that's highly interdependent. Ideally, you should be able to easily reason about how the current file you're editing is connected to the rest of your codebase. The best way to do this is to **limit object dependencies** and to make the required dependencies obvious and visible.

This situation really slows teams down because any time any feature is built or any bug is fixed there's a chance for something to go wrong. If something *does* go wrong, it might be all hands on deck to figure out the root cause. In a really fragile codebase, the change-break-fix cycle can snowball out of control. You end up spending more time fixing issues than improving your app. Not only is this a team velocity problem, it is also a code quality problem. The chances of shipping a bug to users is much higher when the connections between code are hard to see and understand. Code that's hard to understand leads to code that easily breaks when changed. All to say, a good modular architecture can help you avoid accidentally introducing bugs when making changes.

My app exhibits fragile behavior when running

Apps can be complex systems running in complex environments. Things like multi-core programming and sharing data with app extensions contribute to the complexities involved in building iOS apps. Consequently, apps are susceptible to problems that are hard to diagnose such as race conditions and state inconsistency.

For example, you might notice many crash reports arriving due to a race condition associated with some mutable state. This kind of crash can take days to diagnose and fix. Enough of these kinds of issues can really grind a team to a halt. Some architecture patterns and concepts attempt to address these kinds of issues by designing constraints that act as guard rails to help teams avoid the most common pitfalls. They help you stay out of trouble. Therefore, if you find yourself working in a fairly complex environment, try establishing architecture patterns as a means to manage complexity. The more you can make your app behave in deterministic ways, the less likely users are to experience strange bugs and the less time you and your team will have to spend chasing these strange bugs.

My code is hard to re-use

The structure of a codebase determines how much code you can re-use. The structure also determines how easily you can add new behavior to existing code. You might want to focus on this problem if you feel like you're having to make similar decisions over and over again every time you build a new feature. That is, if you feel like you're building each feature from scratch.

Large types can prevent your code from being reusable. For example, a huge 2,000-line class is unlikely to be reusable because you might only need part of the class.

The part you need might be tightly coupled with the rest of the class, making the part you need impossible to use without the rest of the class. Types that are smaller and that have less responsibility are more likely to be reusable.

Writing code takes more time if you can't re-use any code. If you're solving complex UI problems that are applicable in many different ways, it makes sense to spend time to refactor your code to be reusable. Making code reusable not only helps you build new things quicker, it helps you make modifications to existing behaviors. But what if you don't need to re-use most of your code? For example, you probably don't instantiate most of your view controllers from more than one place. This is important: Reusability is not just about being able to re-use code. It's also about being able to move code around when making changes to your app. The more reusable everything is, the easier it is to shuffle code around without needing to do risky refactors.

Also, a codebase with code that's not reusable can result in code quality problems. For instance, say you have field validation logic in several screens where users enter information. The validation error UI logic is duplicated in each screen's view controller. Because similar logic is duplicated, perhaps each screen displays validation errors slightly differently, resulting in an inconsistent user experience. If someone discovers a bug, you'll have to find all the view controllers that show validation errors. You might miss one instance and end up continuing to ship the same bug...! Ultimately, making code reusable allows you to ship a consistent user experience and allows you to tweak your app's behavior easily.

Changes require large code refactors

How many times have you thought a feature change would be simple, yet you found yourself doing a large refactor instead? Architecture patterns not only help you re-use code, they also help you replace parts of your code without needing to do a big refactor. In a well-architected codebase, you should be able to easily make isolated changes without affecting the rest of the codebase. So what makes code hard to replace? Yep, you guessed it: large types and highly interdependent code.

Updating the types in your code to be easily replaceable really speeds up team velocity because it allows multiple people to work on multiple parts of a codebase at the same time.

My teammates step on each other's toes

Your app's architecture also impacts how easily you can work in parallel with your teammates. When a codebase doesn't lend itself to parallel work-streams, teammates either accidentally step on each others toes or become idle waiting for a good time to start committing code again.

Ideally, a codebase has small enough units that each person on a team can write code in a separate file while building a feature. Otherwise, you'll run into issues such as merge conflicts that can take a long time to resolve. For example, if your app's main screen is completely implemented in a single view controller, the developer building the UI's layout will probably conflict with the person building the network refresh. It's amazing when you can meet as a team and self-organize around different aspects of building a feature. Someone can build the layout, someone else can build the networking, someone else can build the caching, someone else can build the validation logic and so on and so forth. Good architecture enables you to do this.

If multiple developers are building the same feature, having small types is not enough because the code that one developer is building might depend on unwritten code from other developers. While developers could hardcode fake data while they wait on other developers, they could move even faster if they agreed on APIs upfront. You can design and write protocols for those dependencies so developers can call into systems that are not built yet. This allows developers to write unit tests and even complete implementations without needing to do a large integration once all systems are built. Also, this guarantees that UI code does not depend on implementation details of networking, caching, etc.

Back in the day, apps were built by one- to five-person teams. Today, many apps are built by twenty or more iOS developers. Some are even built by more than a hundred developers!

Companies who hire lots of developers are looking for ways to maximize the productivity of large development groups by organizing developers into cross-functional feature teams. Many folks call this the "squad model."

The squad model was popularized by Spotify. As your team and company grows, there comes a point where coordinating among teams takes a lot of time. The more dependent one team's code is on another team's code, the more these teams will have to depend on each other in order to ship. Because of this dependency, developers will start stepping on each other's toes. This is where architecture comes into the picture. The trick is to design an app architecture that allows developers to build features in isolation.

An architecture that loosely couples each feature into separate Swift modules. This gives each squad a container that the squad can use to build their feature however they need. In turn, squads can ship features much faster because this kind of architecture gives squads the autonomy they need to move fast.

To summarize, you'll be able to build features much faster if your app's architecture allows your team to easily parallelize work by loosely coupling layers and features that make up your codebase.

My app's codebase is hard to unit test

Code is notoriously hard to unit test because codebases are commonly made up of parts that are tightly coupled together. This makes the different parts impossible to isolate during test. For example, a view controller might persist some data with CoreData. Because the persistence is embedded into the view controller, the persistence and view controller are tightly coupled. This means you won't be able to unit test the view controller without having to stand-up a full CoreData stack. If your unit tests require a ton of set up, or if your unit tests perform uncontrollable side effects such as networking and persistence, then your app's codebase could benefit from an architectural refactor.

My app takes a long time to compile

While building a new feature, how many times do you build and run your app? Several dozen or more, right? A long compile time can really slow you down. A fast feedback loop can really speed things up. That sounds good, but what does compile time have to do with architecture? A modular app architecture helps the Xcode build system from recompiling code that hasn't changed.

Swift language designers made a big decision when designing the Swift language. They decided against using header files. They did this to reduce duplication and to make the language easier to learn. Because Swift does not use header files, the Swift compiler has to read all of the Swift files that make up a Swift module when compiling each file. This means when you change a single file, the Swift compiler might need to parse through *all* the Swift files in the module. If you have lots of Swift files in a single app target, i.e. one Swift module, recompiling your app can take a while, even when you make a small change. How this works in detail is out of scope for this book, but know that the Xcode build system is getting smarter every year. Starting with Xcode 10, Xcode has the ability to do some incremental compilation.

Despite these improvements, breaking your app into several Swift modules can speed up your build times. This is because the Xcode build system doesn't have to recompile modules for which Swift files have not changed. In addition, breaking your app into multiple modules results in smaller modules, i.e., modules with fewer Swift files. This means the Xcode build system has to do less work to build each module. Architectures that enable multi-module apps help you to speed up build times so you can spend less time waiting for your app to run.

Speeding up your local build times is great, but if that's not good enough, you can speed up your build times even more by using a different build system that can use a distributed build cache. Build systems, such as Google's Bazel, let you cache, download and re-use Swift modules that were compiled on someone else's machine. Imagine building a pull request branch you just pulled only to find the app's .ipa downloaded and installed onto your simulator without any source needing to be compiled. All because one of your co-workers already built the code found in this pull request branch. Wouldn't that be amazing? What's better than a zero-compile-time build?

These build time benefits are only possible when you have an architecture that allows for multi-module Swift codebases.

My team has a hard time breaking user stories into tasks

A good architecture can even help you plan software development projects. Breaking user stories into tasks can be very difficult. Breaking user stories into tasks that *everyone on your team understands* is even more difficult. For instance, if you're planning a feature that will be implemented in a single view controller, how will you create clearly defined tasks? An app architecture that categorizes types into responsibilities creates a common vocabulary.

A common vocabulary enables you to build a shared understanding with other teammates about what kinds of objects are used to build features. This allows you to easily break down user stories into the different kinds of objects needed. For example you could break a user story up into tasks for building the `UIView`, the `UIViewController`, the `RemoteAPI` for networking, the `DataStore` for caching and so on. The quicker your team can self organize, the less time your team spends planning, and therefore, the more time your team spends building awesome features.

Increasing code agility

In addition to boosting your team's velocity and strengthening your code's quality, architecture can increase your code's agility. Code that is agile is code that can be easily changed to meet an objective without requiring a massive re-write. Code agility buys you a lot of flexibility. It enables you to quickly respond to changes in the technology landscape. It also enables you to quickly respond to changes in user needs. How do you know if your code is not agile? What problems would you face?

Here are some problems that can be solved with architecture in order to increase your code's agility:

- I find myself locked into a technology.
- I'm forced to make big decisions early in a project.
- Adding feature flags is difficult.

You'll read about each of these problems in this section.

I find myself locked into a technology

Have you ever needed to plan a big migration project to migrate your code from one technology to another? Or have you wanted to migrate your code from one technology to another but couldn't because the effort would be too big? Being locked into technology can put a pause on feature development and can prevent you from taking advantage of the benefits that new technologies have to offer. This problem is especially relevant to mobile development because, as you've experienced, mobile technology is constantly changing.

For example, if you used Parse, a once-popular yet now-defunct mobile backend as a service, you know this pain well. Third parties come and go. Many times, you're expected to respond to these changes quickly. Your app's architecture can help you do so.

You can be locked into technology when your higher-level types, such as view controllers, are tightly coupled to lower-level system implementations. This happens when the higher-level code makes calls into implementation specific types as opposed to making calls to protocol types. For instance, if your view controllers were making direct calls to `NSURLConnection`, pre iOS 7, then you probably had to go into every view controller and update your code to use `NSURLSession`. If you have a very large codebase, you might wait until the last minute possible to migrate because of the effort involved.

This is just one of many possible ways your higher-level code can be tightly coupled to lower-level systems.

You can also be locked into a technology when your higher-level types depend on specific data formats. You typically need to work with data formats when communicating with servers and when persisting information. The server communications data format situation is the trickiest because you probably don't control the server backend. The team that builds and maintains the backend app servers might come knocking on your door one day asking to use a different data format or even a different networking paradigm such as GraphQL.

Say your app servers are sending JSON today and say your view controllers are deserializing and serializing JSON. If your server team decides to use a different format, such as Protocol Buffers, you might need to reimplement every single view controller!

While the previous example is somewhat straight forward, data format issues can be a bit more nuanced though. For instance, the chat app from one of my previous projects needed to relay chat messages from chat servers to the app's UI. Chat messages were encoded using XML. We knew not to pass XML straight to the view controllers. That wasn't enough. The structure of the chat messages were defined by yet another standard called XMPP. We could have easily modeled the `struct` that carries chat messages in a way that mirrors the XMPP spec. We decided to model the `struct` based on the appearance properties of chat messages so that our view controllers would not be tightly coupled to the chat server technology. We didn't want to be locked into XMPP.

These are just a few ways in which your architecture can either lock you into technologies or give you the freedom to easily switch to new technologies.

I'm forced to make big decisions early in a project

Choosing which technologies to use when starting a new project is tempting. Some of these technology choices are big decisions that feel like one-way doors. Once you've made a choice, there's no looking back. As apps get more complex, developers find themselves needing to make more technology decisions. You need a lot of technologies to build modern iOS apps. Wouldn't it be nice to be able to start building apps without having to make all the big decisions up front? You might even find that you didn't need a certain technology after all. A good architecture allows you to make technology decisions at the most opportune time.

The database is the classic example. Have you ever been in a CoreData versus Realm discussion? A lot of the time, these discussions happen before a single line of code is written. The problem is, these database technologies add a lot of complexity. And, if you make this decision early on, chances are good that you'll be locked into one of these technologies. The thing is, you probably don't have all the information you need to make this decision at the beginning of a project. In one of my previous projects we decided to design `DataStore` protocols and use `NSCoding` to serialize Objective-C objects to disk. We did this as a temporary measure until we got time to incorporate CoreData. It turned out we didn't even need CoreData! The simplest solution was good enough. We ended up shipping the app to millions of users and never had any issues with persistence.

Now, we could have just as easily needed a database like CoreData. The point is that you can architect to allow your team to build significant portions of your app without needing to make big, upfront decisions.

Adding feature flags is difficult

Software teams are starting to use data-driven and lean approaches to app development. To take these approaches, developers use feature flags to A/B test features and to toggle unfinished features off. Your app's architecture can make it easy or difficult to incorporate feature flags into your app's codebase. You'll be able to add feature flags easily if your app's codebase is broken down into small loosely coupled pieces. A good app architecture gives you the flexibility needed to switch between behaviors and the flexibility to turn specific things on and off.

Surveying architecture patterns

After you've identified the problems you'd like to solve, a good next step is to survey architecture patterns. The good news is, there are a ton of architecture patterns to chose from. The bad news is, there are a ton of architecture patterns to chose from!

Most of the patterns are very similar to each other. This section provides a guide to help you figure out what order to use when exploring existing architecture patterns.

As you read the following paragraphs, keep in mind that this book covers three of the architectures mentioned. You'll read about why in the following section on putting patterns into practice.

Since `UIKit` is designed with **Model View Controller (MVC)** in mind, any pattern other than MVC will need to be retrofitted into `UIKit`. Therefore, when surveying patterns, MVC is a great place to start.

Once you've looked at MVC, the next place to look are any of the MV- patterns, such as MVVM and MVP. The notable exception is MVI; you'll see why in a bit. MV-patterns are the next natural place to look because these patterns are so similar to MVC. They have models and views, so they map easily to most of `UIKit`'s MVC structure. With non-MVC MV- architectures, you'll have to figure out how to connect view controllers to their equivalent types in whatever MV- pattern you're using. For instance, you'll have to figure out how to map view models to view controllers when using MVVM. You can read more about MVVM in Chapter 5.

Clean Architecture and **Ports & Adapters** is a good place to look next. These concepts by themselves are very high level and abstract. You'll need to do a lot of reading and thinking in order to apply Clean Architecture and Ports & Adapters to iOS app development. If you have time, I recommend you go down this route before jumping into any of the specific patterns derived from these concepts.

A deep understanding will help you tweak any of the derived patterns. If you want to explore the iOS architecture patterns derived from Clean Architecture and Ports & Adapters, check out VIPER and RIBs. RIBs is Uber's take on VIPER. Clean Architecture and Ports & Adapters patterns fit really well into apps that have a lot of local business logic. If your app is presentation heavy and doesn't have a whole lot of local business logic, these patterns might not work well for you.

Next, I recommend looking at **unidirectional architecture** patterns. These patterns are all about reactive UIs and state management. These are probably the hardest patterns to put into practice. However, when applied well, you get a lot of guarantees, such as state consistency, that you don't get out of other patterns. Unidirectional patterns are definitely worth considering. If you're interested, take a look at Flux, Redux, RxFeedback, and Model-View-Intent (MVI). Redux is the unidirectional pattern that I've seen applied the most in iOS app development. Check out Chapter 6 if you want to take a deep dive into Redux.

One of the common properties of all these patterns is the components they define are all interconnected. They're fairly inflexible, i.e., they're not designed to be mixed. You might feel like you have to take one pattern over the other. This is why Josh, my co-author, and I decided to come up with another approach that we call **Elements**.

Elements is a collection of smaller architecture patterns that are designed to be independent. You can adopt one pattern, two patterns, or all of the patterns. They're also designed to work together. Our goal was to take everything we learned about applying architecture patterns to iOS and come up with a flexible approach where developers could apply bits and pieces without having to refactor entire codebases. You can read all about Elements in Chapter 7 and Chapter 8.

This gives you a bird's eye view of some patterns you can use to shape your app's architecture. This is by no means a comprehensive list.

New patterns pop up all the time, so it's worth looking around to see if you can find something else that works best for you.

Selecting a pattern

Once you become familiar with the patterns that look promising, you'll want to decide which pattern(s) to use. Choosing a pattern is not easy because we tend to feel a strong connection with one pattern or another. In all honesty, which pattern you select is less important than how you put the pattern to practice.

I've seen really well-architected MVC iOS apps, and I've seen very poorly architected MVVM iOS apps and vice versa. Yes, view models can be as massive as view controllers. The reality is, many patterns don't go deep into each of their layers. For example, what exactly does a model look like in any of the MV- patterns? There's really not a single way to design a model layer in MV- patterns. It's very open-ended. Not only that, most patterns were not designed with mobile apps in mind — let alone today's complex iOS environment. Therefore, most patterns only scratch the surface. Because of this, selecting the "right" pattern will not automatically result in a well-architected codebase.

Hopefully, this gives you a sense of freedom! The next time you find yourself in a hotly debated discussion about architecture, remember that the patterns themselves aren't *that* important. I'm not suggesting patterns are not important at all, I'm just saying that choosing a particular pattern isn't the single most important decision. You can have a well architected app using any of the patterns.

The best way to decide which pattern to use is to try a couple of the patterns in your codebase. This will give you the best information about how well a pattern will meet your needs. When trying different patterns, don't be afraid to experiment a bit with each. Also, search the internet to see what other people's experience has been with the patterns you're considering.

In addition, don't forget to consider the human aspects. How big is your team? How experienced are your teammates? What patterns are your teammates most familiar with? How tight are your deadlines? And of course, consider the technical aspects such as, what constraints are you looking to design into your codebase? If you're short on time, MVC is probably your best bet when it comes to iOS app development because you won't have to spend time figuring how to incorporate a foreign pattern into `UIKit`'s MVC structure.

Are there any "gotchas" to watch out for while trying out different patterns? Absolutely! Here are some questions based on some of the pain points I've experienced when trying different patterns:

- Do you end up with a lot of boilerplate code? If so, does the boilerplate at least make the code easier to understand?

- Do you end up with a lot of empty files that only proxy method calls to other objects?

- Is the pattern hard to understand?

- How much will you need to refactor to apply the pattern?

- Is the pattern adding a lot of new concepts and vocabulary?

- Will you need to import a library to use the pattern?

These aren't necessarily bad things. They're just things to think about as you survey and compare different patterns. Also, don't feel like you have to pick one pattern over another. Even though these patterns were not designed to be mixed and matched, there's no reason you can't combine them. For example, if you really like unidirectional pattens, but your codebase is built using MVVM, you could easily layer MVVM over something like Redux. Just have your view models dispatch actions and have your view models listening to the Redux store… In case that didn't make any sense — no worries! You learn all about MVVM and Redux in Chapters 5 and 6, respectively. All this to say, architecture is more of an art than science. Go experiment, learn and be creative. There's no right way to do it. Just remember, there are many good ways to architect and there are many not-so-great ways to architect — but not a single right way.

Putting patterns into practice

The rest of this book is all about putting patterns into practice. We currently cover three patterns: **MVVM, Redux and Elements**.

You might be wondering why we cover so few patterns. Remember, how you apply a pattern is more important than which pattern you pick. We wanted to take you on a couple of deep dives into applying patterns. And, we didn't want to shy away from the kind of complexities you'd find in a real app. Instead of scratching the surface with lots of patterns, we opted to focus on a few. We also wanted to cover material not found in other architecture books. For example, many patterns leave out important aspects of app architecture, such as navigation. Most pattern chapters in this book cover navigation, regardless of the pattern's main focus.

You also might be wondering why we selected these three specific patterns. We wanted to cover one pattern from each heritage. For example, MVVM comes from the MV- set of patterns. Redux is a unidirectional pattern. And Elements is rooted in Clean Architecture plus Ports & Adapters. We plan on adding a couple more patterns in future editions of the book. Let us know in the book's forum if there's a particular pattern you'd like to us cover!

In the following chapters, you'll read about the specifics of each pattern in depth. However, you might be wondering what general things to look for when putting any pattern into practice. Here are some to keep in your back pocket:

- **Loosely coupled parts**: Whether you're using MVC, MVVM, Redux, VIPER, etc. make sure your code is broken down into small loosely coupled parts.
- **Cohesive types**: Make sure your types exhibit high cohesion, i.e., the properties and methods that make up each type belong together. If you have small types that have very focused responsibilities, your types probably exhibit high cohesion.
- **Multi-module apps**: Make sure your app is broken down into several Swift modules.
- **Object dependencies**: Make sure you're managing object dependencies using patterns such as Dependency Injection containers and Service Locators. Chapter 4 covers Dependency Injection in depth.

These are the aspects of architecture that make a real difference. We demonstrate all of these aspects in the chapters ahead and in the companion example code.

Key points

- There's no such thing as a perfect universal app architecture.

- You can use architecture to boost your team's velocity, to strengthen your code's quality and to increase your code's agility.

- Selecting the "right" architecture pattern won't guarantee your codebase will be well-architected. Which pattern you select is less important than how you put the pattern to practice.

- Feel free to mix and match different architecture patterns.

- Architecture is more of an art than a science. Go experiment, learn and be creative.

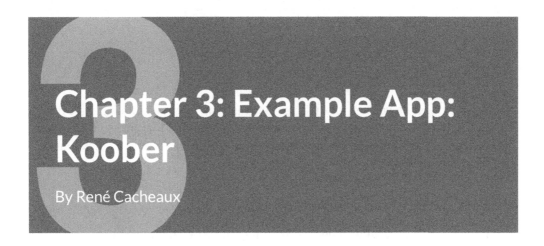

Chapter 3: Example App: Koober

By René Cacheaux

This chapter introduces Koober, the example app used throughout this book. You'll explore all the screens that comprise the app and how they work together. At the end of this chapter, you'll take a quick tour of the Xcode project and source code. A reimplementation of Koober accompanies every chapter so you can compare and contrast different architectures. The material in this book assumes that you have a good understanding of the example app, so make sure to read this chapter before diving into any of the following chapters.

Koober

Imagine a world in which animals are human-like. They speak different languages, live in different countries, go to Mermaidbucks for coffee and so on. In this animal kingdom, smartphones have just hit the market for the first time. All the developers around the world race to build the next big app.

The kangaroo taxi industry in Australia is prime for disruption. Riders are tired of paying in cash and having to physically walk to the street to hail a kangaroo. Plus, some of the kangaroos have been hopping too high, making their passengers sick. Riders have no way to give feedback. A team of developers in Sydney noticed this and decided to launch a new startup company to build Koober, the next big ride-hailing app.

How Koober works

Koober works just like other ride-hailing apps that you might be familiar with from our own human world. Koober has the common components that make up a modern app such as onboarding, sign up, sign in, account profile, etc. Here's a quick tour of all the screens, end to end.

Launching

You'll see the launch screen when you first open the app. This screen comes and goes really quickly, so you might not see it. The app is determining if a user is signed in at the time this screen is presented.

Welcome

If a user is not signed in, the app transitions to the welcome screen.

Signing up

From the welcome screen, you can navigate to the sign-up screen to create a new user account.

Requesting a ride

Once you're signed in, you're taken to the pick-me-up app flow. First, the app determines your current physical location. The location is used as the ride's **pick-up location**. Koober's user location system always returns Sydney, Australia as your current location so you don't have to give your actual location.

Next, you're presented with a map that's annotated with your pick-up location. At the top of the screen, there's a Where to? button for navigating to the **drop-off location** picker.

The drop-off location picker is pre-seeded with locations. You can also perform a search using the UISearchBar.

Once you pick a drop-off location, you're taken back to the map screen wherein the drop-off location is annotated and the ride-option picker is presented at the bottom of the screen.

You use the ride-option picker to pick a **ride option**. A ride option specifies which kind of animal will pick you up. Some animals can carry more riders than others. For example, in Sydney, wallabies, wallaroos and kangaroos want to give rides for Koober.

Wallabies, wallaroos and kangaroos are considered different kinds of kangaroos. The three kinds of kangaroos range from smallest to largest in size, respectively.

This means that wallaroos can cary more weight than wallabies, and they are more expensive to ride.

As soon as you pick a ride option, you can confirm your new ride request. That's how you request a ride with Koober.

Waiting for pick up

Once your new ride request is sent, the app takes you to the waiting-for-pick-up screen. You can start a new ride request from this screen by pressing the Start New Ride button.

Viewing your profile

You can view your user profile by tapping the Profile button located towards the top right-hand corner of all the pick-me-up flow screens.

Signing out

You can sign out of the app from the profile screen.

Signing in

After you sign out, the app presents the welcome screen wherein you can navigate to the sign-in screen. You can always sign in with **johnny@gmail.com** and **password**.

Why Koober?

When planning this book, we wanted to make sure that the example code would be applicable to real projects. We heard from the community that most architecture books oversimplify examples, leaving readers to figure out the real-world application of the theory. So we decided to build an entire app with the complexities of a real app to use as the basis for our examples. We really liked ride hailing because ride-hailing apps have all the complexity of a real-world app without an explosion of screens and UI to build.

Koober demonstrates architectural theory while incorporating aspects such as networking, persistence, authentication and more. We acknowledge this app doesn't cover all of our readers' type of projects; nevertheless, we hope everyone finds the material easy to incorporate into all kinds of projects.

If you try out any of this book's techniques in your current projects, let us know how it goes! We'd love to hear from you in the book's forum.

Getting started with the source

In order to familiarize yourself with the code in the sample app, this section walks you through how the app launches and where you can find the initial view controllers. This section uses the model–view–viewmodel (MVVM) version of the sample app. While following along, don't worry too much about understanding the architecture as you'll explore MVVM in Chapter 5.

Launch sequence

When launching Koober for the very first time, you'll see two screens: the launch screen and the welcome screen.

The launch screen is implemented by `LaunchViewController` and the welcome screen is implemented by `WelcomeViewController`. Keep reading to see how these view controllers get onto the screen.

View controller hierarchy

Koober's root view controller is implemented by `MainViewController`, a custom container view controller.

When the app starts up, the `MainViewController` is installed. `MainViewController` loads by presenting the `LaunchViewController` as a child view controller. When the launch screen is presented, the `MainViewController` and `LaunchViewController` make up the View Controller hierarchy.

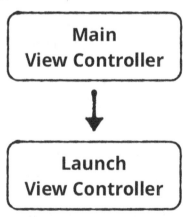

The `LaunchViewController` then determines whether a user is signed in or not. The first time you run Koober, a user will not be signed in, so the `MainViewController` will navigate from the `LaunchViewController` to the `OnboardingViewController`.

`OnboardingViewController` is a `UINavigationController` subclass that starts by presenting the `WelcomeViewController`. When the welcome screen is presented, the `MainViewController`, `OnboardingViewController` and `WelcomeViewController` make up the View Controller hierarchy.

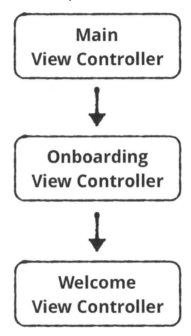

OK, time to fire up Xcode and take a peek at the source.

Opening the source

To view Koober's source, find the **03-example-app/final/KooberApp** directory and open **KooberApp.xcodeproj**. Each chapter has a different version of Koober found inside each chapter's directory.

A single Xcode project contains all the source for Koober, and the source is organized into several targets.

Xcode project targets

- **Koober**: This is the iOS app target for Koober and contains the app delegate and other app-specific resources, such as the info.plist. Other than the app delegate, this target does not contain any source.

- **KooberiOS**: This Swift Package contains all the UI code specific to the Koober iOS app, such as view controllers and views.

- **KooberUIKit**: This Swift Package contains code that depends on `UIKit` and that could be used on other `UIKit` platforms such as `tvOS`.

- **KooberKit**: This last Swift Package contains code that does not depend on `UIKit`. Therefore, this package can be used in any Apple platform.

Presenting MainViewController

To get started tracing the launch sequence in code, inside Xcode's Project navigator, open **Koober/AppDelegate.swift**. On the first line of `application(_:didFinishLaunchingWithOptions:)`, the `MainViewController` is instantiated by the `injectionContainer`.

The `injectionContainer` is a factory that creates instances of objects with their dependencies. In this case, the `injectionContainer` allows the app delegate to create a new instance of `MainViewController` without knowing what other objects `MainViewController` needs in order to be instantiated.

On line 45, the `MainViewController` is set as the window's root view controller. So that's how the `MainViewController` makes its way to the screen.

Presenting the launch screen

Next, open **KooberiOS/Sources/KooberiOS/iOSApp/MainViewController.swift**. You are now in the KooberiOS Swift Package where all the view controller code lives. On line 136, inside the `viewDidLoad` method, `MainViewController` subscribes to `MainViewModel` updates.

Open **KooberKit/Sources/KooberKit/UILayer/MainViewModel.swift**. You are now in the KooberKit package.

On line 35, the view model's `@Published view` property is initialized with a `.launching MainView` enum case.

Because of the initial `.launching` value, when `MainViewController` subscribes to the 'view' property's publisher on `viewDidLoad`, the view model will publish the `.launching` value to the `MainViewController`.

Return to **KooberiOS/Sources/KooberiOS/iOSApp/MainViewController.swift**.

Whenever a new value is published, the subscription to the view model calls the `present(_:)` method on line 70. Because the first value published is `.launching`, the `presentLaunching` method is called inside `present(_:)`, right after `MainViewController` loads. The `presentLaunching` method on line 94 adds the `LaunchViewController` as a child to `MainViewController`, presenting the launch screen.

Getting from launch to onboarding

Make your way to **KooberiOS/Sources/KooberiOS/iOSApp/LaunchViewController.swift**.

On line 47, during `loadView`, `LaunchViewController`'s root view is created with a `LaunchViewModel`.

Go the root view by opening **KooberiOS/Sources/KooberiOS/iOSApp/LaunchRootView.swift**. During initialization, on line 45, the launch view asks the view model to attempt to load a user session to see if a user is signed in.

Open the `LaunchViewModel`'s source located at **KooberKit/Sources/KooberKit/UILayer/LaunchViewModel.swift**.

You can find the `loadUserSession` method on line 56. Once this method finishes querying for a user session, `goToNextScreen(userSession:)` is called.

When you first run Koober, there won't be a signed-in user so the `goToNextScreen(userSession:)` method will be called with `nil`. When `goToNextScreen(userSession:)` determines that a user is not signed in, on line 82 and 83, the `notSignedInResponder`'s `notSignedIn` method is called.

Next, open **KooberKit/Sources/KooberKit/UILayer/MainViewModel.swift**. Notice that this view model conforms to the `NotSignedInResponder` protocol.

Once `LaunchViewModel` determines a user is not logged in, `LaunchViewModel` calls `MainViewModel`'s `notSignedIn` method via the `NotSignedInResponder` protocol. In other words, `MainViewModel` is `LaunchViewModel`'s `notSignedInResponder`. You can read more about this MVVM setup in Chapter 5.

On line 41, inside `notSignedIn`, notice how `MainViewModel` updates the `view` property with a new `MainView` enum case value, `.onboarding`. Since `MainViewController` is subscribed to `view`'s publisher, this update publishes the new `.onboarding` value and tells `MainViewController` to transition from it's current presentation to presenting `OnboardingViewController`. The transition happens in `MainViewController`'s `presentOnboarding` method.

Presenting the Welcome screen

Now that `OnboardingViewController` is on screen, how does `WelcomeViewController` get presented?

Open **KooberiOS/Sources/KooberiOS/iOSApp/Onboarding/OnboardingViewController.swift**.

`OnboardingViewController` loads the same way `MainViewController` loads via view model subscription. On line 63, during `viewDidLoad`, `OnboardingViewController` subscribes to the `OnboardingViewModel`'s `$navigationAction` publisher.

There's some extra complexities in `OnboardingViewController` that you don't need to worry about just yet. The complexity exists because `OnboardingViewController` is a `UINavigationController`, you can read more about this in Chapter 5. The main gist is that right after `OnboardingViewController` loads, `presentWelcome` is called on line 88. This is how the welcome screen gets presented.

Alright! Now that you're familiar with Koober's source code, you'll have no problem following along with the example code in rest of the chapters.

Key points

- Koober, a kangaroo ride-hailing app, is the example app used throughout this book.
- Koober incorporates many of the complexities found in real-world apps, such as authentication and navigation.
- A complete re-implementation of Koober accompanies each architecture chapter.
- The Koober Xcode project consists of four targets: Koober, Koober_iOS, KooberUIKit and KooberKit.
- `MainViewController`, `LaunchViewController` and `OnboardingViewController` coordinate in order to launch Koober.

Chapter 4: Objects & Their Dependencies

By René Cacheaux & Josh Berlin

Ready to dig deep into object-oriented programming? Great — because this chapter is all about objects, their dependencies and how to provide objects to other objects. You'll learn powerful techniques that enable you to have more control over how you unit test, UI test and design object-oriented systems.

Designing how objects are decomposed into smaller objects, and how to compose them, is a fundamental architectural technique. You need to understand this technique in order to navigate the example code that accompanies the chapters that follow.

In this chapter, you'll first learn the benefits of managing object dependencies. Then, you'll take a quick look at common dependency patterns. Finally, you'll spend the rest of the chapter taking a deep dive into Dependency Injection, one of the common dependency patterns. Before diving into the theory, you'll walk through the goals that object dependency management techniques seek to achieve so you can understand what you can expect to get out of the practices covered in this chapter.

Establishing the goals

These are the qualities you can expect to see when putting this chapter's dependency techniques into practice:

- **Maintainability**: The ability to easily change a code-base without introducing defects, i.e., the ability to reimplement part of a code-base without adversely affecting the rest of the code-base.

- **Testability**: Deterministic unit and UI tests, i.e., tests that don't rely on things you can't control, such as the network.

- **Substitutability**: The ability to substitute the implementation of a dependency at compile-time and at runtime. This quality is useful for A/B testing, for gating features using feature flags, for replacing side-effect implementations with fake implementations during a test, for temporarily swapping in a diagnostic version of an object during development and more.

- **Deferability**: Having the ability to defer big decisions such as selecting a database technology.

- **Parallel work streams**: Being able to have multiple developers work independently on the same feature at the same time without stepping on each others toes.

- **Control during development**: A code-base that developers can quickly iterate on by controlling build and run behavior, e.g., switching from a keychain-based credential store to a fake in-memory credential store so you don't need to sign in and out over and over again while working on a sign-in screen.

- **Minimizing object lifetimes**: For any given app, the less state a developer has to manage at once, the more predictably an app behaves. Therefore, you want to have the least amount of objects in-memory at once.

- **Reusability**: Building a code-base out of components that can be easily reused across multiple features and multiple apps.

Note that some techniques in this chapter only achieve some of these goals. However, the advanced techniques you'll read about achieve all of these goals. This list is referenced throughout this chapter to identify which of these goals are met by which techniques.

Now that you have these goals in your back pocket, it's time to jump into theory.

Learning the lingo

It's difficult to explain how to design objects and their dependencies without agreeing on a vocabulary. Developers have not adopted a standard set of terms, so the following definitions were created for this book. Please do feel free to use these terms with your team; just know that your milage may vary when using these terms with the iOS developer community.

Typically, when app developers use the term dependency, they are talking about libraries. However, in this chapter, a **dependency** is an object that another object depends on in order to do some work.

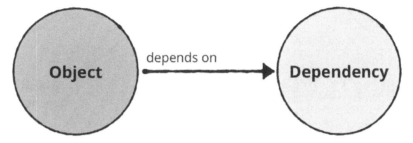

A dependency can *also* depend on other objects. These other objects are called **transitive dependencies**.

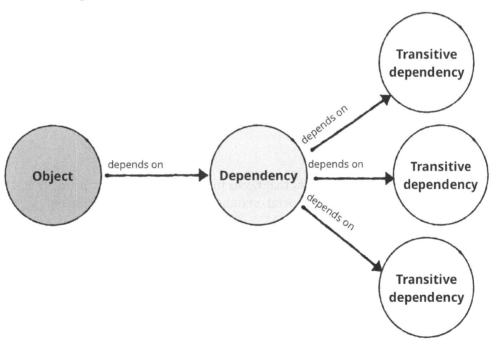

The **object-under-construction** is the object that depends on dependencies.

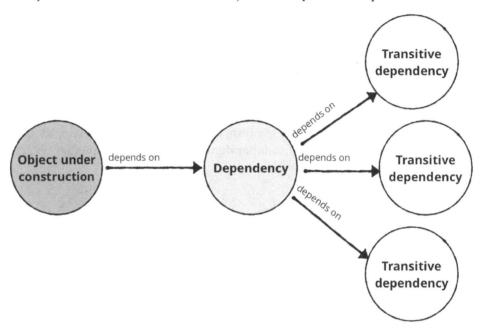

The reason an object goes under construction is to be used by yet another object — the **consumer**.

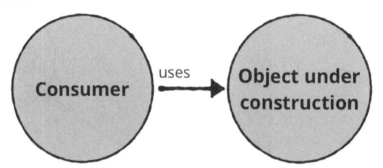

All together, you have a consumer that needs the object-under-construction that depends on dependencies that depend on transitive dependencies and so on.

The relationships between these objects form an **object graph**.

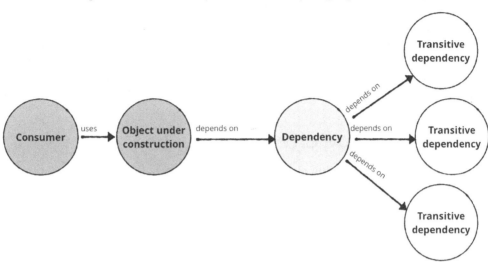

While reading about dependency patterns in the following sections, you'll see the terms **outside** and **inside**. Outside refers to code that exists outside the object-under-construction. Inside refers to the code that exists inside the object-under-construction. As you'll see, this distinction is architecturally significant.

That's the terminology you'll need to know to follow along this deep and winding object-dependency journey. Reviewing when and how dependencies are created will help you understand why dependencies exist in the first place, so that's next.

Creating dependencies

How do dependencies materialize in the first place? Here's a couple of common scenarios.

Refactoring massive classes

You've all seen them — the massive classes that appear to be infinitely long. Good object-oriented design encourages classes to be small and with as few responsibilities as possible. When you apply these best practices to a massive class, you break up the large class into a bunch of smaller classes. Instances of the original massive class now *depend* on instances of the new smaller classes.

Removing duplicate code

Say you have a couple of view controllers that you analyze. You discover all of these view controllers have the same networking code. You extract the networking code into a separate class. The view controllers now *depend* on the new networking class. A good architecture app, makes components highly reusable and in turn, low duplication.

Controlling side effects

Most of the time, these smaller classes perform side effects that cannot be controlled during development and during tests. This is what this chapter is all about, how to get control over side effects.

How you do this refactoring has a direct impact on how many of the outlined goals you can achieve. There are three fundamental considerations that will help you achieve the goals.

The fundamental considerations

When you design objects that depend on each other, you have to decide how the object-under-construction will get access to its dependencies. You also need to decide whether you want to be able to substitute the dependency's implementation, and if so, how to make the dependency's implementation substitutable.

Accessing dependencies

The object-under-construction needs to get access to its dependencies in order to call methods on those dependencies. Here are the ways an object-under-construction can get a hold of its dependencies.

From the inside:

- **Global property**: The object-under-construction can simply access any visible global property.

- **Instantiation**: If a dependency is ephemeral, i.e. the dependency doesn't need to live longer than the object-under-construction, the object-under-construction can instantiate the dependency.

From the outside:

- **Initializer argument**: A dependency can be provided to the object-under-construction as an initializer argument.

- **Mutable stored-property**: A dependency can be provided to an already created object-under-construction by setting a visible mutable stored-property on the object-under-construction.

- **Method**: Dependencies can be provided to the object-under-construction through visible methods of the object-under-construction.

Determining substitutability

Not all dependencies need to have substitutable implementations. For example, you probably don't need to substitute the implementation of a dependency that has no side effects, i.e. it only contains pure business logic. However, if the dependency writes something to disk, makes a network call, sends analytic events, navigates the user to another screen, etc. then you probably want to substitute the dependency's implementation during development or during testing.

Designing substitutability

If you *do* need to substitute a dependency's implementation then you need to decide if you need to substitute the implementation at compile-time, at runtime or both. To illustrate, you'll probably need runtime substitutability when you need to provide a different experience to different users for A/B testing. On the other hand, for testing, developers typically rely on compile-time substitutability.

You have the goals, the vocabulary and the main considerations — what's next? You might be wondering why there's so much talk about testing in an architecture book. That's the next stop on this journey.

Why is this architecture?

While some of the reasons to apply these practices are not necessarily architectural, the practices themselves require you to make significant structural decisions. That's why this material is in an architecture book.

In theory, you can design a good architecture without the techniques in this chapter. However, if you're writing software using industry best practices, such as unit testing, you'll definitely need to know about these techniques. On the flip side, these techniques are not a silver bullet. It's also possible to design a poor architecture while using these techniques. This chapter is just one of many puzzle pieces you must master in order to design great software.

You're now ready to learn how to take control of your objects' dependencies. There are several patterns you can use to design objects and their dependencies. This chapter focuses on one of those patterns, but it's worth taking a quick look at all the different patterns first.

Dependency patterns

Dependency Injection and Service Locator are the most-used patterns in software engineering.

- **Dependency Injection**: This is the pattern you'll learn *all* about in this chapter. The basic idea of the pattern is to provide all dependencies outside the object-under-construction. More on this later.

- **Service Locator**: A **Service Locator** is an object that can create dependencies and hold onto dependencies. You provide the object-under-construction with a Service Locator. Whenever the object-under-construction needs a dependency, the object-under-construction can simply ask the Service Locator to create or provide the dependency. This pattern is easier to use than Dependency Injection but results in more work when harnessing automated tests. Many developers use this pattern to successfully achieve the goals outlined in this chapter.

Here are other patterns you can use that have been created by the Swift community:

- **Environment**: An environment is a mutable struct that provides all the dependencies needed by objects-under-construction. This pattern is very similar to Service Locator; the only difference is an environment is accessed inside objects-under-construction, and a Service Locator is provided to the object-under-construction. This is a neat lightweight approach to managing object dependencies. To learn more, check out the Point Free Swift video series (https://www.fewbutripe.com/swift/functional/programming/2018/01/27/point-free.html) by Brandon Williams and Stephen Celis.
- **Protocol Extension**: This pattern uses Swift's protocol extensions to allow the object-under-construction to get access to its dependencies. To learn more about this pattern, see Daniel Hall's article, A Swift-y Approach to Dependency Injection (http://danielhall.io/a-swift-y-approach-to-dependency-injection).

Now, the stage is set. You've got everything you need. It's time to take a deep dive into the world of Dependency Injection.

Dependency Injection

The main goal of **Dependency Injection** is to provide dependencies to the object-under-construction from the outside of the object-under-construction as opposed to querying for dependencies from within the object-under-construction. Dependencies are "injected" into the object-under-construction.

Externalizing dependencies allows you to control dependencies outside the object-under-construction — in a test, for example. By externalizing dependencies, you can easily see *what* dependencies an object has by looking at the object's public API. This helps other developers reason about your code, including your future self!

When developers hear "Dependency Injection," they commonly think about Dependency Injection frameworks. However, Dependency Injection is first and foremost a pattern that you can follow with or without a framework. The best way to learn Dependency Injection is without using a framework. That's why this book does not use a framework for Dependency Injection.

From here, you can learn about the history behind Dependency Injection or you can skip ahead and jump into the details.

History

Dependency injection, or DI, is not a new concept. Ask any Android developer if they are familiar with DI, and they will likely tell you DI is essential to building well-architected apps. Dependency injection is also heavily used when building Java backend applications. So, it's no surprise that Java developers take advantage of the design pattern when moving to Android.

DI is intimately built into the core of some popular frameworks like AngularJS. The official AngularJS documentation has an entire section on the topic. The authors of the documents stressing that DI is "pervasive throughout Angular."

The object-oriented theory behind DI has been around for a while. DI is based on the Dependency Inversion Principle, also known as Inversion of Control. According to Martin Fowler, Inversion of Control was first written about in 1988 in a paper titled Designing Reusable Classes (http://www.laputan.org/drc/drc.html) by Johnson and Foote. Arguably, the concept was popularized by Robert Martin's paper, Object Oriented Design Quality Metrics: An Analysis of Dependencies (https://linux.ime.usp.br/~joaomm/mac499/arquivos/referencias/oodmetrics.pdf) published in 1994. These papers are worth a read if you want to dig deep into the roots of object-oriented design.

The term Dependency Injection was coined by Fowler in his January 14, 2004, post titled, Inversion of Control Containers and the Dependency Injection Pattern (https://martinfowler.com/articles/injection.html). The increasing popularity of Agile and Test-Driven Development motivated developers to find ways to easily test object-oriented code. As a result, to meet testability needs, developers invented Inversion of Control and, more specifically, DI. As you'll see, using Dependency Injection is key to building testable and maintainable iOS apps.

Types of injection

There are three types of injection:

- **Initializer**: The consumer provides dependencies to the object-under-construction's initializer when instantiating the object-under-construction. To enable this, you add dependencies to the object-under-construction's initializer parameter list. This is the best injection type because the object-under-construction can store the dependency in an immutable stored-property. The object-under-construction doesn't need to handle the case in which dependencies are nil and doesn't have to handle the case in which dependencies change. Initializer injection isn't always an option, so that's when you would use property injection, the next injection type.

- **Property**: After instantiating the object-under-construction, the consumer provides a dependency to the object-under-construction by setting a stored-property on the object-under-construction with the dependency. If you don't have a default implementation for a property-injected-dependency, then you'll need to make the property type `Optional`. This injection type is usually used in Interface Builder-backed view controllers because you don't have control over which initializer UIKit uses to create Interface Builder-backed view controllers.

- **Method**: The consumer provides dependencies to the object-under-construction when calling a method on the object-under-construction. Method injection is rarely used; however, it's another option at your disposal. If a dependency is only used within a single method, then you could use method injection to provide the dependency. This way, the object-under-construction doesn't need to hold onto the dependency. Remember, the less state an object has, the better. The shorter an object's lifetime, the better.

A good rule of thumb: When the object-under-construction cannot function without a dependency, use initializer injection. If the object-under-construction can function without a dependency, you can use any type of injection, preferably initializer injection.

Circular dependencies

Sometimes, two objects are so closely related to each other that they need to depend on one another. For this case to work when using Dependency Injection, you have to use property or method injection in one of the two objects that are in the circular dependency. That's because you cannot initialize both objects with each other; you have to create one first and then create the second object with the first object via initializer injection, then set a property on the first object with the second. Also, remember to avoid retain cycles by making one reference weak or unowned.

Substituting dependency implementations

Using injection is not enough to get all of the testability benefits and flexibility benefits. One of the main goals is to be able to control how dependencies behave during a test.

Say you have a dependency class that stores and retrieves data from a database. Injecting this database object, i.e., dependency, into a view controller does not give you control over how the database object behaves during a test. This is true because the view controller depends on a specific implementation of the database dependency that cannot be substituted at runtime. In order to control this dependency, the view controller should be able to accept a different implementation of the database object so that a fake implementation, which you control, can be injected during a test.

Therefore, injection alone does not enable substitutability. To enable substitutability, you need to define protocols for dependencies so the consumer can inject different classes that conform to the dependency's protocol. When designing an object-under-construction, use protocol types for dependencies.

Recall that you can make dependency implementations substitutable at compile-time, at runtime or both. Each dependency is instantiated *somewhere*. In order to substitute a dependency's implementation, you wrap the dependency's instantiation with an `if-else` statement. In one condition you can instantiate a fake type for testing and, in another condition, you can instantiate a production type for running the app. Writing this `if-else` statement is different for compile-time substitution versus runtime substitution.

Compile-time substitution

To conditionally compile code in Swift, you add **compilation condition identifiers** to Xcode's **active compilation conditions** build setting. Once you add custom identifiers to the active compilation condition's build setting, you use the identifiers in `#if` and `#elseif` compilation directives.

You can use conditional compilation to change the dependency implementation that you want for a specific build configuration. For example, if you want to use a fake remote API implementation during tests:

- Create a **Test** build configuration.

- Change your target scheme's **Test** scheme action's build configuration to the **Test** build configuration created in the previous step.

- Add a TEST identifier to your target's **active compilation conditions** build setting for the **Test** build configuration.

- Find the line of code wherein the consumer is creating a real remote API instance.

- Write an `#if TEST` compilation directive and, under the `if` statement, instantiate a fake remote API.

- Write an `#else` compilation directive and instantiate a real remote API under the `else`.

- Write an `#endif` compilation directive on the next line to close the conditional compilation block.

When you run the **Test** action in Xcode, to run unit and UI tests, the Swift compiler will compile the code that instantiates a fake remote API. When you run any other build action, such as **Run**, the Swift compiler will compile the code that instantiates a real remote API. Cool! Say goodbye to those flakey tests that try to make real network calls.

Runtime substitution

Sometimes you want to substitute a dependency's implementation at runtime. For instance, if you want to run different logic for your beta testers who are using Testflight, you'll need to use runtime substitution since the build that Testflight uses is the exact same build distributed to end users via the App Store. Therefore, you can't use compile-time substitution for this situation. The Testflight use case is just one example.

To substitute an implementation at runtime, you write an `if` statement around the dependency instantiation. You need to decide where to get a value that you can use to compare in the `if` statement. For example, you can use a remote-feature flag service, or you can key off local values, such as the app's version number.

Another neat trick is to use launch arguments to substitute dependencies at runtime. This is useful when you're developing an app in Xcode. This is neat because you don't need to recompile the app to change dependency implementations. Simply grab the launch arguments from `UserDefaults` and wrap your dependency instantiations with `if` statements that check launch argument values. You can use this trick during development or even during a continuous integration test.

OK — you've got the fundamentals. There are several approaches to putting Dependency Injection into practice. You'll start learning the most basic approach and gradually move onto more difficult, real-world approaches. These are the Dependency Injection approaches you'll learn in this chapter:

- **On-demand**: In this approach, you create dependency graphs when needed in a decentralized fashion. This approach is simple yet not very practical. You can use this approach to solidify your understanding of the fundamentals and to feel some of the pain addressed by more advanced approaches.

- **Factories**: Here, you begin to centralize initialization logic. This approach is also fairly simple and is designed to help you learn the fundamentals.

- **Single container**: This approach packages all the initialization logic together into one container. Since there's state involved, it's a bit more difficult to put into practice than the previous two approaches.

- **Container hierarchy**: One of the problems with centralizing all the initialization logic is you end up with one massive class. You can break a single container down into a hierarchy of containers. That's what this approach is all about.

Alright, time to get started by jumping into the on-demand approach.

On-demand approach

This approach is designed for learning DI and for using DI in trivial situations. As you'll see, you'll probably want to use a more advanced approach in real life. In the **on-demand approach**, whenever a consumer needs a new object-under-construction, the consumer creates or finds the dependencies needed by the object-under-construction *at the time the consumer instantiates the object-under-construction*. In other words, the consumer is responsible for gathering all dependencies and is responsible for providing those dependencies to the object-under-construction via the initializer, a stored-property or a method.

Initializing ephemeral dependencies

If dependencies don't need to live longer than the object-under-construction, and can therefore be owned by the object-under-construction, then the consumer can simply initialize the dependencies and provide those dependencies to the object-under-construction. These dependencies are **ephemeral dependencies** because they're created and destroyed alongside the object-under-construction.

In this case, because the consumer is initializing all the dependencies, the consumer needs to know which concrete implementation to use when initializing a dependency. As long as *the object-under-construction* uses protocol types for its dependencies, the object-under-construction won't know what concrete implementation the consumer used to create the dependencies, and that's what you want.

Finding long-lived dependencies

If a dependency needs to live longer than the object-under-construction, then the consumer needs to find a reference to the dependency. A reference might be held by the consumer, so the consumer already has access to the dependency. Or a parent of the consumer might be holding on to a reference.

Substituting dependency implementations

That takes care of providing dependencies. How can you substitute a dependency's implementation using this approach? Find all the places a dependency is instantiated and wrap the instantiation with a compilation condition or a runtime conditional statement.

These are the mechanics to the on-demand approach. What are the pros and cons?

Pros of the on-demand approach

- This approach is relatively easy to explain and to understand.

- Your code is testable because you can substitute nondeterministic side effect dependencies with deterministic fake implementations.

- You can defer decisions. For example, you can use an in-memory data store implementation while you decide on a database technology. Changing from the in-memory implementation to the database implementation is easy because you can find all the in-memory instantiations and replace them with the database instantiations. This can be a bit tedious, so this is also a con that's addressed in more advanced approaches.

- Your team can work on the same feature at the same time because one developer can build an object-under-construction while another builds the dependencies. The developer building the object-under-construction can use fake implementations of the dependencies while the other developer builds the real implementations of the dependencies.

Cons of the on-demand approach

- Dependency instantiations are decentralized. The same initialization logic can be duplicated many times.

- Consumers need to know how to build the entire dependency graph for an object-under-construction. Dependencies can also have dependencies and so on. The consumer might have to instantiate a lot of dependencies. This is not ideal because multiple consumers using the same object-under-construction class will have to duplicate the dependency graph instantiation logic.

These cons can be addressed by taking a **factories approach**. You'll learn this approach next.

Factories approach

Instantiating dependencies on-demand is a decentralized approach that doesn't scale well. That's because you'll end up writing a lot of duplicate dependency instantiation logic as your dependency graph gets larger and more complex. The factories approach is all about *centralizing* dependency instantiation.

This approach works for ephemeral dependencies, i.e., dependencies that can be instantiated at the same time as the object-under-construction. This approach does not address managing long-lived dependencies such as singletons.

You'll learn how to manage long-lived dependencies in the upcoming containers-approach section.

To take the factories approach, you create a **factories class**. What does a factories class look like?

Factories class

A factories class is made up of a bunch of factory methods. Some of the methods create *dependencies* and some of the methods create *objects-under-construction*. Also, a factories class has no state, i.e., the class should not have any stored properties.

One goal of creating a factories class is to make it possible for consumers to create objects-under-construction without having to know how to build dependency graphs required to instantiate objects-under-construction. This makes it super easy for any part of your code to get a hold of any object needed regardless of how much the object in question is broken down into smaller objects.

Next, you'll learn how to design the different kinds of factory methods that make up a factories class.

Dependency factory methods

The responsibility of a **dependency factory method** is to know how to create a new dependency instance.

Creating and getting transitive dependencies

Since dependencies themselves can have *their own* dependencies, these factory methods need to get transitive dependencies before instantiating a dependency. Transitive dependencies might be ephemeral or long-lived.

To create an **ephemeral transitive dependency**, a dependency factory method can simply call another dependency factory included in the factories class.

To get a reference to a **long-lived transitive dependency**, a dependency factory method should include a parameter for the transitive dependency. By adding parameters, long-lived transitive dependencies can be provided to the dependency factory method.

Resolving protocol dependencies

Dependency factory methods typically have a protocol return type to enable substitutability. When this is true, dependency factory methods encapsulate the mapping between protocol and concrete types.

This is typically called **resolution** because a dependency factory method is *resolving* which implementation to create for a particular protocol dependency. In other words, these methods know which concrete initializer to use.

To illustrate, say you have a `UserProfileDataStore` protocol. Say this protocol is a dependency. The factories class encapsulates the logic that knows to use a `DatabaseUserProfileDataStore` for objects-under-construction that need a `UserProfileDataStore`. You would place this logic into a single factory method inside the factories class.

This centralizes the dependency resolution so that you only have once place in your codebase that knows how to resolve the `UserProfileDataStore` dependency. This is awesome because you can change what kind of data store your *entire app* uses by changing one line of code.

Object-under-construction factory methods

The responsibility of an **object-under-construction factory method** is to create the dependency graph needed to instantiate an object-under-construction. Object-under-construction factory methods look just like dependency factory methods. The only difference is object-under-construction factory methods are called from the outside of a factories class, whereas dependency factory methods are called within a factories class.

Getting runtime values

Sometimes, objects-under-construction, and even dependencies, need values that can only be determined at runtime. For example, a REST client might need a user ID to function. These runtime values are typically called **runtime factory arguments**. As the name suggests, you handle this situation by adding a parameter, for each runtime value, to the object-under-construction's or dependency's factory method. At runtime, the factory method caller will need to provide the required values as arguments.

Substituting dependency implementations

To enable substitution in a factories class, use the same technique as you saw in the on-demand approach, i.e., wrap dependency resolutions with a conditional statement. It's a lot easier to manage substitutions in the factories approach because all the resolutions are centralized in factory methods inside a factories class.

This means you don't have to duplicate conditional statements inside every consumer; you write the conditional statement once, and only once, for each dependency resolution. This is a big win.

Injecting factories

What if the object-under-construction needs to create multiple instances of a dependency? What if the object-under-construction is a view controller that needs to create a dependency every time a user presses a button or types a character into a text field?

Factory methods return a single instance of a dependency — so, Houston, we have a problem. The trick is to find a way to give the object-under-construction the power to invoke a factory method *multiple times*, whenever the object-under-construction needs to create a new dependency instance.

Your first instinct might be to simply create an instance of the factories class within the object-under-construction.

The object-under-construction would then have access to every single factory method. While this is a very simple approach, the problem is that the object-under-construction becomes harder to unit test. That's because all dependencies are no longer injected from the outside. With this approach, you'd need to work with the factories class in order to substitute real implementations with fake implementations.

The goal is to be able to unit test an object-under-construction without needing the factories class at all. Therefore, it's important to give objects-under-construction the ability to create multiple instances of dependencies from the outside.

You can give this power to objects-under-construction from the outside using one of two Swift features: closures or protocols.

Using closures

One option is to add a factory closure stored-property to the object-under-construction. Here are the steps:

- Declare a stored-property in the object-under-construction with a signature such as: `let makeUseCase: () -> UseCase`.

- Add an initializer parameter to the object-under-construction with the same closure type.

- Go to the factories class and find the factory method that creates the object-under-construction.

- Use initializer injection, in the object-under-construction factory method, to inject a closure that creates a new dependency. To do this, open a closure in the object-under-construction's initializer call. Inside the closure, call the dependency factory method for the dependency in question and return the new instance. The closure captures the factories class instance so the object-under-construction essentially holds on to the factories object without knowing.

- Now, the object-under-construction can easily create a new instance of a dependency by invoking the factory closure, whenever.

This is *so* cool because the object-under-construction can create as many instances without needing to know all the transitive dependencies behind the dependency created in the factory closure. This means you can change the entire dependency structure without having to change a single line of code in the object-under-construction.

That's one option; the other option is to declare a factory protocol.

Using protocols

The other option is to declare a factory protocol so the object-under-construction can delegate the creation of a dependency to the factories class. Here are the steps:

- Declare a new factory protocol that contains a single method for the dependency that the object-under-construction needs to create.

- The factories class will already conform to this protocol because the dependency factory method in the protocol should match the implemented factory method in the factories class. Simply declare conformance in the factories class.

- Add a stored-property and initializer parameter of the factory protocol type to the object-under-construction. This allows you to inject the factories object into the object-under-construction; *however*, the object-under-construction will only see the single factory method defined in the protocol. The object-under-construction does not know it is injected with the factories object because the protocol restricts the object-under-construction's view.

- Go into the object-under-construction's factory method in the factories class and update the initialization line to inject `self`. `self` is the factories object which conforms to the new factory protocol you declared.

The object-under-construction now has the power to create new dependency instances whenever, while not having access to all the factories in the factories class. You get the same benefits with this approach as the closure approach. This decision comes down to style preference.

That's all there is to injecting factories. It's time to take a quick look at when and how to create instances of the factories class.

Creating a factories object

Since a factories class is stateless, you can create an instance of a factories class at any time. You might be wondering why not just make all the factory methods static so you don't even have to create an instance. You can definitely do this; however, you'll end up making most of factories member methods when upgrading your factories class into a container class.

You'll learn about this next, after checking out the pros and cons to this factories approach.

Pros of the factories approach

- Ephemeral dependencies are *created* in a central place. This gives you a lot of power to switch out entire subsystems by changing a couple of lines of code.

- Substituting a large amount of dependencies during a functional UI test is much easier because all your dependencies are initialized in one class. Developers typically want to fake out the entire networking and persistence stack during UI tests because developers want deterministic tests so their builds don't constantly break with false positives.

- Consumers are more resilient to change because they no longer need to know how to build dependency graphs. That's one less responsibility for all consumers. This helps your team work in parallel because code is more loosely coupled.

- Code is generally easier to read because all of the initialization boilerplate is moved out of the classes that do interesting work.

Cons of the factories approach

- In a large app, a single factories class can become extremely large. You can break up large factories classes into multiple classes.

- This approach only works for ephemeral objects. Longer-lived objects need to be held somewhere. Ideally, all dependencies should be centrally managed regardless of lifespan. You'll learn how to do this in the next section.

In practice, a factories class is not enough. You'll most likely need to convert the factories class into a container class.

This factories section is here in order to help you take small steps because there's so much to learn about DI.

When refactoring a codebase to use DI, feel free to take this factories approach to get a feel for the pattern. As you'll see in the next section, you can easily update your code to go from this factories approach to the container approach.

Single-container approach

A **container** is like a factories class that can hold onto long-lived dependencies. A container is a stateful version of a factories class.

What are some examples of long-lived dependencies? A data store is a perfect example. A data store is a container for data that is needed to render screens. Since this data can probably change, you want a single copy of this data. Therefore, you don't want to create a new data store instance every time an object needs a data store. You probably want a single instance to live as long as the app's process, i.e., you need a singleton. To keep a data store instance alive, you need an object to hold onto this singleton so that ARC doesn't de-allocate the data store.

Keep reading to see how to design a container class.

Container class

A container class looks just like a factories class except with stored properties that hold onto long-lived dependencies. You can either initialize constant stored properties during the container's initialization or you can create the properties lazily if the properties use a lot of resources. However, lazy properties have to be variables so constant properties are better by default.

Having long-lived dependencies co-located with factories changes how factories access these long-lived dependencies. You'll soon explore this more.

Dependency factory methods

Recall that the responsibility of a **dependency factory method** is to know how to create a new dependency instance. Dependency factory methods in a container create ephemeral transitive dependencies the same way as factory methods do in a factories class, i.e., by calling another dependency factory.

How dependency factory methods get ahold of long-lived dependencies in a container, though, is different than in a factories class.

To get a reference to a long-lived transitive dependency, a dependency factory method gets the dependency from a stored property. This is nice because it removes the need to add parameters to factory methods.

All factory methods can be invoked without any inputs. The fact that these methods can have zero parameters is super powerful. You take a dependency with a complex initializer such as `init(remoteAPI: UserRemoteAPI, dataStore: UserDataStore)` and reduce it down to a factory method, such as `makeProfileViewModel()`.

The above is true except for runtime value parameters. Since runtime values are provided outside of the container, and because runtime values are not long-lived dependencies, factory methods in a container are still much easier to invoke. As you'll see later, this comes in handy when injecting factories.

Object-under-construction factory methods

Factory methods that create objects-under-construction can also use the stored properties to inject long-lived dependencies into objects-under-construction.

Just like dependency factory methods from above, these factory methods also don't need to have parameters for long-lived dependencies. This is a *huge* benefit for consumers because consumers don't have to manage anything in order to create objects-under-construction. They simply invoke the empty argument factory method or provide runtime values.

Consumers can now create objects-under-construction without having to know anything about the dependency graphs behind these objects. This gives your code flexibility because one developer can change the dependency graph without affecting the developer building the code around the consumer.

That takes care of linking a container's stored properties to factory method implementations. Next, you'll see how to substitute implementations of the long-lived dependencies held by stored properties.

Substituting long-lived dependency implementations

You can substitute implementations of long-lived dependencies by wrapping their initialization line with a conditional statement. This is possible as long as the long-lived stored properties use a protocol type. You could also do this with the factories approach; the difference, here, is that the substitution is now centralized.

Easy peasy. At this point, you probably want to know when and how to create a container.

Creating and holding a container

Unlike factories, you should only ever create one instance of a container. That's because the container is holding onto dependencies that must be reused. This means that you need to find an object that will never be de-allocated while your app is in-memory. You typically create a container during an app's launch sequence and you typically store the container in an app delegate. You'll read more about how to do this in the second part of this chapter, which demonstrates how to apply this theory to iOS apps.

Going from learning how to build a factories class to learning how to build a single container is not a huge leap. However, the theory behind containers gets interesting when you need to break a single container into a container hierarchy. You'll learn about this next, after going through the pros and cons of the single-container approach.

Pros of the single-container approach

- A container can manage an app's entire dependency graph. This removes the need for other code to know how to build object graphs.

- Containers manage singletons; therefore, you won't have singleton references floating in global space. Singletons can now be managed centrally by a container.

- You can change an object's dependency graph without having to change code outside the container class.

Cons of the single-container approach

- Putting all the long-lived dependencies and all the factory methods needed by an app into a single container class can result in a massive container class. This is the most common issue when using DI. The good news is that you can break this massive container up into smaller containers.

Designing container hierarchies

So far, you've read about ephemeral objects that don't need to be reused and long-lived objects that stay alive throughout the app's lifetime. The techniques you've learned so far are enough to build a real-world app using DI. Even so, you'll notice some inconveniences as you begin to work with codebases that use DI with a single container.

Reviewing issues with a single container

The first thing you'll notice is a growing container class — as you add more features to your app, you'll need more and more dependencies. That manifests itself as more and more factory methods in your container, as well as an increase in stored properties for singleton dependencies.

You'll also notice a lot of optional conditional unwrapping. Most apps have many dependencies that need to know about the currently signed-in user to do things like authenticate HTTP requests.

If all the reusable dependencies live as long as an app lives, the container logic will need to handle optional cases because the user can be signed out while the app is running.

Based on the container design thus far, there's nothing stopping any consumer from asking the container for dependencies that require the user to be signed in.

Ideally, consumers would only have access to these reusable dependencies when a user is signed in. This is just one of many examples of optional case handling that sneaks into your singe-dependency container.

In this section, you'll learn how to use advanced DI techniques address these undesirable qualities.

Object scopes

The trick to solving these issues is to design object **scopes**. To do this, think about at what point in time dependencies should be created and destroyed. Every object has a lifetime. You want to explicitly design when objects come and go. For example, objects in a user scope are created when a user signs in and are destroyed when a user signs out. Objects in a view controller scope are created when the view controller loads and are destroyed when the view controller is de-allocated.

Here are the typical scopes you find in most apps:

- **App scope**: Traditional singletons fall under this scope. Objects in the app scope are created when the app launches and are destroyed when the app is killed. Typical dependencies you find in this scope include authentication stores, analytics trackers, logging systems, etc.

- **User scope**: User scope objects are created when a user signs in, and they're destroyed when a user signs out. Some apps allow users to sign in to multiple accounts. In this case, the app could have multiple user scopes alive at the same time. Most dependencies, such as remote API's and data stores, are usually found in this scope. This scope also typically contains more specific versions of dependencies found in the app scope. For instance, the app scope could have an anonymous analytics tracker while a user scope could have a user specific analytics tracker.

Scopes are very powerful because they help convert a bunch of mutable state into immutable state. For that reason, you can go even further with scopes by designing shorter lived scopes. Here are a couple of examples.

- **Feature scope**: Objects in a feature scope are created when the user navigates to a feature and are destroyed when the user navigates away. Feature scopes are handy when a feature needs to share data amongst many objects that make up the feature.

For example, in Koober, the pick-me-up feature needs to know the user's current location. The user's current location is fetched once and then is not retrieved again; the current location is immutable from the pick-me-up feature's point of view.

Many different view controllers and objects with business logic need to utilize the current location value in order to function.

Imagine having to pass this value around from object to object. By creating a feature scope, the current location can be injected into all of these objects.

The objects don't need to worry about how to get the value. As far as the objects in the feature are concerned, the location value is immutable even though the user can still ask for a new ride, and a new current location will be fetched. This works because, every time a user starts a new ride, an entirely new object graph is created with the current static location value.

- **Interaction scope**: Objects in an interaction scope are created when a gesture is recognized and are destroyed when the gesture ends. This is handy when you are building a complex user interaction. This is an example of a very short-lived scope.

Once you've designed the scopes that you need, and once you've identified which dependencies should live in which scopes, the next step is to break up the single container into a container hierarchy.

Container hierarchy

A container manages the lifetime of the dependencies it holds. Because of this, each scope maps to a container. A user scope would have a user-scoped container. The user-scoped container is created when the user signs in and so forth. This is how the dependencies that are in the user scope are all created and destroyed at the same time, because the scoped container owns these objects.

For every scope you design, you create a container class. When you do this, you'll notice that scoped containers will want to have access to factory methods and stored properties from other containers. To do this, you build a **container hierarchy**.

Designing a container hierarchy

There's one simple rule to building container hierarchies: A child container can ask for dependencies from its parent container including the parent's parents and so on, all the way to the root container. A parent container cannot ask for a dependency from a child container.

The app scoped container is always the root container. If you think about how the hierarchy maps to length of object lifetimes, the rule makes a lot of sense. Parent containers live longer than child containers. If the parent was allowed to ask for a dependency from a child container, the child container might no longer be alive. So that's the rationale for the rule.

Are you ready for some meta?

The container hierarchy is an object graph itself; therefore, you can use initializer injection to provide child containers with parent containers.

As with all DI conventions, this sounds more complicated than it really is. The child container's initializer needs to have a parameter for the parent container. The child container can then hold a reference to the parent container in a stored-property. This gives the child access to all the factory methods and stored properties in the parent container.

As an example, say you have a `UserProfileViewModel`. This view model needs a `Logger` in order to log events. `Logger` needs to live as long as the app is alive because you want to be able to log messages regardless of whether or not a user is signed in. So the logger goes into an `AppDependencyContainer`.

The `UserProfileViewModel`, however, is specific to a signed-in user, so this object is scoped to the signed-in user. The view model goes into a `UserDependencyContainer`. The view model needs the logger but the logger lives in a different container.

To solve this, you add a `AppDependencyContainer` parameter to `UserDependencyContainer`'s initializer. That way, `UserDependencyContainer`, the child container, can ask `AppDependencyContainer`, the parent container, for a logger when initializing a new `UserProfileViewModel`.

Capturing data

Breaking up a container into a container hierarchy takes care of the first inconvenience. What about the second inconvenience — the one about handling optionals?

Besides managing the lifetime of dependencies, a container can also capture data model values. This is helpful if the data model value is immutable for the lifetime of the container. Capturing data in a container is a way to convert mutable values into immutable values. This makes the code inside a container more deterministic because the logic does not have to consider a change in the captured value.

To illustrate, say you have an app-scoped container named `AppContainer`. `AppContainer` has a `UserSessionDataStore` that contains a user session only if a user is signed in. Say you have a user-scoped container named `UserContainer`. `UserContainer` is initialized with an `AppContainer` *and* the currently signed-in user session object — not the data store, but the actual session.

This is important because a user container *cannot exist* without a user session. This takes away the optional case handling related to signed-in user.

Moving forward with the example, inside `UserContainer`, say you have a factory method for creating a `UserProfileRemoteAPI`. The remote API needs the user session in order to function. That's easy — the remote API factory method can access the user session stored-property.

Remember the factory and the stored-property are both inside the same `UserContainer` class. The days of having to check if there's a signed-in user all over a codebase are gone!

Pros of the container hierarchy

- Scoping allows you to design dependencies that don't have to be singletons.
- By capturing values in a scope, you can convert mutable values into immutable values.
- Container classes are shorter when you divide container classes into scoped container classes.

Cons of the container hierarchy

- Container hierarchies are more complex than a single-container solution. Developers that join your team might encounter a learning curve.
- Even when containers are broken up into scoped containers, complex apps might still end up with really long container classes.

By this point, you've learned *a lot* about DI, and you're on your way to mastering object-oriented design. This is all the theory you'll need to understand how Koober, the example app, uses DI. In this book, you'll encounter different versions of Koober that are built using different architectures. DI is such a universal approach that every version of Koober you'll see uses the same DI pattern as DI can support all kinds of different architectures.

Most of the theory you've read is applicable to iOS without any special considerations. However, there are a couple of iOS-specific decisions that you'll need make when using DI in your iOS codebases. It's time to go from theory to practice.

Applying DI theory to iOS apps

In this section, you'll see how the theory you just learned is applied in Koober so that you can see what DI looks like in a real-world app. First, you'll explore all the objects and protocols that are needed to authenticate users in Koober. Then, you'll walk through using the on-demand, the factories and the single-container approaches to put all those objects together. Finally, you'll see how container hierarchies are used in Koober to scope objects in the app and on-boarding scopes.

Object graphs and iOS apps

Because Cocoa Touch is an object-oriented SDK, every iOS app consists of an object graph at runtime. An instance of `UIApplication` is the root of an app's object graph. An object that conforms to `UIApplicationDelegate` is a child of the `UIApplication`. Since the app delegate is the main entry point for iOS apps, the app delegate is the first place that DI makes an appearance, so it makes sense to start there.

One of the first objects you typically instantiate is a root view controller. Koober's root view controller is the first object-under-construction example that you'll explore. The root view controller is the root of the object graph that you design when building iOS apps. The ultimate goal is to learn how to use DI containers to construct this object graph. In the rest of this chapter, you'll work towards this goal.

To set the stage, the following section walks you through the object graph required to authenticate users in Koober.

Learning Koober's authentication object graph

In a typical iOS app, developers design many different objects that need to coordinate with each other in order to check whether a user is signed in and in order to correctly route the user to the initial screen. Here are the objects and protocols Koober uses to authenticate users:

UserSessionRepository's dependency graph

Here are all the protocols and objects needed to create a `KooberUserSessionRepository`:

- **AuthRemoteAPI**: The `AuthRemoteAPI` protocol represents the networking layer of Koober's user authentication system. Implementations of this protocol are responsible for talking to Koober's cloud services to sign in existing users and sign up new users. In exchange for a successful authentication attempt, Koober Cloud returns a token that should be used for making authenticated HTTP requests.

  > The example code uses `FakeAuthRemoteAPI` so you don't need to have a network connection or a local server to use Koober. All implementations of `AuthRemoteAPI` do not depend on any other objects.

- **UserSessionCoding**: The object that implements this `UserSessionCoding` protocol is responsible for encoding a `UserSession` object into `Data` and for decoding `Data` into a `UserSession` object. Koober's `KeychainUserSessionDataStore` uses this for storing a `UserSession` as `Data` in the keychain.

- **UserSessionDataStore**: Implementations of `UserSessionDataStore` are responsible for storing a user session for the signed-in user. Koober includes many different implementations of this protocol.

  For example, you can use `FileUserSessionDataStore` during development to be able to sign out the current user by deleting the app in the simulator. `KeychainUserSessionDataStore` is designed to be used in an app store build so that Koober can store real user credentials in the Keychain. `KeychainUserSessionDataStore` depends on a user session coder that conforms to `UserSessionCoding`.

- **UserSessionRepository**: This repository is a create, read, update and delete protocol for managing user sessions. It's used to determine whether or not a user is signed in when Koober launches, it's used to sign in an existing user and it's used to sign up a new user. KooberUserSessionRepository implements this protocol and is the default implementation used in Koober. KooberUserSessionRepository is stateful, this object must be a long-lived dependency that lives as long as the app.

This is KooberUserSessionRepository's dependency graph:

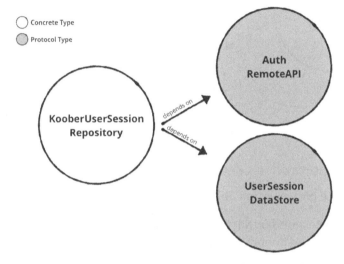

Here's what KooberUserSessionRepository's dependency graph looks like once UserSessionDataStore is resolved:

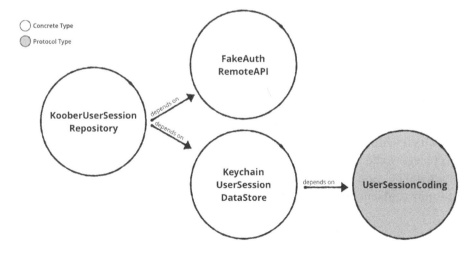

Finally, this is what KooberUserSessionRepository's fully materialized dependency graph looks like:

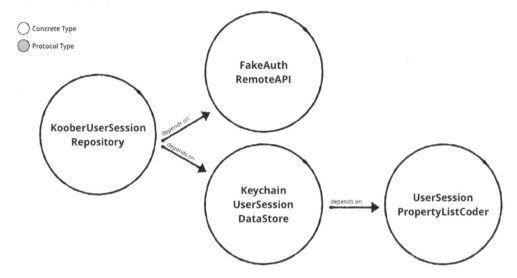

LaunchViewController's dependency graph

These are all the protocols and objects needed to create a LaunchViewController:

- **NotSignedInResponder**: NotSignedInResponder is a user authentication protocol. Objects in Koober call into this protocol when they determine that a user is not signed in.

This can happen during launch or when a user signs out. The object that implements this protocol is responsible for navigating the user to the OnboardingViewController. MainViewModel implements this protocol.

- **SignedInResponder**: SignedInResponder is also a user authentication protocol. This protocol is used when objects in Koober determine that a user is signed in.

This can occur on launch or after a user successfully signs in or signs up. MainViewModel implements this protocol.

- **LaunchViewModel**: This view model holds UI state for a LaunchViewController. This object would normally be a long-lived dependency but, in Koober, it is ephemeral because Koober only ever creates one LaunchViewController because apps only cold launch one time in a process lifetime.

- **LaunchViewController**: When Koober launches for the first time, Koober needs to start up all the subsystems and needs to determine if a user is signed in. While Koober is launching, LaunchViewController begins looking for a signed-in user and presents a splash screen. LaunchViewController depends on a LaunchViewModel in order to begin searching for a signed-in user.

This is LaunchViewController's dependency graph:

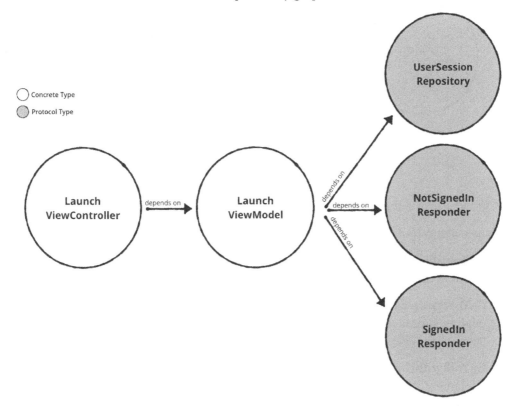

Here's what `LaunchViewController`'s fully materialized dependency graph looks like:

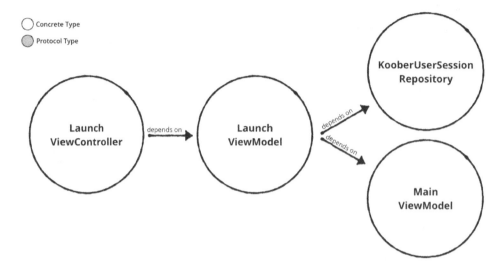

OnboardingViewController's dependency graph

`OnboardingViewController` depends on the following protocols and objects:

- **OnboardingViewModel**: This holds UI state for an `OnboardingViewController`. This object is a long-lived dependency that lives while the user is signed out.

- **GoToSignUpNavigator**: `GoToSignUpNavigator` is a UI navigation protocol. The implementor is responsible for taking the user to the sign-up screen. `OnboardingViewModel` implements this protocol.

- **GoToSignInNavigator**: `GoToSignInNavigator` is a UI navigation protocol. The implementor is responsible for taking the user to the sign-in screen. `OnboardingViewModel` implements this protocol.

- **WelcomeViewModel**: This view model holds UI state for a `WelcomeViewController`.

- **WelcomeViewController**: This view controller renders the welcome screen where a user can either go to the sign-up screen or the sign-in screen.

- **SignInViewModel**: This holds UI state for a `SignInViewController`.

- **SignInViewController**: Users sign in to Koober using this view controller.

- **SignUpViewModel**: This view model holds UI state for a `SignUpViewController`.

- **SignUpViewController**: Users create a new Koober account using this view controller.

- **OnboardingViewController**: If a user is not signed in, Koober's `MainViewController` presents an `OnboardingViewController`.

  `OnboardingViewController` is a container view controller that is responsible for managing the navigation between the welcome screen and the sign-in and sign-up screens. This controller should only be alive as long as a user is not signed in.

This is `OnboardingViewController`'s dependency graph:

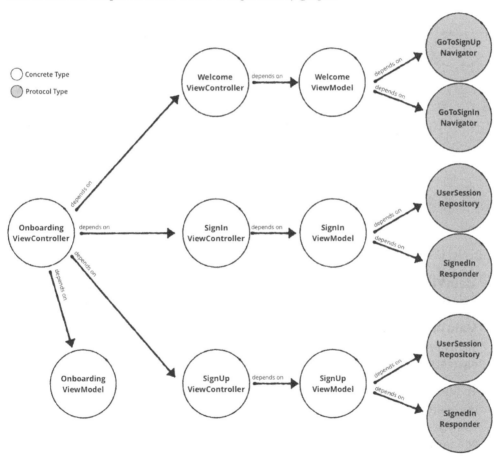

Here's what `OnboardingViewController`'s fully materialized dependency graph looks like:

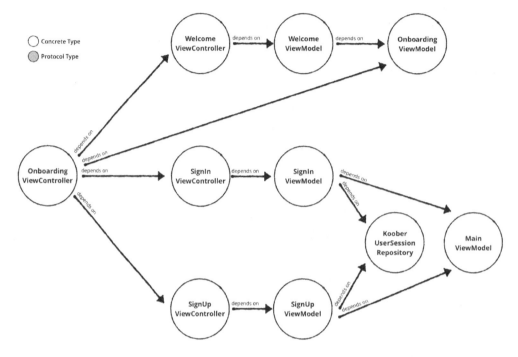

MainViewController's dependency graph

Finally, here are the protocols and objects `MainViewController` depends on:

- **MainViewModel**: The `MainViewModel` holds UI state for a `MainViewController`. This object is stateful; therefore, it needs to be a long lived dependency.

- **MainViewController**: `MainViewController` is Koober's root view controller. `MainViewController` is a container view controller that manages top-level navigation.

  To illustrate, `MainViewController` presents and dismisses the launch screen, the on-boarding screens and the signed-in screens. `MainViewController` depends on view controller factory methods in order to create `LaunchViewControllers`, `OnboardingViewControllers` and `SignedInViewControllers`.

Here's what `MainViewController`'s fully materialized dependency graph looks like:

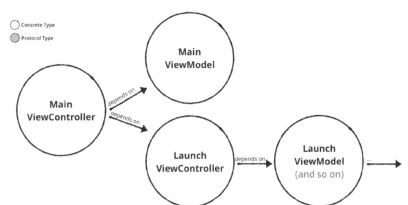

Now that you're familiar with Koober's top-level object graph, you'll see how to use the on-demand approach to build this graph.

Applying the on-demand approach

`MainViewController` is Koober's root view controller's class. `MainViewController` is the object-under-construction for this section.

Tracing MainViewController's dependencies

In order to instantiate the `MainViewController`, you'll first need to instantiate `MainViewController`'s dependencies. Here's `MainViewController`'s initializer's method signature. The real initializer in Koober is a bit more complex; this is a simplified version to demonstrate the on-demand DI approach:

```
public init(viewModel: MainViewModel,
            launchViewController: LaunchViewController)
```

`MainViewController` has two dependencies, a `MainViewModel` and a `LaunchViewController`. Creating a `MainViewModel` is easy:

```
let mainViewModel = MainViewModel()
```

However, creating a `LaunchViewController` is more complicated because `LaunchViewController` has its own dependency graph. The objects of this graph are considered `MainViewController`'s transitive dependencies.

Here's `LaunchViewController`'s initializer's method signature.

```
public init(viewModel: LaunchViewModel)
```

To create a `LaunchViewController` you need to first create a `LaunchViewModel` using `LaunchViewModel`'s initializer:

```
public init(userSessionRepository: UserSessionRepository,
            notSignedInResponder: NotSignedInResponder,
            signedInResponder: SignedInResponder)
```

`LaunchViewModel` has three dependencies, a `UserSessionRepository`, a `NotSignedInResponder` and a `SignedInResponder`.

As you can see, decomposing large objects into single-responsibility objects results in deep object graphs. For this reason, you'll find the on-demand approach is not practical for real-world apps that have large and deep object graphs.

The on-demand approach is good for teaching DI and for using Dependency Injection in small apps. Nevertheless, it's worth taking a look at how to build `MainViewController`'s dependency graph using the on-demand approach as a stepping stone to learning the factories approach.

Creating a shared UserSessionRepository

The first step is to look at how to make the `UserSessionRepository`. Remember the main objective is to create a `MainViewController`. Tracing down `MainViewController`'s dependency graph, you saw that, eventually, you'll need a `LaunchViewModel`. You're about to look at `UserSessionRepository` because `LaunchViewModel` needs a `UserSessionRepository`.

`UserSessionRepository` is a protocol, so you need to resolve to an implementation. Koober uses a default implementation named `KooberUserSessionRepository`. `KooberUserSessionRepository` is stateful; therefore, a new instance should not be instantiated when another object needs this dependency. You need to create this object once and hold it so that all objects-under-construction can use the same `KooberUserSessionRepository` instance.

A free global constant is a good place to hold this object since it needs to live as long as the app is running. Here's how to set this up:

```
// This code is global, it's not in any type.
public let GlobalUserSessionRepository:
  UserSessionRepository = {

  let userSessionCoder =
    UserSessionPropertyListCoder()

  let userSessionDataStore =
    KeychainUserSessionDataStore(
      userSessionCoder: userSessionCoder)

  let authRemoteAPI =
    FakeAuthRemoteAPI()

  return KooberUserSessionRepository(
    dataStore: userSessionDataStore,
    remoteAPI: authRemoteAPI)
}()
```

Even though `KooberUserSessionRepository` has a relatively simple dependency graph, a lot of code is required to build its dependency graph.

If `KooberUserSessionRepository` *could* be instantiated multiple times, you would have to duplicate all this code every time you needed a new `KooberUserSessionRepository` when using the on-demand approach. This duplication is the main downside to the on-demand approach and is the reason this approach is not practical in real life.

Substituting the UserSessionDataStore

Say you want to avoid using the keychain when developing Koober's sign-in and sign-up screens. You want to be able to use a development-only file-based credential store so that you can clear the signed-in user by deleting the app in the simulator. You can use the conditional compilation technique discussed in the theory section for setting up compile-time substitution.

Here's an example demonstrating how to do this by updating the previous code example with conditional compilation:

```
// This code is global, it's not in any type.
public let GlobalUserSessionRepository:
  UserSessionRepository = {

  #if USER_SESSION_DATASTORE_FILEBASED
```

```
    let userSessionDataStore =
      FileUserSessionDataStore()

  #else
  let userSessionCoder =
    UserSessionPropertyListCoder()

  let userSessionDataStore =
    KeychainUserSessionDataStore(
      userSessionCoder: userSessionCoder)
  #endif

  let authRemoteAPI =
    FakeAuthRemoteAPI()

  return KooberUserSessionRepository(
    dataStore: userSessionDataStore,
    remoteAPI: authRemoteAPI)
}()
```

This example switches which `UserSessionDataStore` is initialized based on the `USER_SESSION_DATASTORE_FILEBASED` identifier. If the current scheme's **active compilation conditions** build setting includes this identifier, the compiler will compile the code that initializes a `FileUserSessionDataStore`. Otherwise, the code that initializes a `KeychainUserSessionDataStore` is compiled.

Same as before, if you *could* create more than one `UserSessionDataStore`, you would have to duplicate the conditional compilation if you want to use the same `UserSessionDataStore` implementation across your codebase. This is inconvenient and undesirable. Substitution is much more powerful when used alongside the factories and containers approach.

That wraps up creating the `UserSessionDataStore`. The example will use this code to create a `MainViewController` in the next section.

Creating a MainViewController

`UserSessionRepository` is the only shared instance needed to ultimately create a `MainViewController`.

Now that you've seen how to set up a shared instance dependency, it's time to go into `application(_:didFinishLaunchingWithOptions:)` to see how the `MainViewController` is created and installed:

```
func application(
  _ application: UIApplication,
  didFinishLaunchingWithOptions launchOptions:
    [UIApplication.LaunchOptionsKey: Any]?) -> Bool {

  let mainViewModel = MainViewModel()

  let launchViewModel =
    LaunchViewModel(
      userSessionRepository: GlobalUserSessionRepository,
      notSignedInResponder: mainViewModel,
      signedInResponder: mainViewModel)

  let launchViewController =
    LaunchViewController(viewModel: launchViewModel)

  let mainViewController =
    MainViewController(
      viewModel: mainViewModel,
      launchViewController: launchViewController)

  window.frame = UIScreen.main.bounds
  window.makeKeyAndVisible()
  window.rootViewController = mainViewController

  return true
}
```

Notice how the `GlobalUserSessionRepository` shared instance is used to create a `LaunchViewModel`. All the other dependencies in this example are created inside `application(_:didFinishLaunchingWithOptions:)`. Voila — the `MainViewController` is finally instantiated towards the end before being installed as the root view controller.

So far, you've seen how to use the on-demand approach to build the root view controller's object graph. The app delegate isn't the only place an app needs to create new objects. Next, you'll visit the `MainViewController`'s implementation to see how the on-demand approach works when a parent view controller needs to create a new instance of a child view controller.

Creating an OnboardingViewController on-demand

The main challenge when using the on-demand approach outside the app delegate is accessing shared instance dependencies. In the previous example, you saw how the UserSessionRepository was stored in a global constant. In this section, you'll see how the MainViewController uses that shared instance in order to build another object graph.

Using global references in this way is not ideal. Later in this chapter, you'll see how to use a container instead of global references to store shared instances.

The following example shows how MainViewController creates an OnboardingViewController. During a cold start, if the LaunchViewController has determined a user is not signed in, the MainViewController will instantiate an OnboardingViewController.

Because OnboardingViewController depends on a graph of objects, MainViewController needs to create all of OnboardingViewController's dependencies.

The following method, is from MainViewController's implementation and shows how the OnboardingViewController is created:

```
public func presentOnboarding() {

  let onboardingViewModel = OnboardingViewModel()

  let welcomeViewModel =
    WelcomeViewModel(goToSignUpNavigator: onboardingViewModel,
                     goToSignInNavigator: onboardingViewModel)

  let welcomeViewController =
    WelcomeViewController(viewModel: welcomeViewModel)

  let signInViewModel =
    SignInViewModel(
      userSessionRepository: GlobalUserSessionRepository,
      signedInResponder: self.viewModel)

  let signInViewController =
    SignInViewController(viewModel: signInViewModel)

  let signUpViewModel =
    SignUpViewModel(
      userSessionRepository: GlobalUserSessionRepository,
      signedInResponder: self.viewModel)
```

```
    let signUpViewController =
      SignUpViewController(viewModel: signUpViewModel)

    let onboardingViewController =
      OnboardingViewController(
        viewModel: onboardingViewModel,
        welcomeViewController: welcomeViewController,
        signInViewController: signInViewController,
        signUpViewController: signUpViewController)

    onboardingViewController.modalPresentationStyle = .fullScreen
    present(onboardingViewController, animated: true) { ... }
    self.onboardingViewController = onboardingViewController
  }
```

The method above is fairly self explanatory. It creates and presents an `OnboardingViewController`. By the way, that's one long method! Herein lies the problem with the on-demand approach. If you use the on-demand approach in a complex app, you'll find long methods like this all over the place. This *is* better than nothing because your objects are now testable. However, as you saw in the theory section, there's a better way.

Applying the factories approach

You've seen how to apply the on-demand approach to Koober. You saw how object graphs are assembled all over the place. Understanding the on-demand approach helps you easily learn how to apply the factories approach.

In this section, you'll learn how to create the same objects from the last section using a factories class named `KooberObjectFactories`.

You'll begin by looking at the methods needed to create a `UserSessionRepository`. Then, you'll see how `KooberObjectFactories` is used to create a shared global `UserSessionRepository`. From there, you'll walk through the methods needed to create a `MainViewController`.

You'll see how to give `MainViewController` the power to create `OnboardingViewControllers` by injecting a factory closure. You'll wrap up this example by learning how `KooberObjectFactories` is used within Koober's app delegate and by taking a look at how `MainViewController` invokes the factory closure when it needs to create a new `OnboardingViewController`.

Creating a shared UserSessionRepository

The following code example demonstrates how to build a simple factories class that can create a `UserSessionRepository` and all the objects in `UserSessionRepository`'s dependency graph:

```swift
class KooberObjectFactories {

  // Factories needed to create a UserSessionRepository.

  func makeUserSessionRepository() -> UserSessionRepository {
    let dataStore = makeUserSessionDataStore()
    let remoteAPI = makeAuthRemoteAPI()
    return KooberUserSessionRepository(dataStore: dataStore,
                                       remoteAPI: remoteAPI)
  }

  func makeUserSessionDataStore() -> UserSessionDataStore {
    #if USER_SESSION_DATASTORE_FILEBASED
    return FileUserSessionDataStore()

    #else
    let coder = makeUserSessionCoder()

    return KeychainUserSessionDataStore(userSessionCoder: coder)
    #endif
  }

  func makeUserSessionCoder() -> UserSessionCoding {
    return UserSessionPropertyListCoder()
  }

  func makeAuthRemoteAPI() -> AuthRemoteAPI {
    return FakeAuthRemoteAPI()
  }
}
```

This example takes all the code that was in the `GlobalUserSessionRepository`'s declaration from the previous on-demand approach example and distributes object initializations into factory methods, one for each dependency.

One nice thing about factory methods is that they can hide implementation substitutions. For example, look at `makeUserSessionDataStore()` in the above code. The caller of this method has no idea they may get a `FileUserSessionDataStore` or a `KeychainUserSessionDataStore`.

This is great because it gives you the flexibility to change which data store to use by changing one method without needing to change any of the calling code.

Now the factories class is set up, take a look below at how
`GlobalUserSessionRepository` is declared:

```
// This code is global, it's not in any type.
public let GlobalUserSessionRepository:
  UserSessionRepository = {

  let objectFactories =
    KooberObjectFactories()

  let userSessionRepository =
    objectFactories.makeUserSessionRepository()

  return userSessionRepository
}()
```

This is *a lot* less code than the same declaration you saw in the on-demand approach example. The factories approach moves a ton of boilerplate code away from object usage sites into the centralized factories class. This helps you and other developers read code because you don't have to reason about how object graphs are assembled. If you need to see how an object is constructed, the factories class is always a Command-click away.

Alright, that's how the global shared `UserSessionRepository` is created using the factories approach. Next, you'll see how this code is used to create a `MainViewController`.

Creating a MainViewController

Recall the `MainViewController` initializer you saw in the on-demand example.

```
public init(viewModel: MainViewModel,
            launchViewController: LaunchViewController)
```

This is a simplified initializer; the one in Koober is more complex. The initializer used in Koober needs a couple of factory closures because `MainViewController` needs to be able to create view controllers after it's created.

Here's the initializer used in Koober:

```
init(viewModel: MainViewModel,
     launchViewController: LaunchViewController,
     // Closure that creates an OnboardingViewController
     onboardingViewControllerFactory:
       @escaping () -> OnboardingViewController,
     // Closure that creates a SignedInViewController
     signedInViewControllerFactory:
       @escaping (UserSession) -> SignedInViewController)
```

Considering that this adds quite a bit of complexity, you'll first walk through a factories example that uses the same simple initializer from the on-demand approach, and then you'll explore the code necessary to use the more complex initializer.

Since `MainViewController` needs a `MainViewModel`, you'll first look at how the factories approach creates a `MainViewModel`. The following code adds a `MainViewModel` factory method to `KooberObjectFactories`:

```
class KooberObjectFactories {

  // Factories needed to create a UserSessionRepository.

  ...

  // Factories needed to create a MainViewController.

  func makeMainViewModel() -> MainViewModel {
    return MainViewModel()
  }
}
```

There's not much to say about this code; it adds a simple factory method. You'll later see where it's used.

Since `MainViewModel` is stateful, the factory setup should only create one `MainViewModel` instance. For this reason, you need a global constant such as the one below:

```
// This code is global, it's not in any type.
public let GlobalMainViewModel: MainViewModel = {
  let objectFactories = KooberObjectFactories()
  let mainViewModel = objectFactories.makeMainViewModel()

  return mainViewModel
}()
```

This example is also pretty straightforward. Putting a shared `MainViewModel` into a global constant gives `KooberObjectFactories` access to this shared instance.

Now that `KooberObjectFactories` can create and access a shared `MainViewModel`, it's time to give `KooberObjectFactories` the ability to create a `MainViewController`:

```swift
class KooberObjectFactories {

  // Factories needed to create a UserSessionRepository.

  ...

  // Factories needed to create a MainViewController.

  func makeMainViewModel() -> MainViewModel {
    return MainViewModel()
  }

  // New code starts here.
  // 1
  func makeMainViewController(
    viewModel: MainViewModel,
    userSessionRepository: UserSessionRepository)
    -> MainViewController {

    let launchViewController = makeLaunchViewController(
      userSessionRepository: userSessionRepository,
      notSignedInResponder: mainViewModel,
      signedInResponder: mainViewModel)

    return MainViewController(
      viewModel: mainViewModel,
      launchViewController: launchViewController)
  }

  func makeLaunchViewController(
    userSessionRepository: UserSessionRepository,
    notSignedInResponder: NotSignedInResponder,
    signedInResponder: SignedInResponder)
    -> LaunchViewController {

    let viewModel = makeLaunchViewModel(
      userSessionRepository: userSessionRepository,
      notSignedInResponder: notSignedInResponder,
      signedInResponder: signedInResponder)

    return LaunchViewController(viewModel: viewModel)
  }

  // 2
  func makeLaunchViewModel(
```

```
    userSessionRepository: UserSessionRepository,
    notSignedInResponder: NotSignedInResponder,
    signedInResponder: SignedInResponder) -> LaunchViewModel {

    return LaunchViewModel(
      userSessionRepository: userSessionRepository,
      notSignedInResponder: notSignedInResponder,
      signedInResponder: signedInResponder)
  }
}
```

Again, the factories approach is about centralizing dependency and object-under-construction instantiation into a factories class. Here are a couple things to note about the above code:

1. Notice how this factory method has a couple of parameters. Because KooberObjectFactories is stateless and has no idea where long-lived dependencies are held, you have to pass long-lived dependencies into factory methods in the factories approach. In this line, both the viewModel and userSessionRepository parameters are long-lived.

2. This is another factory method that needs to have dependencies passed in from the outside. LaunchViewModel needs objects that conform to NotSignedInResponder and SignedInResponder. You and I know that MainViewModel conforms to this, but KooberObjectFactories does not know because KooberObjectFactories does not manage long-lived dependencies and MainViewModel is a long-lived dependency. Therefore, KooberObjectFactories cannot create a NotSignedInResponder nor a SignedInResponder.

In the on-demand example, the equivalent code was in application(_:didFinishLaunchingWithOptions:). Speaking of application(_:didFinishLaunchingWithOptions:), now that the instantiations are centralized, what does this method look like?

```
func application(
  _ application: UIApplication,
  didFinishLaunchingWithOptions launchOptions:
      [UIApplication.LaunchOptionsKey: Any]?) -> Bool {

  let sharedMainViewModel = GlobalMainViewModel
  let sharedUserSessionRepository = GlobalUserSessionRepository
  let objectFactories = KooberObjectFactories()

  let mainViewController =
    objectFactories.makeMainViewController(
      viewModel: sharedMainViewModel,
      userSessionRepository: sharedUserSessionRepository)
```

```
    window.frame = UIScreen.main.bounds
    window.makeKeyAndVisible()
    window.rootViewController = mainViewController

    return true
}
```

The above code gets shared instances needed to create a `MainViewController`, creates a factories class instance, and finally creates a `MainViewController` using the factories class instance.

No matter how complicated `MainViewController`'s dependency graph gets, the above code, for the most part, stays the same.

For instance, if `MainViewController` needed five more ephemeral dependencies, the above code wouldn't change, at all. That's because the code responsible for building ephemeral dependencies needed by `MainViewController`'s dependency graph is no longer in `application(_:didFinishLaunchingWithOptions:)`, it's now in `KooberObjectFactories`.

On the other hand, if `MainViewController` needed more long-lived dependencies, the above code would need to change a little bit in order to access the long-lived dependencies. As you'll see later, this won't be the case when upgrading a factories class to a container class.

Remember, a factories class is stateless. You can instantiate the class whenever you need to invoke a factory method. Just remember that doing this inside any object other than the app delegate can make your objects harder to unit test.

Great! You now know how to design a simple factories class. What about that complex initializer you saw earlier? What code would need to be added? This example is going to go from using the following `MainViewController` initializer:

```
public init(viewModel: MainViewModel,
            launchViewController: LaunchViewController)
```

To the following initializer:

```
public init(viewModel: MainViewModel,
            launchViewController: LaunchViewController,
            onboardingViewControllerFactory:
                @escaping () -> OnboardingViewController)
```

If you recall Koober's real `MainViewController` initializer you saw earlier, you'll notice this new version isn't *exactly* the same. This version is missing the last factory closure parameter. That's because walking through adding the last factory closure parameter would take *forever*.

The good news: If you understand how the version above works, you'll understand how the real version works as well!

Also, here's the updated dependency graph that corresponds:

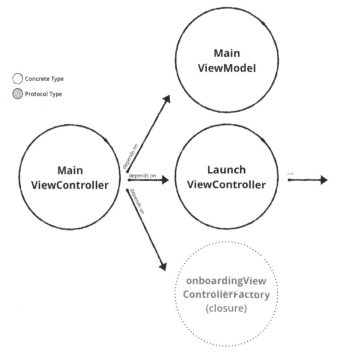

The next part of this example demonstrates how to apply the theory about injecting factories into an object-under-construction. Here's the first bit of code:

```
class KooberObjectFactories {

  // Factories needed to create a UserSessionRepository.

  ...

  // Factories needed to create a MainViewController.

  func makeMainViewController(
    viewModel: MainViewModel,
    userSessionRepository: UserSessionRepository)
    -> MainViewController {
```

```
    let launchViewController = makeLaunchViewController(
      userSessionRepository: userSessionRepository,
      notSignedInResponder: mainViewModel,
      signedInResponder: mainViewModel)

    // The type of this constant is
    // () -> OnboardingViewController.
    // The compiler will infer this type once the closure
    // is implemented.
    let onboardingViewControllerFactory = {
      // Return a new on-boarding view controller here.
      ...
    }

    return MainViewController(
      viewModel: mainViewModel,
      launchViewController: launchViewController,
      // New factory closure argument:
      onboardingViewControllerFactory:
        onboardingViewControllerFactory)
  }
  ...
}
```

The above code modifies `MainViewController`'s factory method to account for the factory injected version of `MainViewController`'s initializer. Notice how the example adds a closure constant named onboardingViewControllerFactory. This factory closure is injected into `MainViewController` via initialization.

The body of onboardingViewControllerFactory should create and return a new OnboardingViewController. The body is empty in the example above because KooberObjectFactories is missing factory methods for creating OnboardingViewControllers.

The following code adds those factory methods:

```
class KooberObjectFactories {

  // Factories needed to create a UserSessionRepository.

  ...

  // Factories needed to create a MainViewController.

  ...

  // Factories needed to create an OnboardingViewController.

  func makeOnboardingViewController(
```

```swift
    userSessionRepository: UserSessionRepository,
    signedInResponder: SignedInResponder)
    -> OnboardingViewController {

    let onboardingViewModel = makeOnboardingViewModel()

    let welcomeViewController = makeWelcomeViewController(
      goToSignUpNavigator: onboardingViewModel,
      goToSignInNavigator: onboardingViewModel)

    let signInViewController = makeSignInViewController(
      userSessionRepository: userSessionRepository,
      signedInResponder: signedInResponder)

    let signUpViewController = makeSignUpViewController(
      userSessionRepository: userSessionRepository,
      signedInResponder: signedInResponder)

    return OnboardingViewController(
      viewModel: onboardingViewModel,
      welcomeViewController: welcomeViewController,
      signInViewController: signInViewController,
      signUpViewController: signUpViewController)
}

func makeOnboardingViewModel() -> OnboardingViewModel {
    return OnboardingViewModel()
}

func makeWelcomeViewController(
  goToSignUpNavigator: GoToSignUpNavigator,
  goToSignInNavigator: GoToSignInNavigator)
  -> WelcomeViewController {

    let viewModel = makeWelcomeViewModel(
      goToSignUpNavigator: goToSignUpNavigator,
      goToSignInNavigator: goToSignInNavigator)

    return WelcomeViewController(viewModel: viewModel)
}

func makeWelcomeViewModel(
  goToSignUpNavigator: GoToSignUpNavigator,
  goToSignInNavigator: GoToSignInNavigator)
  -> WelcomeViewModel {

    return WelcomeViewModel(
      goToSignUpNavigator: goToSignUpNavigator,
      goToSignInNavigator: goToSignInNavigator)
}

func makeSignInViewController(
  userSessionRepository: UserSessionRepository,
```

```swift
      signedInResponder: SignedInResponder)
    -> SignInViewController {

    let viewModel = makeSignInViewModel(
      userSessionRepository: userSessionRepository,
      signedInResponder: signedInResponder)

    return SignInViewController(viewModel: viewModel)
  }

  func makeSignInViewModel(
    userSessionRepository: UserSessionRepository,
    signedInResponder: SignedInResponder)
    -> SignInViewModel {

    return SignInViewModel(
      userSessionRepository: userSessionRepository,
      signedInResponder: signedInResponder)
  }

  func makeSignUpViewController(
    userSessionRepository: UserSessionRepository,
    signedInResponder: SignedInResponder)
    -> SignUpViewController {

    let viewModel = makeSignUpViewModel(
      userSessionRepository: userSessionRepository,
      signedInResponder: signedInResponder)

    return SignUpViewController(viewModel: viewModel)
  }

  func makeSignUpViewModel(
    userSessionRepository: UserSessionRepository,
    signedInResponder: SignedInResponder)
    -> SignUpViewModel {

    return SignUpViewModel(
      userSessionRepository: userSessionRepository,
      signedInResponder: signedInResponder)
  }
}
```

Wow — `OnboardingViewController` has quite a dependency graph. The above code was previously in `MainViewController`'s `presentOnboarding()` method in the on-demand version of this example. The complexity of assembling `OnboardingViewController`'s object graph has now moved outside of `MainViewController`. This allows `MainViewController` to focus on being a great view controller.

`KooberObjectFactories` now has the ability to create `OnboardingViewControllers`. The following example illustrates how to use this ability inside the `onboardingViewControllerFactory` closure:

```swift
class KooberObjectFactories {

  // Factories needed to create a UserSessionRepository.

  ...

  // Factories needed to create a MainViewController.

  func makeMainViewController(
    viewModel: MainViewModel,
    userSessionRepository: UserSessionRepository)
    -> MainViewController {

    let launchViewController = makeLaunchViewController(
      userSessionRepository: userSessionRepository,
      notSignedInResponder: mainViewModel,
      signedInResponder: mainViewModel)

    // Closure factory now implemented:
    let onboardingViewControllerFactory = {
      // Factories class is stateless, therefore
      // there's no chance for a retain cycle here.
      return self.makeOnboardingViewController(
        userSessionRepository: userSessionRepository,
        signedInResponder: mainViewModel)
    }

    return MainViewController(
      viewModel: mainViewModel,
      launchViewController: launchViewController,
      onboardingViewControllerFactory:
        onboardingViewControllerFactory)
  }

  ...

  // Factories needed to create an OnboardingViewController.

  ...
}
```

In the example above, the `onboardingViewControllerFactory` closure simply invokes the `OnboardingViewController` factory method from earlier. The closure captures the `userSessionRepository` and `mainViewModel` arguments passed into `MainViewController`'s factory method.

These objects are used to invoke `OnboardingViewController`'s factory method. The closure also captures `self`, i.e., the `KooberObjectFactories` instance.

So, in an indirect way, `MainViewController` holds a reference to `KooberObjectFactories` and that's OK because `KooberObjectFactories` is stateless. There's no chance for a retain cycle to materialize.

That's how you inject factories! There was a lot of changes necessary in order to give `MainViewController` the power to create `OnboardingViewControllers`. Take a look at how `application(_:didFinishLaunchingWithOptions:)` needs to change to account for all this:

```
func application(
  _ application: UIApplication,
  didFinishLaunchingWithOptions launchOptions:
      [UIApplication.LaunchOptionsKey: Any]?) -> Bool {

  let sharedMainViewModel = GlobalMainViewModel
  let sharedUserSessionRepository = GlobalUserSessionRepository
  let objectFactories = KooberObjectFactories()

  let mainViewController =
    objectFactories.makeMainViewController(
      viewModel: sharedMainViewModel,
      userSessionRepository: sharedUserSessionRepository)

  window.frame = UIScreen.main.bounds
  window.makeKeyAndVisible()
  window.rootViewController = mainViewController

  return true
}
```

Wait a second... that's right: **nothing** changed. You've now witnessed the awesome power of DI. Also, remember that *very* long `presentOnboarding()` method from the on-boarding example?

Take a look at that method now:

```
public func presentOnboarding() {
  let onboardingViewController = makeOnboardingViewController()

  onboardingViewController.modalPresentationStyle = .fullScreen
  present(onboardingViewController, animated: true) { ... }
  self.onboardingViewController = onboardingViewController
}
```

In order to create a new `OnboardingViewController`, `MainViewController` just has to invoke the empty argument `makeOnboardingViewController` closure property.

`MainViewController` doesn't have to know *anything* about the dependency graph needed to create a new `OnboardingViewController`. Cool!

You're starting to become a DI guru. But wait — there's more. The one problem with `KooberObjectFactories` is you have to create global constants for long-lived dependencies. You probably don't want these objects just hanging out in global space. To solve this, you'll see how you can upgrade `KooberObjectFactories` to a `KooberAppDependencyContainer` in the next section.

Applying the single-container approach

In order to convert `KooberObjectFactories` into a dependency container, `KooberObjectFactories` needs to go from being stateless to being stateful. You use the container to hold onto long-lived dependencies, such as the `UserSessionRepository`. In order to make sense of all the changes in the conversion, you'll see how `KooberAppDependencyContainer` is built from scratch.

The first order of business is to create and store the shared `UserSessionRepository`:

```
class KooberAppDependencyContainer {

  // MARK: - Properties
  // 1
  let sharedUserSessionRepository: UserSessionRepository

  // MARK: - Methods
  init() {
    // 2
    func makeUserSessionRepository() -> UserSessionRepository {
      let dataStore = makeUserSessionDataStore()
      let remoteAPI = makeAuthRemoteAPI()
      return KooberUserSessionRepository(dataStore: dataStore,
                                         remoteAPI: remoteAPI)
    }

    func makeUserSessionDataStore() -> UserSessionDataStore {
      #if USER_SESSION_DATASTORE_FILEBASED
      return FileUserSessionDataStore()

      #else
      let coder = makeUserSessionCoder()
      return KeychainUserSessionDataStore(
        userSessionCoder: coder)
      #endif
    }
```

```
    func makeUserSessionCoder() -> UserSessionCoding {
      return UserSessionPropertyListCoder()
    }

    func makeAuthRemoteAPI() -> AuthRemoteAPI {
      return FakeAuthRemoteAPI()
    }

    // 3
    self.sharedUserSessionRepository =
      makeUserSessionRepository()
  }
}
```

Here's what each part does:

1. This declares a constant stored property. This property holds onto the shared UserSessionRepository instance that should be used when creating an object-under-construction that depends on a UserSessionRepository.

2. Notice how these factory methods are *inside* the container's initializer. These factory methods cannot be instance methods because Swift does not allow an initializer to call a method on self until all stored properties are initialized. In this case, you need these methods *to* initialize a stored property.

3. The shared UserSessionRepository stored property is initialized with a UserSessionRepository created by the inlined factory methods.

The example above gives the container the ability to fully create and store a shared UserSessionRepository. Next, you'll look at how to give the container the ability to create a MainViewController.

MainViewController needs three big things in order to be instantiated: A shared MainViewModel, an OnboardingViewController factory closure, and a LaunchViewController. You'll add factory methods for these dependencies in this order.

MainViewModel is first. The shared MainViewModel is another global long-lived dependency that needs to move into the container. The following code adds the sharedMainViewModel into KooberAppDependencyContainer:

```
class KooberAppDependencyContainer {

  // MARK: - Properties
  let sharedUserSessionRepository: UserSessionRepository
  // 1
  let sharedMainViewModel: MainViewModel
```

```
  // MARK: - Methods
  init() {
    func makeUserSessionRepository() -> UserSessionRepository {
      let dataStore = makeUserSessionDataStore()
      let remoteAPI = makeAuthRemoteAPI()
      return KooberUserSessionRepository(dataStore: dataStore,
                                         remoteAPI: remoteAPI)
    }

    func makeUserSessionDataStore() -> UserSessionDataStore {
      #if USER_SESSION_DATASTORE_FILEBASED
      return FileUserSessionDataStore()

      #else
      let coder = makeUserSessionCoder()
      return KeychainUserSessionDataStore(
        userSessionCoder: coder)
      #endif
    }

    func makeUserSessionCoder() -> UserSessionCoding {
      return UserSessionPropertyListCoder()
    }

    func makeAuthRemoteAPI() -> AuthRemoteAPI {
      return FakeAuthRemoteAPI()
    }

    // 2
    // Because `MainViewModel` is a concrete type
    //  and because `MainViewModel`'s initializer has
    //  no parameters, you don't need this inline
    //  factory method, you can also initialize the
    //  `sharedMainViewModel` property on the
    //  declaration line like this:
    //  `let sharedMainViewModel = MainViewModel()`.
    //  Which option to use is a style preference.
    func makeMainViewModel() -> MainViewModel {
      return MainViewModel()
    }

    self.sharedUserSessionRepository =
      makeUserSessionRepository()

    // 3
    self.sharedMainViewModel =
      makeMainViewModel()
  }
}
```

Here's what each part does:

1. This line adds a constant stored property to hold onto a shared `MainViewModel`. The container will use this instance any time an object-under-construction needs a `MainViewModel`.
2. This block adds a new inlined `MainViewModel` factory method to `init`. One neat thing is this design guarantees that another `MainViewModel` won't be accidentally created because this factory method is inaccessible outside `init`.
3. The shared `MainViewModel` is created and used to initialize the `sharedMainViewModel` property.

That's the `MainViewModel` dependency, next is `OnboardingViewController`:

```swift
class KooberAppDependencyContainer {

  // MARK: - Properties
  let sharedUserSessionRepository: UserSessionRepository
  let sharedMainViewModel: MainViewModel
  // 1
  var sharedOnboardingViewModel: OnboardingViewModel?

  // MARK: - Methods
  init() {
    ...
  }

  // 2
  // On-boarding (signed-out)
  // Factories needed to create an OnboardingViewController.

  func makeOnboardingViewController()
    -> OnboardingViewController {

    // 3
    self.sharedOnboardingViewModel = makeOnboardingViewModel()

    let welcomeViewController = makeWelcomeViewController()
    let signInViewController = makeSignInViewController()
    let signUpViewController = makeSignUpViewController()

    // 4
    return OnboardingViewController(
      viewModel: self.sharedOnboardingViewModel!,
      welcomeViewController: welcomeViewController,
      signInViewController: signInViewController,
      signUpViewController: signUpViewController)
  }

  func makeOnboardingViewModel() -> OnboardingViewModel {
```

```swift
    return OnboardingViewModel()
  }

  func makeWelcomeViewController() -> WelcomeViewController {
    let viewModel = makeWelcomeViewModel()
    return WelcomeViewController(viewModel: viewModel)
  }

  func makeWelcomeViewModel() -> WelcomeViewModel {
    return WelcomeViewModel(
      goToSignUpNavigator: self.sharedOnboardingViewModel!,
      goToSignInNavigator: self.sharedOnboardingViewModel!)
  }

  func makeSignInViewController() -> SignInViewController {
    let viewModel = makeSignInViewModel()
    return SignInViewController(viewModel: viewModel)
  }

  func makeSignInViewModel() -> SignInViewModel {
    return SignInViewModel(
      userSessionRepository: self.sharedUserSessionRepository,
      signedInResponder: self.sharedMainViewModel)
  }

  func makeSignUpViewController() -> SignUpViewController {
    let viewModel = makeSignUpViewModel()
    return SignUpViewController(viewModel: viewModel)
  }

  func makeSignUpViewModel() -> SignUpViewModel {
    return SignUpViewModel(
      userSessionRepository: self.sharedUserSessionRepository,
      signedInResponder: self.sharedMainViewModel)
  }
}
```

Notice how the factory methods don't have parameters anymore! That's because factory methods in a container can use other factory methods to create ephemeral dependencies and because factory methods in a container can access the container's properties to get long-lived dependencies. Containers have everything they need to assemble entire dependency graphs.

Here are some additional things to note about the above code:

1. This adds an optional stored property to hold onto a shared `OnboardingViewModel`. This property is optional because an `OnboardingViewModel` is only needed when a user is *not* signed in to Koober. This property starts out with a nil value.

2. All the factory methods for all dependencies in `OnboardingViewController`'s dependency graph are added here.

3. This line creates a new `OnboardingViewModel` every time a new `OnboardingViewController` is created. This `OnboardingViewModel` is stored in the container's `sharedOnboardingViewModel`. `OboardingViewModel`s are stateful and therefore, the same view model instance should be used for the lifetime of the `OnboardingViewController` instance created in this factory method. Later, you'll see how to improve this by separating the on-boarding factory methods into a scoped container.

4. This line creates a new `OnboardingViewController` by using the `sharedOnboardingViewModel` as well as all the view controllers the `OnboardingViewController` needs. Yes, the force unwrap is ugly. You'll see how to get rid of this later when learning how to separate this logic into a scoped container.

`MainViewModel`? Check. `OnboardingViewController`? Check. It's time to look at `LaunchViewController`:

```
class KooberAppDependencyContainer {

  // MARK: - Properties
  let sharedUserSessionRepository: UserSessionRepository
  let sharedMainViewModel: MainViewModel
  var sharedOnboardingViewModel: OnboardingViewModel?

  // MARK: - Methods
  init() {
    ...
  }

  // On-boarding (signed-out)
  // Factories needed to create an OnboardingViewController.

  ...

  // Main
  // Factories needed to create a MainViewController.
```

```
    func makeLaunchViewController() -> LaunchViewController {
      let viewModel = makeLaunchViewModel()
      return LaunchViewController(viewModel: viewModel)
    }

    func makeLaunchViewModel() -> LaunchViewModel {
      return LaunchViewModel(
        userSessionRepository: self.sharedUserSessionRepository,
        notSignedInResponder: self.sharedMainViewModel,
        signedInResponder: self.sharedMainViewModel)
    }
  }
```

There's nothing too surprising, here. The above code adds two factory methods: one to create a `LaunchViewModel`, which is then used to create a `LaunchViewController` in the other factory method.

All the setup is complete. The only thing missing is a factory method that can create a `MainViewController`:

```
class KooberAppDependencyContainer {

  // MARK: - Properties
  let sharedUserSessionRepository: UserSessionRepository
  let sharedMainViewModel: MainViewModel
  var sharedOnboardingViewModel: OnboardingViewModel?

  // MARK: - Methods
  init() {
    ...
  }

  // On-boarding (signed-out)
  // Factories needed to create an OnboardingViewController.

  ...

  // Main
  // Factories needed to create a MainViewController.

  func makeMainViewController() -> MainViewController {
    // 1
    let launchViewController = makeLaunchViewController()

    // 2
    let onboardingViewControllerFactory = {
      return self.makeOnboardingViewController()
    }

    // 3
    return MainViewController(
```

```
      viewModel: self.sharedMainViewModel,
      launchViewController: launchViewController,
      onboardingViewControllerFactory:
        onboardingViewControllerFactory)
  }
  ...
}
```

Here's what each part does:

1. This line creates a `LaunchViewController`.

2. Look how simple the `OnboardingViewController` factory closure is, now that the `OnboardingViewController` factory method takes no arguments.

3. This is what you've been waiting for: the line that creates the `MainViewController`. This line uses a long-lived dependency, a newly created dependency *and* a factory closure to create a `MainViewController`. All the big concepts, wrapped up into a single line.

OK, the container is setup and ready to build Koober's object graph. It's time for the very final step — making a `MainViewController` and its entire graph when Koober launches:

```
@UIApplicationMain
class AppDelegate: UIResponder, UIApplicationDelegate {

  // MARK: - Properties
  // 1
  let appContainer = KooberAppDependencyContainer()
  let window = UIWindow()

  // MARK: - Methods
  func application(
    _ application: UIApplication,
    didFinishLaunchingWithOptions launchOptions:
      [UIApplication.LaunchOptionsKey: Any]?) -> Bool {

    // 2
    let mainVC = appContainer.makeMainViewController()

    window.frame = UIScreen.main.bounds
    window.makeKeyAndVisible()
    window.rootViewController = mainVC

    return true
  }
}
```

It only takes two steps to create Koober's entire dependency graph. With the above code, you:

1. Create the app container and store it in a constant inside the app delegate. Creating this container is easy because the initializer doesn't have any parameters. Remember, you should only create one instance of a container because containers are stateful unlike a factories class.
2. Create the root object, in this case a `MainViewController`, by invoking the root object's factory method on the container. This single line creates and sets up everything Koober needs in order to run. All dependencies are provided from the outside.

The awesome thing about all this is that all of the classes inside Koober have no idea about the dependency containers. It's not like using DI will introduce a bunch of things into your existing code that you might want to get rid of later.

What a journey it's been. You've seen all big three approaches used in practice. You're almost at the finish line! The only pesky thing that needs addressing is the optional `sharedOnboardingViewModel`. Don't you hate it when you find yourself needing to force unwrap something? I know I do. In the next section, you'll see how to address this issue by separating the on-boarding factory logic into a separate scoped container.

Applying the container hierarchy approach

The first step to creating a scoped container for the on-boarding logic is to remove all the on-boarding factory methods from `KooberAppDependencyContainer`:

```
class KooberAppDependencyContainer {

  // MARK: - Properties

  // Long-lived dependencies
  let sharedUserSessionRepository: UserSessionRepository
  let sharedMainViewModel: MainViewModel

  // MARK: - Methods
  init() {
    func makeUserSessionRepository() -> UserSessionRepository {
      let dataStore = makeUserSessionDataStore()
      let remoteAPI = makeAuthRemoteAPI()
```

```swift
    return KooberUserSessionRepository(dataStore: dataStore,
                                       remoteAPI: remoteAPI)
  }

  func makeUserSessionDataStore() -> UserSessionDataStore {
    #if USER_SESSION_DATASTORE_FILEBASED
    return FileUserSessionDataStore()

    #else
    let coder = makeUserSessionCoder()
    return KeychainUserSessionDataStore(
      userSessionCoder: coder)
    #endif
  }

  func makeUserSessionCoder() -> UserSessionCoding {
    return UserSessionPropertyListCoder()
  }

  func makeAuthRemoteAPI() -> AuthRemoteAPI {
    return FakeAuthRemoteAPI()
  }

  func makeMainViewModel() -> MainViewModel {
    return MainViewModel()
  }

  self.sharedUserSessionRepository =
    makeUserSessionRepository()

  self.sharedMainViewModel =
    makeMainViewModel()
}

// Main
// Factories needed to create a MainViewController.

func makeMainViewController() -> MainViewController {
  let launchViewController = makeLaunchViewController()

  let onboardingViewControllerFactory = {
    return self.makeOnboardingViewController()
  }

  return MainViewController(
    viewModel: self.sharedMainViewModel,
    launchViewController: launchViewController,
    onboardingViewControllerFactory:
      onboardingViewControllerFactory)
}

// Launching
```

```swift
  func makeLaunchViewController() -> LaunchViewController {
    let viewModel = makeLaunchViewModel()
    return LaunchViewController(viewModel: viewModel)
  }

  func makeLaunchViewModel() -> LaunchViewModel {
    return LaunchViewModel(
      userSessionRepository: self.sharedUserSessionRepository,
      notSignedInResponder: self.sharedMainViewModel,
      signedInResponder: self.sharedMainViewModel)
  }

  // On-boarding (signed-out)
  // Factories needed to create an OnboardingViewController.

  func makeOnboardingViewController()
    -> OnboardingViewController {

    fatalError("This method needs to be implemented.")
  }
}
```

The above code is the exact same KooberAppDependencyContainer from before except without all the on-boarding factory methods barring the primary OnboardingViewController factory method, makeOnboardingViewController().

This method will use the child on-boarding dependency container in order to create an OnboardingViewController. You'll see the implementation of this method at the end of this example once you've explored the child on-boarding container's class.

Next, you'll explore a *new* container class that represents the on-boarding scope. Koober transitions into the on-boarding scope when Koober determines a user is not signed in. This could occur at launch or when a user signs out.

Here's what the on-boarding scoped container class looks like:

```swift
class KooberOnboardingDependencyContainer {

  // MARK: - Properties
  // 1
  // From parent container
  let sharedUserSessionRepository: UserSessionRepository
  let sharedMainViewModel: MainViewModel
  // 2
  // Long-lived dependencies
  let sharedOnboardingViewModel: OnboardingViewModel

  // MARK: - Methods
  // 3
  init(appDependencyContainer: KooberAppDependencyContainer) {
```

```
  // 4
  func makeOnboardingViewModel() -> OnboardingViewModel {
    return OnboardingViewModel()
  }

  // 5
  self.sharedUserSessionRepository =
    appDependencyContainer.sharedUserSessionRepository

  self.sharedMainViewModel =
    appDependencyContainer.sharedMainViewModel

  // 6
  self.sharedOnboardingViewModel =
    makeOnboardingViewModel()
}

// 7
// On-boarding (signed-out)
// Factories needed to create an OnboardingViewController.

func makeOnboardingViewController()
  -> OnboardingViewController {

  let welcomeViewController = makeWelcomeViewController()
  let signInViewController = makeSignInViewController()
  let signUpViewController = makeSignUpViewController()

  return OnboardingViewController(
    viewModel: self.sharedOnboardingViewModel,
    welcomeViewController: welcomeViewController,
    signInViewController: signInViewController,
    signUpViewController: signUpViewController)
}

func makeWelcomeViewController() -> WelcomeViewController {
  let viewModel = makeWelcomeViewModel()

  return WelcomeViewController(viewModel: viewModel)
}

func makeWelcomeViewModel() -> WelcomeViewModel {
  return WelcomeViewModel(
    goToSignUpNavigator: self.sharedOnboardingViewModel,
    goToSignInNavigator: self.sharedOnboardingViewModel)
}

func makeSignInViewController() -> SignInViewController {
  let viewModel = makeSignInViewModel()
  return SignInViewController(viewModel: viewModel)
}

func makeSignInViewModel() -> SignInViewModel {
```

```
    return SignInViewModel(
      userSessionRepository: self.sharedUserSessionRepository,
      signedInResponder: self.sharedMainViewModel)
  }

  func makeSignUpViewController() -> SignUpViewController {
    let viewModel = makeSignUpViewModel()
    return SignUpViewController(viewModel: viewModel)
  }

  func makeSignUpViewModel() -> SignUpViewModel {
    return SignUpViewModel(
      userSessionRepository: self.sharedUserSessionRepository,
      signedInResponder: self.sharedMainViewModel)
  }
}
```

Here's what each part does:

1. These two long-lived dependencies are held by the app dependency container. Instead of holding onto the app dependency container, this example holds onto the long-lived dependencies themselves. This is so the factory methods in this on-boarding container can have easy access to the long-lived dependencies without needing to know how to fish for the dependencies out of the app dependency container.

2. This line declares the scoped `sharedOnboardingViewModel` long-lived dependency. This long-lived dependency only lives as long as this container lives. Most importantly, notice how this property is a constant *and not optional*.

3. This is the container's initializer. Notice how the app dependency container is required in order to create this on-boarding container. That's because the objects, that this container creates, need long-lived dependencies held by the app dependency container. The app dependency container is the on-boarding container's **parent container**.

4. This adds an inline factory method that creates a shared `OnboardingViewModel`. `OnboardingViewModel` is stateful and therefore needs to be stored in a property. Since the property needs to be set in the initializer, `OnboardingViewModel`'s factory method needs to be inlined inside the initializer.

5. These lines find the long-lived dependencies held by the parent app dependency container and uses those dependencies to set corresponding properties on this child container. The properties are needed so that the on-boarding dependency container can hold onto these long-lived dependencies. Holding dependencies from a parent container is OK because parent containers outlive child containers. There's no chance this child container is holding onto something for longer than it should.
6. The shared `OnboardingViewModel` is created here, using the inlined factory method.
7. Here are all the factory methods that used to be in the app dependency container. The only difference here is that `sharedOnboardingViewModel` is no longer forced unwrapped.

There's one step left. Recall that `MainViewController`'s factory method needs to be able to create a new `OnboardingViewController` inside the factory closure that gets injected into `MainViewController`.

To do this, the factory closure needs `KooberAppDependencyContainer`'s `makeOnboardingViewController()` to be implemented.

Here's what `makeOnboardingViewController()`'s implementation looks like:

```
class KooberAppDependencyContainer {

  // MARK: - Properties
  let sharedUserSessionRepository: UserSessionRepository
  let sharedMainViewModel: MainViewModel

  // MARK: - Methods
  init() {
    ...
  }

  // Factories needed to create a MainViewController.

  ...

  // Factories needed to create an OnboardingViewController.

  func makeOnboardingViewController()
    -> OnboardingViewController {

    // 1
    let onboardingDependencyContainer =
      KooberOnboardingDependencyContainer(
        appDependencyContainer: self)
```

```
    // 2
    return onboardingDependencyContainer
             .makeOnboardingViewController()
  }
}
```

Making a new `OnboardingViewController` from the app dependency container is a two-step process:

1. First, you need to create the child on-boarding dependency container using `self`, the parent app dependency container.

2. Finally, you use the child container to create and return a new `OnboardingViewController`.

OK — the container hierarchy is set up and ready to build Koober's object graph. It's time for the very final step — making a `MainViewController` and its entire graph when Koober launches:

```
@UIApplicationMain
class AppDelegate: UIResponder, UIApplicationDelegate {

  // MARK: - Properties
  let appContainer = KooberAppDependencyContainer()
  let window = UIWindow()

  // MARK: - Methods
  func application(
    _ application: UIApplication,
    didFinishLaunchingWithOptions launchOptions:
      [UIApplication.LaunchOptionsKey: Any]?) -> Bool {

    let mainVC = appContainer.makeMainViewController()

    window.frame = UIScreen.main.bounds
    window.makeKeyAndVisible()
    window.rootViewController = mainVC

    return true
  }
}
```

Yup, this code hasn't changed at all. Refactoring the single container into a container hierarchy did not affect the consuming code. Cool, right? And that wraps up going through Koober's use of DI!

Congratulations; you made it to the end! By practicing all the techniques you saw in this chapter, you'll become a DI master in no time. Everything you learned in this chapter is the foundation needed to design well-architected object-oriented software. That's right — you'll even be able to use these techniques outside of mobile development. Taking the time to solidify your comfort level with DI will pay off big time. Make sure you have a good understanding of DI before moving on to the next chapters so that you can easily navigate the sample codebases.

Key points

- The iOS SDK is object oriented; therefore, you use object-oriented techniques to design well-architected iOS apps.
- There are many beneficial goals including **testability** and **maintainability** that can be achieved by managing object dependencies.
- **Consumers** need **objects-under-construction** and objects-under-construction need **transitive dependencies**. Together, these objects form an **object graph**.
- **Accessing dependencies**, **determining substitutability** and **designing substitutability** form the basis of the three fundamental questions you need to answer to reap the benefits of managing object dependencies.
- **Dependency Injection**, **Service Locator**, **Environment** and **Protocol extensions** are the main dependency patterns used by iOS app developers.
- Dependency Injection (DI) is all about providing dependencies from the outside of objects.
- There are three types of DI: **Initializer**, **property** and **method** injection.
- You saw how to apply DI four ways: **On-demand**, **Factories**, **Single Container** and **Container Hierarchy**.
- When applying the DI pattern, your goal is to construct a flow, or a screen, entire object graph upfront.
- When an object-under-construction needs to create multiple instances of a dependency, you inject a **factory closure** or you inject an object that conforms to a **factory protocol**.

Where to go from here?

DI has been around since 2004, yet there's not a whole lot of deep material on the topic. Most of the content you'll find teaches you how to use a DI library. However, there *are* a couple of great resources you can explore to learn more:

- Inversion of Control Containers and the Dependency Injection pattern (https://martinfowler.com/articles/injection.html) by Martin Fowler. This is *the* original post that introduces DI. It's a great read if you want to get a sense for the origin of the pattern and why it came to be.

- Dependency Injection in .NET (https://www.manning.com/books/dependency-injection-in-dot-net) by Mark Seemann. Although this book uses .NET for example code, the material is applicable to any object-oriented language. This is probably the most thorough treatment of DI available.

If you're interested in learning how to apply DI using a library, check out Gemma Barlow's tutorial on Swinject: Swinject Tutorial for iOS: Getting Started (https://www.raywenderlich.com/17-swinject-tutorial-for-ios-getting-started).

Which chapter should you read next? Since the next chapters do not build upon each other, it's really up to you which chapter you dive into next. Enjoy!

Chapter 5: Architecture: MVVM

By René Cacheaux & Josh Berlin

Model-View-ViewModel (MVVM) is the new trend in the iOS community, but its roots date back to the early 2000s at Microsoft. Yes, you read that correctly! Microsoft. Microsoft architects introduced MVVM to simplify design and development using Extensible Application Markup Language (XAML) platforms, such as Silverlight.

Prior to MVVM, designers would drag and drop user interface components to create views, and developers would write code for each view specifically. This resulted in the tight coupling between views and business logic — changing one typically required changing the other. Designers lost freedom due to this workflow: They became hesitant to change view layouts because, doing so, often required massive code rewrites.

Microsoft specifically introduced MVVM to decouple views and business logic. This alleviated pain points for designers: They could now change the user interface, and developers wouldn't have to change too much code.

Fast forward to iOS today, and you'll find that iOS designers usually don't modify Xcode storyboards or auto layout constraints directly. Rather, they create designs using graphical editors such as Adobe Photoshop. They hand these designs to developers, who, in turn, create both the views and code. Thereby, the goals of MVVM are different for iOS.

MVVM isn't intended to allow designers to create views via Xcode directly. Rather, iOS developers use MVVM to decouple views from models. But the benefits are the same: iOS designers can freely change the user interface, and iOS developers won't need to change much business logic code.

What is it?

MVVM is a "reactive" architecture. The view reacts to changes on the view model, and the view model updates its state based on data from the model.

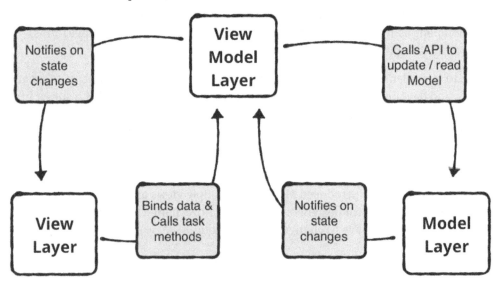

MVVM involves three layers:

- The **model layer** contains data access objects and validation logic. It knows how to read and write data, and it notifies the view model when data changes.

- The **view model layer** contains the state of the view and has methods to handle user interaction. It calls methods on the model layer to read and write data, and it notifies the view when the model's data changes.

- The **view layer** styles and displays on-screen elements. It doesn't contain business or validation logic. Instead, it binds its visual elements to properties on the view model. It also receives user inputs and interaction, and it calls methods on the view model in response.

As a result, the view layer and model layer are completely decoupled. The view layer and model layer only communicate with the view model layer.

Next, you'll go into the each of these layers in depth.

Model layer

The model layer is responsible for all create, read, update and delete (CRUD) operations.

You can design the model layer in many different ways; yet, two of the most common are **push-and-pull** and **observe-and-push** designs:

- **Push-and-pull** designs require consumers to ask for data and wait for the response, which is the "pull" part. Consumers can also update model data and tell the model layer to send it, which is the "push" part.

- **Observe-and-push** designs require consumers to "observe" the model layer, instead of asking for data directly. Like push-and-pull designs, consumers can also update model data and tell the model layer to "push" it.

Koober uses a push-and-pull design. Specifically, it uses an implementation of the **repository pattern**. You'll go into more detail about this, next.

Repository pattern

Repositories contain data access objects that can call out to a server or read from disk.

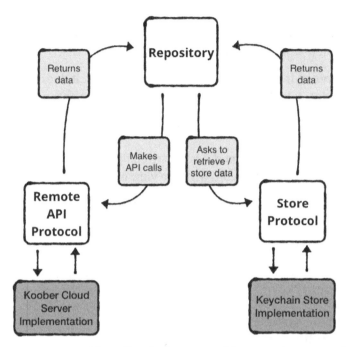

The repository pattern provides a façade for networking, persistence and in-memory caching. This façade creates, reads, updates and deletes data on disk and in the cloud. The repository doesn't expose to consumers how it retrieves or stores the data.

When combined with MVVM, view models use the repository façade, instead of performing these operations themselves. In turn, view models transform and expose model data to views to display on-screen.

Repository structure

The repository provides a set of asynchronous CRUD methods. The underlying implementations can be either stateless or stateful. Stateless implementations don't keep data around after retrieving it, whereas stateful implementations save data for later. The components are usually stateful and keep data in-memory for quick access.

Under the hood, the repository has multiple layers of data access. Each implementation of a repository may implement all or only one of these layers:

- The **cloud-remote-API layer** makes calls to a server to read and update data. This may make REST calls, get data from a socket connection or another means. The data at this layer always comes from outside of the app.

- The **persistent-store layer** puts data in a local database. The database can be Core Data, Realm or a Plist file on disk. The data at this layer always comes from the app. The data gets persisted after the app closes.

- The **in-memory-cache layer** stores data in objects that stay around for the lifetime of the repository. The cache doesn't persist between app sessions. The in-memory cache is useful for showing pre-fetched data before making a network call to the cloud.

Example: KooberUserSessionRepository

In Koober, signing up or signing in creates a new session. The session contains the current user's authentication token and metadata, such as name and avatar.

The `KooberUserSessionRepository` handles all user-related activity in the Koober app, including signing up, signing in, signing out and getting the current user.

When a new user signs up, the `KooberUserSessionRepository` calls out to the Koober Cloud REST API, creates a user session from the response, and finally saves the user session to a persistent store.

This all happens under the covers. `KooberUserSessionRepository` exposes none of the internal implementation to its consumers. In particular, `KooberUserSessionRepository` API exposes nothing about where the data comes from. The underlying implementation could change to call out to a different REST API and store the data in-memory only. If it did, the API would still stay the same and consumers wouldn't be impacted.

The sign-in API takes in an email and password, and asynchronously returns a user session object. The API's caller only cares that they get the most up-to-date user session. They don't care whether or not the user session comes from an in-memory store, a cloud API or a persistent store.

Repositories allow flexibility in your implementations, while keeping the user interface layer stable. Repository implementations can change due to new project requirements. The callers of the user repository methods never change, regardless of the implementation. If your company asks you to switch from REST to Protocol Buffers, do you panic or do you keep calm and refactor? The flexibility makes your app more stable, less prone to bugs and requires less refactoring when implementations do inevitably change.

View layer

A view is a user interface for a screen. In MVVM, the view layer reacts to state changes through bindings to view model properties. It also notifies the view model of user interaction, like button taps or text input updates.

The purpose of the view is to render the screen. It knows how to layout and style the user interface elements, but doesn't know anything about business logic.

In MVVM, you use one-way data binding to bind the UI elements from the view to the view model. This means the view model is the single source of truth. The view doesn't update until the view model changes its state.

The view layer contains a hierarchy of views. Each parent view knows about its children and has access to their properties.

View model layer

The view model is the life of the party in this chapter. It contains a view's state, methods for handling user interaction and bindings to different user interface elements.

The view model knows how to handle user interactions, like button taps. User interactions map to methods in the view model. The methods do some work, like making an API call, and then change the state of the view model. The state update causes the view to react.

The purpose of the view model is to decouple the view controller from the view. Ever heard of the "massive view controller problem"? Does your view controller file seem to scroll forever? View models are here to help. They are completely separate from the view controller, and they know nothing about its implementation.

You can replace your entire view with a different layout without changing the view model. View models give MVVM big wins in testability, since you can test them without a user interface.

Kickstarter wrote its iOS app using view models. It has over 1,000 view model tests. On its blog, Kickstarter writes, "We write these as a pure mapping of input signals to output signals, and test them heavily, including tests for localization, accessibility, and event tracking." This idea of "pure mapping" is at the core of MVVM. View models take input signals and produce output signals, providing a clear boundary between view models and views.

Next, you'll learn about the structure of a view model in more depth.

- **View State** is stored in the view model. The state is made up of `@Published` properties. Using `Combine`, the user interface subscribes to the publishers when the view model is created.

- **Task Methods** perform tasks in response to user interactions. The methods do some work, such as calling a sign-in API, and then updating the view model's state. The view knows if the state changes because the publishers signal new data. You usually mark task methods as `@objc` methods, because you have to target-action pair on a UI Control.

- **Dependencies** are passed to the view model through initializer injection. Task methods rely on the dependencies to communicate with other subsystems in the app, such as a REST API or persistent store. View models know how to use the dependencies, but have no knowledge of the underlying implementations.

View models sometimes use other view models to change state across the app. In this case, other view models are injected using initializer injection. You'll cover how to signal out to other view models in the code example sections.

Example: Koober sign-in view model

The sign-in view model contains business logic for signing in to Koober and publishers to update state.

The view model depends on a `UserSessionRespository` and a `SignedInResponder`, which the initializing object injects through the initializer.

- The `UserSessionRespository` calls the Koober sign-in API to authenticate with an email and password.

- The `SignedInResponder` handles a successful sign in. It signals out to switch app state from onboarding to signed in.

The view model contains two values:

- The `email` and `password` variables update each time you enter new text in the text fields. These variables are bound to the text fields in the sign-in view.

The view model also contains publishers:

- The `emailInputEnabled` and `passwordInputEnabled` publishers bind to the text fields in the view. They update each time you enter new text in the text fields.

- The `errorMessagePublisher` publisher sends `ErrorMessage` objects. The view presents the error each time the publisher sends a new one.

The only task method in the sign-in view model is `signIn()`. The method asks the `UserSessionRespository` to sign in using values in `email` and `password`. If sign in succeeds, the view model gives the `SignedInResponder` the new user session. If the sign in fails, the view model adds the error to `errorMessages` and the view displays the error.

Creating the view

The view knows how to style and layout its subviews, as well as hook up user interface elements to the view model publishers. In Koober, view controllers create the view and the view model inside `loadView()`. The view controller creates the view model first and passes it to the view. Since Koober creates view layouts in code, views can have a custom initializer.

If you use Interface Builder to create view controllers and views, view controllers would contain implicitly unwrapped view model variables. Dependency containers would inject view models into view controllers using property injection instead of initializer injection. View controllers would pass the view model to the View inside `viewDidLoad()` or `awakeFromNib()`.

Container views

Each screen in Koober has a container view — a top-level view that contains other child views. The container view's purpose is to build a complex screen out of modular views. Instead of throwing all the user interface into one massive view, keep your views small, focused and reusable.

The "view" in container view refers to a `UIViewController` and its `UIView`.

Structuring container views

A dependency container initializes a container view with its child views. A container view adds and displays child views in its view hierarchy. Child views limit the responsibility of the top-level container view. The number of child views needed depends on the screen's complexity. Each child view is reusable and performs all its work independently.

Why not throw everything in one massive container view? What if you don't need to reuse the view anywhere else in the app? It doesn't matter if the view is reusable. What's important is moving the coordination of view code out of the view model. This lets you change the structure of the app without having to change code inside every view model.

A view model shouldn't know how things work at a higher level. It shouldn't make assumptions or tightly couple itself to coordination code. This makes view coordination code easier to change and allows developers to work together without stepping on each other's toes.

This allows one developer to work on a single screen while another developer works on coordinator screens. They can even make changes in parallel, which is pretty cool!

Example: Koober ride request

The pick-me-up screen contains the meat of the Koober app — the map, the available ride options, and pick-up and drop-off location selections. This is a ton of functionality. If we wrote all this functionality in one view controller, the file would be massive.

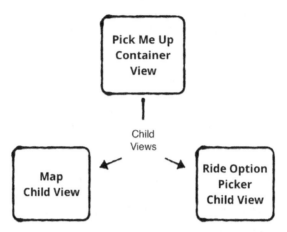

Container views help us organize all the functionality and design each piece independently.

The map and ride-option picker are child views that can live on their own. In Koober, they only live in the pick-me-up screen, but they get the advantage modular view design. One developer could build out the entire map screen while another builds the ride-option picker. Then, the pick-me-up screen adds them to the view hierarchy in the proper place.

Communicating amongst view models

Sometimes, view models need to signal out to the rest of the app when state changes. If a task is outside of the responsibility of one view model, the application may need to notify another view model to take over.

When view models signal out, they communicate what occurred rather than what to do. The application decides what to do. This provides flexibility — you can change how the app responds without changing the view model.

Collaborating view models

Normally state changes in a view model update a view. Sometimes, those state changes affect the entire app. View models don't know how to post app-wide notifications; they take inputs and produce outputs. One way for view models to communicate with the app is to call into another view model, forming a graph of view models.

View models have three ways to collaborate with each other:

- **Closures**: For signaling out, view models take a closure as an initializer argument. The view model calls the closure when an event occurs.

- **Protocols**: Each output signal is modeled with a single method protocol. Other view models that want to respond to outgoing signals must conform to the protocol. You should use a single protocol per signal; otherwise, you force the conformer to place all response logic into a single object.

- **Publishers**: For outgoing signals, a view model exposes a publisher that other view models can modify by updating the publisher's value.

Navigating

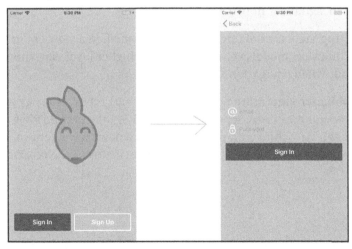

For the onboarding flow in Koober, tapping the Sign In button pushes the sign-in screen onto the navigation stack.

In an architecture like Model-View-Controller (MVC), navigating this flow is straightforward: The Sign In button tap fires a method in the welcome view controller, which creates the sign-in view controller and pushes it onto the navigation stack.

In MVVM, the same flow is more complicated. Remember, the view calls task methods on the view model to get work done — even navigation. The Sign In button tap tells the view model what happened. Next, the view model circles back and tells the view to navigate to the sign-in screen. This indirection is weird but, in pure MVVM, view models handle user interaction.

In this section, you'll look at how to drive navigation between screens, manage view state during navigation and manage scopes when navigating.

Model-driven navigation

In model-driven navigation, view models contain a view enum describing all possible navigation states. The system observes this and navigates to the next screen when the value changes.

Container views and container view models handle navigation for their children. Child view models signal out to the container view model that handles navigation at the top level.

Child views can signal out in two ways:

- **Collaborating view models** signal to each other when a view enum value changes. Child view models get injected with a higher level view model and call task methods when navigation should occur.
- **Shared publisher view state** holds a mutable `Publisher` property with the current view enum value. A dependency container injects child view models with the `Publisher`. Any child view model can push a new view enum value. The container view model observes the value and navigates to the next screen when it changes.

System-driven navigation

System-driven navigation is any navigation managed by the system. For example, gestures that trigger scroll view page navigation, or tapping a Back button in a navigation stack, automatically navigate the user to the previous screen.

In pure MVVM, you override all these gestures, and the view model handles the user interaction. For most apps, this is overkill. A better option is to work with the system and leverage what's already designed for you by Apple. As soon as an MVVM implementation causes friction with the built-in system paradigms, consider using an MVVM implementation that combines model-driven navigation and system-driven navigation.

Combination

You can use built-in, system-driven navigation to your advantage, while still implementing an MVVM architecture. For example, you can use model-driven navigation to move a navigation stack forwards and use system-driven navigation to move backwards.

Koober's onboarding flow uses a combination of model-driven and system-driven navigation.

The onboarding view model switches between three states: welcome, sign in, and sign up. Tapping the Sign In button on the welcome screen changes the view model state to "sign in." The onboarding view reacts to the change, and it pushes the sign-in screen onto the navigation stack. Tapping the Back button on the sign-in screen's navigation bar uses system-driven navigation to pop the screen from the stack.

Managing state

Some navigation schemes create new views when navigating, and other schemes hold onto views and reuse them.

Creating new views on navigation

Creating a new view each time a view is presented is easier to manage. The view and view model aren't held in memory when the view is offscreen.

The system deallocates views each time the application dismisses them. When the application creates them again, the view model populates the view with the correct initial state.

With this option, you don't need to worry about state changes when the view is offscreen.

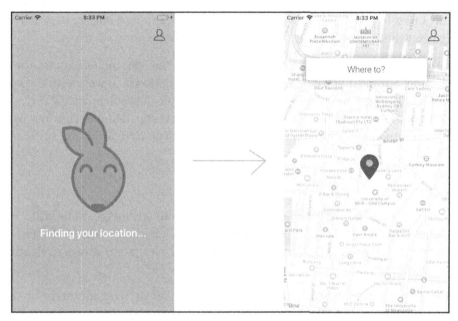

In Koober, you get the user's current location before showing the map screen.

That operation might take a couple seconds, so you show the finding-your-location screen while it's in progress.

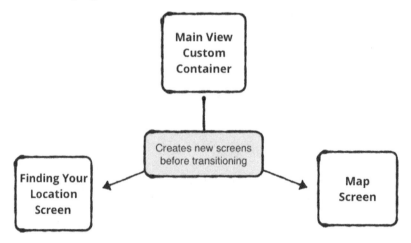

The main-view-custom-container handles the transition between the finding-your-location screen and the map screen. It creates the finding-your-location and the map screens right before any transitions. After presenting the map, it destroys and deallocates the finding-your-location screen.

Reusing views on navigation

Reusing views makes sense when they need to preserve their state. System containers, like tab bars and navigation controllers, reuse views on navigation.

Tab bars hold onto a list of view controllers that live in memory. Navigation controllers reuse views when moving backwards in the stack.

Applying theory to iOS apps

Congratulations for making it to the code examples - the kangaroos are proud! You've just learned a ton of theory about MVVM.

Now that you know the core MVVM concepts, you'll have much more fun in the code example section.

The code example section covers three important real-world use cases for MVVM:

- In **Building a view**, you'll learn how to create the Koober sign-in screen's model layer, view model layer, and view layer.

- In **Composing views**, you'll learn how to request a Koober ride on the map screen. You'll learn how to build the ride option selector, the map screen, and how they communicate with each other using view models.

- In **Navigating**, you'll learn how to drive navigation with view models, and how the map screen navigates between views. Also, you'll learn how the user's profile info is modally presented from the map screen.

Time to dive into the code!

Building a view

The sign-in screen allows you to authenticate with Koober. The initial state shows placeholders for empty email and password fields. The Sign In button is always active, even when the text fields are empty. Tapping the button validates the email and password, and shows an error if either field is empty or if the API call returns an error.

While the sign-in API request is in progress, the screen displays a spinner and disables the user interface.

> **Note**: Most of the code snippets are subsets of the full files. Feel free to open **05-architecture-mvvm/final/KooberApp/KooberApp.xcodeproj** while reading if you'd like to follow along and check out the full source.

Model layer

The sign-in model layer does most of the authentication work. It authenticates with the Koober server and persists the user session. The repositories are in **KooberKit/DataLayer/Repositories** and the models are in **KooberKit/DataLayer/Model**.

The sign-in model layer uses the repository pattern for accessing data — specifically, the UserSessionRepository protocol:

```
public protocol UserSessionRepository {
  func readUserSession() -> Promise<UserSession?>
  func signUp(newAccount: NewAccount) -> Promise<UserSession>
  func signIn(
    email: String, password: String) -> Promise<UserSession>
  func signOut(
    userSession: UserSession) -> Promise<UserSession>
}
```

UserSessionRepository has methods for reading the user session and authenticating a user. For the sign-in screen, you'll call signIn(email: password:).

All the Repository methods return a promise with a `UserSession` object. You use
`PromiseKit`, a third-party framework, to create promises. A promise allows the caller
to return from the method immediately and expect either a success or failure. You'll
learn more about how to use promises in the **View model layer** section below.

```
public class UserSession: Codable {
  public let profile: UserProfile
  public let remoteSession: RemoteUserSession
}

public struct UserProfile: Codable {
  public let name: String
  public let email: String
  public let mobileNumber: String
  public let avatar: URL
}

public struct RemoteUserSession: Codable {
  let token: AuthToken
}
```

`UserSession` is a simple class that contains a profile and a user session.
`UserProfile` contains metadata about the user. `RemoteUserSession` contains an
`AuthToken`, a typealisased `String`.

That's it for the model layer! The repository pattern is awesome because the actual
underlying implementation of the `UserSessionRepository` doesn't matter to the
callers of the protocol methods.

You can see the implementation in **KooberKit/DataLayer/Repositories/
KooberUserSessionRepository.swift**. The repository calls out to a remote API, and
stores the data in a data store. You could swap that out with a fake remote API and
in-memory store, and the `UserSessionRepository` protocol wouldn't change.

View model layer

`SignInViewModel` is where all the reactive magic happens in the sign-in screen. It holds all the view's state, and it signs the user in.

You can find the view model in **KooberKit/UILayer/Onboard/SignIn/SignInViewModel.swift**.

```
public class SignInViewModel {

  // MARK: - Properties
  let userSessionRepository: UserSessionRepository
  let signedInResponder: SignedInResponder

  // MARK: - Methods
  public init(userSessionRepository: UserSessionRepository,
              signedInResponder: SignedInResponder) {
    self.userSessionRepository = userSessionRepository
    self.signedInResponder = signedInResponder
  }

  public var email = ""
  public var password: Secret = ""

  // Publishers go here
  // Task Methods go here
}
```

And you can find the sign in responder protocol in **KooberKit/UILayer/SignedInResponder.swift**.

```
protocol SignedInResponder {
  func signedIn(to userSession: UserSession)
}
```

First, take a look at the dependencies:

- `UserSessionRepository` authenticates the user as you saw above in the **Model layer** section.

- `SignedInResponder` handles a successful sign-in by switching the app state from onboarding to signed in. This causes the app to dismiss the onboarding flow and show the map screen. The sign-in view model doesn't care how the switch happens — it just tells the responder what happened.

The view model also contains `email` and `password` variables. These variables are bound to the email and password input fields in the view layer. You'll see how that's done below in **View layer**.

Next, take a look at the publishers:

```
// SignInViewModel's Publishers
public var errorMessagePublisher:
  AnyPublisher<ErrorMessage, Never> {
    errorMessagesSubject.eraseToAnyPublisher()
}
private let errorMessagesSubject =
  PassthroughSubject<ErrorMessage, Never>()

@Published public private(set)
  var emailInputEnabled = true
@Published public private(set)
  var passwordInputEnabled = true
@Published public private(set)
  var signInButtonEnabled = true
@Published public private(set)
  var signInActivityIndicatorAnimating = false
```

`SignInViewModel` contains the entire state of the sign-in view. The view binds its user interface elements to the publishers, and the view model updates them internally.

The `$emailInputEnabled` and `$passwordInputEnabled` publishers are bound to the view's email and password input fields. To sign in, they both must contain non-empty values.

This diagram shows the sign-in flow:

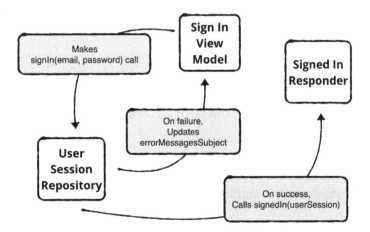

The view model tells the user-session repository to sign in using the email and password values. On success, the view model notifies the signed in responder of the new user session object. On error, the view model updates the `errorMessagesSubject` `PassthroughSubject` publisher with the error message.

Next, look at how the sign-in view model implements task methods:

```
@objc
public func signIn() {
  indicateSigningIn()
  userSessionRepository.signIn(
      email: email,
      password: password)
    .done(signedInResponder.signedIn(to:))
    .catch(indicateErrorSigningIn)
}
```

The sign-in view calls the `signIn()` task method when the user taps the Sign In button. The method is marked `@objc` since the view adds a target / action pair to this selector for its Sign In button.

First, the method calls `indicateSigningIn()`.

```
func indicateSigningIn() {
  emailInputEnabled = false
  passwordInputEnabled = false
  signInButtonEnabled = false
  signInActivityIndicatorAnimating = true
}
```

The `indicateSigningIn` method disables all the user interface controls by setting their values to `false`, and shows the spinner by updating `signInActivityIndicatorAnimating` to `true`.

The view model doesn't care how the sign-in view reacts to these state changes. The view can contain a `UIActivityIndicatorView` or custom spinner.

This is cool because the sign-in business logic is completely separate from the user interface implementation.

Next, the method asks the `UserSessionRepository` to sign the user in using the `email` and `password` values. `signIn()` immediately method returns a promise that will eventually resolve with a valid `UserSession` or fail with an `Error`.

In the success case, `signedInResponder` updates the app with the new `UserSession`.

In the error case, `indicateErrorSigningIn()` updates the view model state using the generated `Error`.

The error will appear with this Sign In Failed dialog:

```
func indicateErrorSigningIn(_ error: Error) {
  errorMessagesSubject.send(
    ErrorMessage(
      title: "Sign In Failed",
      message: "Could not sign in.\nPlease try again."))

  emailInputEnabled = true
  passwordInputEnabled = true
  signInButtonEnabled = true
  signInActivityIndicatorAnimating = false
}
```

This method re-enables all the user interface controls and hides the spinner.

The method also publishes a sign-in error through the `errorMessagesSubject`.

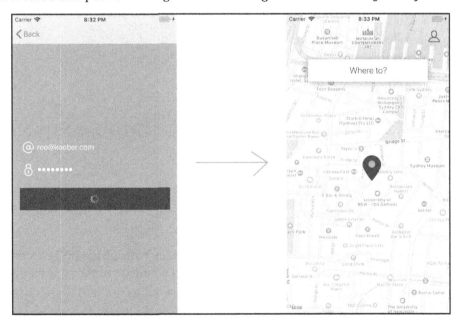

That's the entire view model!

One more thing: You'll notice, when looking at the view model files in the sample project, that none of them import UIKit and are completely independent of UIKit. This ensures you can test the view model logic without access to any UIKit elements.

View layer

We created all Koober root views in code instead of using storyboards. The kangaroos made us do it! No, really, there's a valid reason for this. Root views get a view model injected on initialization. Using storyboards, this would be impossible. Also, in-code constraint creation is a lot easier these days. But that's a debate for another day.

In this section, you'll learn how to create the SignInRootView in the SignInViewController.

SignInRootView is a UIView subclass that contains all the sign-in UI: email and password text fields, the Sign In button and an activity-indicator spinner.

You can find the View files in **Koober_iOS/iOSApp/Onboarding/SignIn**.

```swift
public class SignInViewController : NiblessViewController {

  // MARK: - Properties
  let viewModelFactory: SignInViewModelFactory
  let viewModel: SignInViewModel
  private var subscriptions = Set<AnyCancellable>()

  // MARK: - Methods
  init(viewModelFactory: SignInViewModelFactory) {
    self.viewModelFactory = viewModelFactory
    self.viewModel = viewModelFactory.makeSignInViewModel()
    super.init()
  }

  public override func loadView() {
    self.view = SignInRootView(viewModel: viewModel)
  }
}
```

SignInViewController initializes its SignInRootView with a SignInViewModel in loadView(). The root view knows how to bind its UI elements to the view model's publishers.

```swift
protocol SignInViewModelFactory {
  func makeSignInViewModel() -> SignInViewModel
}
```

`SignInViewModelFactory` protocol has a single responsibility: create a sign-in view model. The `makeSignInViewModel` method returns a ready-to-use `SignInViewModel`.

View controllers don't know how to create view models. View models have dependencies that are outside of the view controller's scope. So you inject factories into view controllers that know how to create view models.

> **Note**: Creating view model factories is out of the scope for this chapter. But, if you'd like to explore the code, the `SignInViewModelFactory` implementation is in **Koober_iOS/iOSApp/Onboarding/KooberOnboardingDependencyContainer.swift**.

That's it for the view controller's responsibility in MVVM. The root view handles the user interface updates, and the view controller manages the view's lifecycle.

Next, look at the sign-in root view:

```
class SignInRootView: NiblessView {

  // MARK: - Properties
  let viewModel: SignInViewModel

  //...

  // MARK: - Methods
  init(frame: CGRect = .zero,
       viewModel: SignInViewModel) {
    self.viewModel = viewModel
    super.init(frame: frame)
    bindTextFieldsToViewModel()
    bindViewModelToViews()
  }

  //...
}
```

`SignInRootView` has a custom initializer that takes a frame and a view model. It uses the injected `SignInViewModel` to bind its UI elements to publishers in initialization.

```
// SignInRootView

// ...

func bindTextFieldsToViewModel() {
  bindEmailField()
```

```
    bindPasswordField()
}

func bindEmailField() {
  emailField
    .publisher(for: \.text)
    .map { $0 ?? "" }
    .assign(to: \.email, on: viewModel)
    .store(in: &subscriptions)
}
func bindPasswordField() {
  passwordField
    .publisher(for: \.text)
    .map { $0 ?? "" }
    .assign(to: \.password, on: viewModel)
    .store(in: &subscriptions)
}

// ...
```

The `bindEmailField()` method binds the `emailField` text variable to the view model's `email` value. Anytime the user enters text in the email text field, the `email` value changes. The `passwordField` behaves the same way.

The bind methods use the text field's `text` variable to drive the view model's corresponding values. Binding the text field to the view model's value means the view model always contains a valid text value. The map function returns an empty string if the text is `nil` to ensure the value is always valid.

Next, let's look at how the view binds the view model's publishers to its views.

```
// SignInRootView
// ...

// MARK: - Dynamic behavior
extension SignInRootView {

  func bindViewModelToViews() {
    bindViewModelToEmailField()
    bindViewModelToPasswordField()
    bindViewModelToSignInButton()
    bindViewModelToSignInActivityIndicator()
  }

  func bindViewModelToEmailField() {
    viewModel
      .$emailInputEnabled
      .receive(on: DispatchQueue.main)
      .assign(to: \.isEnabled, on: emailField)
```

```
      .store(in: &subscriptions)
  }
// ...
```

The binding is pretty simple. The view binds the view model's `$emailInputEnabled` publisher to the `isEnabled` flag on the view's `emailField`. When `emailInputEnabled` changes, `emailField` enables or disables.

`SignInRootView` has one more thing remaining to complete its set up: Bind the Sign In button action to the view model's sign-in task method:

```
// SignInRootView
// ...

func wireController() {
  signInButton.addTarget(
    viewModel,
    action: #selector(SignInViewModel.signIn),
    for: .touchUpInside)
}

// ...
```

The `wireController()` method gets called in the view's `didMoveToWindow()` lifecycle method. The view knows which task method in the view model to wire the `signInButton` touch event. That's the entire view.

The view controller and root view work together to make up the "View" in MVVM. The view controller configures the view with its dependencies. The view lays out and styles the user interface, and it knows how to bind the user inputs to the right publishers.

Composing views

The pick-me-up screen is the heart of the Koober app. This is where the 'roos hop around and fulfill their ride-sharing destinies.

Here, you select where you want a Koober to take you and select your Koober ride option. The map displays pins for your pick-up and drop-off locations, and the bottom container shows the ride-option picker.

In this example, you'll look at the flow of selecting a ride option after you select a drop-off location.

You can find the pick-me-up view models in **KooberKit/iOSApp/UILayer/SignedIn/ PickMeUp** and the UI in **Koober_iOS/iOSApp/SignedIn/PickMeUp**.

Pick-me-up container view

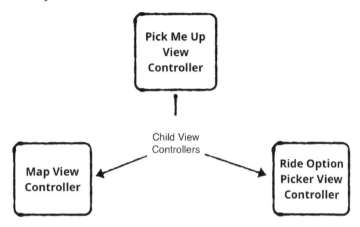

The `PickMeUpViewController` is a container with three children: `PickMeUpMapViewController`, `RideOptionPickerViewController` and `SendingRideRequestViewController`:

```swift
public class PickMeUpViewController: NiblessViewController {

  // MARK: - Properties
  // View Model
  let viewModel: PickMeUpViewModel

  // Child View Controllers
  let mapViewController: PickMeUpMapViewController
  let rideOptionPickerViewController:
    RideOptionPickerViewController
  let sendingRideRequestViewController:
    SendingRideRequestViewController

  // ...

  // MARK: - Methods
  init(viewModel:
         PickMeUpViewModel,
       mapViewController:
         PickMeUpMapViewController,
       rideOptionPickerViewController:
         RideOptionPickerViewController,
       sendingRideRequestViewController:
         SendingRideRequestViewController,
       viewControllerFactory:
         PickMeUpViewControllerFactory) {
    self.viewModel =
      viewModel
    self.mapViewController =
```

```
      mapViewController
    self.rideOptionPickerViewController =
      rideOptionPickerViewController
    self.sendingRideRequestViewController =
      sendingRideRequestViewController
    self.viewControllerFactory =
      viewControllerFactory

    super.init()
  }

  public override func loadView() {
    view = PickMeUpRootView(viewModel: viewModel)
  }

  // ...
}
```

`PickMeUpViewController` gets its child view controllers and `PickMeUpViewModel` on initialization through initializer injection. It adds the children to the view hierarchy, but it knows nothing about their implementations. It's only responsible for laying them out.

The children notify `PickMeUpViewModel` when the user interacts with their views. They don't communicate directly with the parent container view.

Next, look at how `RideOptionPickerViewController` loads ride options based on the user's pick-up location.

Ride-option picker view controller

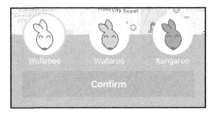

`RideOptionPickerViewController` shows available ride options at the user's pick-up location and a **Confirm** button.

```
public class RideOptionPickerViewController:
  NiblessViewController {

  // ...

  // MARK: - Methods
  init(pickupLocation: Location,
       imageCache: ImageCache,
       viewModelFactory: RideOptionPickerViewModelFactory) {
    self.pickupLocation = pickupLocation
    self.imageCache = imageCache
    self.viewModel =
      viewModelFactory.makeRideOptionPickerViewModel()
    super.init()
  }

  // ...
}
```

`RideOptionPickerViewController` has three dependencies:

- The pick-up `Location` to load the ride options at a specific coordinate.
- An `ImageCache` to get the Koober ride option icons.
- A `RideOptionPickerViewModelFactory` to create the `RideOptionPickerViewModel`.

`RideOptionPickerViewController` uses the dependencies from above to load the ride options:

```
public class RideOptionPickerViewController:
  NiblessViewController {

  // ...

  public override func viewDidLoad() {
```

```
    super.viewDidLoad()
    rideOptionSegmentedControl
      .loadRideOptions(availableAt: pickupLocation)
    observeErrorMessages()
  }

  // ...
}
```

On `loadView()`, the custom segmented control gets set as the screen's root view. On `viewDidLoad()`, the custom segmented control loads the available ride options from the network based on the user's pick-up location.

That's it for the view controller. It creates its root view and loads the ride options.

All the user interaction happens in the root view, which communicates with the view model.

Ride-option picker segmented control

`RideOptionSegmentedControl` displays a button for each Koober ride option:

```
class RideOptionSegmentedControl: UIControl {

  // MARK: - Properties
  let mvvmViewModel: RideOptionPickerViewModel

  // ...

  private func makeRideOptionButton(
    forSegment segment:
    RideOptionSegmentViewModel) ->
    (RideOptionID, RideOptionButton) {

    let button = RideOptionButton(segment: segment)
    button.didSelectRideOption = { [weak self] id in
      self?.mvvmViewModel.select(rideOptionID: id)
    }
    return (segment.id, button)
  }

  // ...
}
```

The segmented control configures each ride-option button ride to notify the `RideOptionPickerViewModel` when the ride option selection changes. Each button's `didSelectRideOption` closure fires on tap, and calls the `func` `select(rideOptionID: RideOptionID)` with the new id.

Since the view model gets injected into the view, it has no clue how the underlying method implementation works. The segmented control only knows how to make calls to the view model's select ride-option task method.

Ride-option picker view model

Next, you'll go into the view model in more depth.

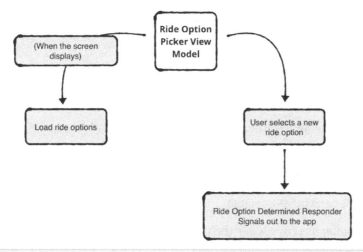

```
public class RideOptionPickerViewModel {

  // MARK: - Properties
  let repository: RideOptionRepository

  @Published public private(set) var pickerSegments =
    RideOptionSegmentedControlViewModel()
  let rideOptionDeterminedResponder:
    RideOptionDeterminedResponder

  public var errorMessages:
    AnyPublisher<ErrorMessage, Never> {
    errorMessagesSubject.eraseToAnyPublisher()
  }
  private let errorMessagesSubject =
    PassthroughSubject<ErrorMessage, Never>()

  // MARK: - Methods
  public init(repository: RideOptionRepository,
              rideOptionDeterminedResponder:
                RideOptionDeterminedResponder) {
    self.repository = repository
    self.rideOptionDeterminedResponder =
      rideOptionDeterminedResponder
  }
```

```swift
public func loadRideOptions(
    availableAt pickupLocation: Location,
    screenScale: CGFloat) {
    // Call loadRideOptions on repository here
    // and show ride options

        // ...
}
public func select(rideOptionID: RideOptionID) {
  var segments = pickerSegments.segments
  for (index, segment) in segments.enumerated() {
    segments[index].isSelected =
      (segment.id == rideOptionID)
  }
  pickerSegments = RideOptionSegmentedControlViewModel(
      segments: segments
  )
  rideOptionDeterminedResponder.pickUpUser(in: rideOptionID)
}
}
```

`RideOptionPickerViewModel` has two dependencies: `RideOptionRepository` and `RideOptionDeterminedResponder`.

- `RideOptionRepository` loads the ride options from the server.

- `RideOptionDeterminedResponder` updates the pick-me-up view state with the new ride-option selections.

When a ride option button calls `select(rideOption: RideOptionID)`, the method updates the `isSelected` state of the ride-option buttons and publishes the new segments. Then, it tells the responder that you selected a new ride option:

```swift
protocol RideOptionDeterminedResponder {
  func pickUpUser(in rideOptionID: RideOptionID)
}
```

The `RideOptionDeterminedResponder` is a protocol with a single method to handle selection. Under the hood, the `RideOptionDeterminedResponder` is the `PickMeUpViewModel` that implements the protocol. Using a protocol to signal out of means that you don't have to pass entire view models to each other and expose extra functionality.

Next, circle back to the `PickMeUpViewModel` and see how you use the responder to update the pick-me-up screen.

Pick-me-up view model

`PickMeUpViewModel` describes the state of the pick-me-up screen using enums:

```
public enum PickMeUpView {
  case initial
  case selectDropoffLocation
  case selectRideOption
  case confirmRequest
  case sendingRideRequest
  case final
}
```

`PickMeUpView` captures every possible state of the pick-me-up screen.

1. `initial` displays the map with an initial hardcoded pick-up location. Koober currently supports one pick-up spot. The select ride-option picker is hidden in this state.

2. `selectDropoffLocation` displays the select drop-off-location picker with a list of predefined drop-off locations.

3. `selectRideOption` displays the select ride-option picker. The Confirm Ride button is initially hidden until you select a ride option.

4. `confirmRequest` displays the select ride-option picker with one option highlighted, as well as the Confirm button.

5. `sendingRideRequest` displays the Requesting Ride screen.

6. `final` dismisses the Requesting Ride screen.

```
enum PickMeUpRequestProgress {
  case initial(pickupLocation: Location)
  case waypointsDetermined(waypoints: NewRideWaypoints)
  case rideRequestReady(rideRequest: NewRideRequest)
}

public struct NewRideRequest: Codable {
  public let waypoints: NewRideWaypoints
  public let rideOptionID: RideOptionID
}

public struct NewRideWaypoints: Codable {
  let pickupLocation: Location
  let dropoffLocation: Location
}
```

`PickMeUpRequestProgress` determines the user's pre-ride request state.

1. `initial(pickupLocation: Location)` configures the initial state with a pick-up location.
2. `waypointsDetermined(waypoints: NewRideWaypoints)` stores the pick-up and drop-off location once a user selects a drop-off location from the list.
3. `rideRequestReady(rideRequest: NewRideRequest)` stores the ride-option selection along with the waypoints in a `NewRideRequest` object.

For ride-option selection, take an in-depth look at the transition from `selectRideOption` state to `confirmRequest` state.

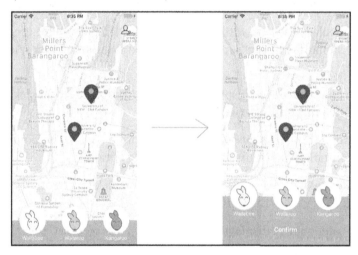

`PickMeUpViewModel` makes the state transition as soon as the user selects one of the ride options.

```
public class PickMeUpViewModel:
  DropoffLocationDeterminedResponder,
  RideOptionDeterminedResponder,
  CancelDropoffLocationSelectionResponder {

  // MARK: - Properties
  var progress: PickMeUpRequestProgress
  let newRideRepository: NewRideRepository
  let newRideRequestAcceptedResponder:
    NewRideRequestAcceptedResponder
  let mapViewModel: PickMeUpMapViewModel

  @Published public private(set) var view: PickMeUpView
  @Published public private(set) var shouldDisplayWhereTo = true
```

```
// ...
func pickUpUser(in rideOptionID: RideOptionID) {
  if case let .waypointsDetermined(waypoints) = progress {
    // 1
    let rideRequest = NewRideRequest(
                    waypoints: waypoints,
                    rideOptionID: rideOptionID)
    // 2
    progress = .rideRequestReady(rideRequest: rideRequest)
    // 3
    view = .confirmRequest
  } else if case
       let .rideRequestReady(oldRideRequest) = progress {
    let rideRequest = NewRideRequest(
                    waypoints: oldRideRequest.waypoints,
                    rideOptionID: rideOptionID)
    progress = .rideRequestReady(rideRequest: rideRequest)
    view = .confirmRequest
  } else {
    fatalError()
  }
}

// ...
}
```

The pick-me-up view model contains a `PickMeUpView` publisher, a `shouldDisplayWhereTo` publisher, and a `PickMeUpRequestProgress` variable.

The `pickUpUser(in: RideOptionID)` handles ride-option selection in three steps:

1. Creates a `NewRideRequest` with the selected ride option and waypoints

2. Updates the internal progress state with the new data.

3. Updates the `PickMeUpView` variable to the `.confirmRequest` state which publishes the new value.

The View reacts to the state change, and it displays the Confirm button.

Here's a diagram showing the entire confirm request flow:

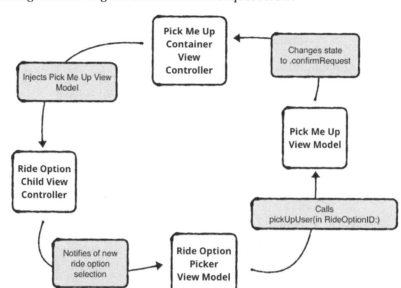

Let's go through the steps one by one:

1. `PickMeUpViewController` injects its `PickMeUpViewModel` into `RideOptionPickerViewController`. `RideOptionPickerViewController` creates a `RideOptionSegmentedControl` with the `PickMeUpViewModel`.

2. `RideOptionSegmentedControl` tells its `RideOptionPickerViewModel` when the user selects a ride option.

3. `RideOptionPickerViewModel` calls `pickUpUser(in rideOptionID: RideOptionID)` on its `PickMeUpViewModel`.

4. `PickMeUpViewModel` changes its state to `.confirmRequest` and `PickMeUpViewController` displays the Confirm button.

That's it for the pick-me-up screen! `PickMeUpViewController` screen relies on its `RideOptionPickerViewController` child to signal out to the view model when the ride-option selection changes. This separation of responsibilities lets the `PickMeUpViewController` focus on higher-level tasks, such as laying out the children on screen and presenting the correct user interface when the `PickMeUpViewModel` state changes.

Navigating

This section is all about navigation. You'll learn different techniques for driving navigation, how to manage initial view state on navigation and managing scopes when transitioning from onboarding to signed in.

Driving navigation

Koober uses three main techniques for driving navigation:

- Model-driven navigation: View model state changes drive transitions in the user interface.
- System-driven navigation: Built-in UIKit components drive navigation.
- Combination of both model- and system-driven navigation.

Model-driven navigation

The transitions from the map to the drop-off selection screen and drop-off selection screen back to the map use model-driven navigation.

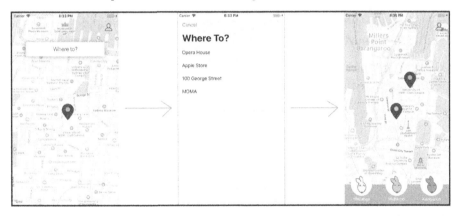

In the initial state, the pick-me-up screen shows your pick-up location, but no drop-off location. Tapping the Where to? button brings up a screen to select the drop-off location.

After you select a location, the screen dismisses, and the pick-me-up screen shows the selected drop-off location along with the ride-option picker.

You can find the pick-me-up view models in **KooberKit/iOSApp/UILayer/SignedIn/PickMeUp** and the user interface in **Koober_iOS/iOSApp/SignedIn/PickMeUp**.

The pick-me-up view model changes the current view state, and the view performs the navigation. You might remember the `PickMeUpView` enum from the **Composing views** section:

```
public enum PickMeUpView {
  case initial
  case selectDropoffLocation
  case selectRideOption
  case confirmRequest
  case sendingRideRequest
  case final
}

public class PickMeUpViewModel:
  DropoffLocationDeterminedResponder,
  RideOptionDeterminedResponder,
  CancelDropoffLocationSelectionResponder {

  // MARK: - Properties
  // ...
  @Published public private(set) var view: PickMeUpView

  // ...
}
```

`PickMeUpViewModel` contains a `PickMeUpView` publisher that gets updated on view state changes. `PickMeUpViewController` observes the changes and reacts by navigating to the next screen.

The view model's pick-me-up view starts in the `initial` state, and switches to `selectDropoffLocation` when the user taps the Where to? button.

```
class PickMeUpRootView: NiblessView {

  // MARK: - Properties
  let viewModel: PickMeUpViewModel
  private var subscriptions = Set<AnyCancellable>()
  let whereToButton: UIButton = {
    // Create and return button here
    // ...
  }()

  // ...

  func bindWhereToButtonToViewModel() {
    whereToButton.addTarget(
      viewModel,
      action: #selector(
        PickMeUpViewModel.
          showSelectDropoffLocationView),
```

```
      for: .touchUpInside)
  }

  // ...
}
```

The View binds the Where to? button to the view model's `showSelectDropoffLocationView()` method.

```
public class PickMeUpViewModel:
  DropoffLocationDeterminedResponder,
  RideOptionDeterminedResponder,
  CancelDropoffLocationSelectionResponder {

  // ...

  @Published public private(set) var view: PickMeUpView

  // ...

  @objc
  public func showSelectDropoffLocationView() {
    view = .selectDropoffLocation
  }

  // ...
}
```

`showSelectDropoffLocationView()` updates the view model's view to `.selectDropoffLocation` which publishes the new value.

Next, let's look at how the view controller observes the state changes.

```
public class PickMeUpViewController: NiblessViewController {

  // MARK: - Properties
  // View Model
  let viewModel: PickMeUpViewModel

  // Child View Controllers
  let mapViewController:
    PickMeUpMapViewController
  let rideOptionPickerViewController:
    RideOptionPickerViewController
  let sendingRideRequestViewController:
    SendingRideRequestViewController

  // State
  private var subscriptions = Set<AnyCancellable>()

  // Factories
```

```swift
  let viewControllerFactory: PickMeUpViewControllerFactory

  // MARK: - Methods
  // ...

  public override func viewDidLoad() {
    addFullScreen(childViewController: mapViewController)
    super.viewDidLoad()
    subscribe(to: viewModel.$view.eraseToAnyPublisher())
    observeErrorMessages()
  }

  func subscribe(to publisher:
    AnyPublisher<PickMeUpView, Never>) {

    publisher
      .receive(on: DispatchQueue.main)
      .sink { [weak self] view in
        self?.present(view)
      }.store(in: &subscriptions)
  }

  func present(_ view: PickMeUpView) {
    switch view {
    case .initial:
      presentInitialState()
    case .selectDropoffLocation:
      presentDropoffLocationPicker()
    case .selectRideOption:
      dropoffLocationSelected()
      // Handle other states
      // ...
    }
  }

  // ...

  func presentDropoffLocationPicker() {
    let viewController =
      viewControllerFactory.
        makeDropoffLocationPickerViewController()
    present(viewController, animated: true)
  }

  // ...
}
```

`PickMeUpViewController` subscribes to the `view` publisher, and calls `present(_ view: PickMeUpView)` on state changes.

When view state switches to selectDropoffLocation, the view controller calls presentDropoffLocationPicker(). It creates and presents a new DropoffLocationPickerViewController.

That's it! View models update the view's current state, and the view reacts to state changes. Dismissing DropoffLocationPickerViewController follows the same model-driven navigation pattern:

```swift
class DropoffLocationPickerContentRootView: NiblessView {

  // MARK: - Properties
  let viewModel: DropoffLocationPickerViewModel

  // ...

  // MARK: - Methods
  init(frame: CGRect = .zero,
       viewModel: DropoffLocationPickerViewModel) {
    // ...
  }

  // ...
}

// ...

extension DropoffLocationPickerContentRootView:
  UITableViewDelegate {

  func tableView(_ tableView: UITableView,
                 didSelectRowAt indexPath: IndexPath) {
    let selectedLocation = searchResults[indexPath.row]
    viewModel.select(dropoffLocation: selectedLocation)
  }
}
```

DropoffLocationPickerContentRootView gets initialized with a DropoffLocationPickerViewModel.

The view model has a task method to select a drop-off location: select(dropoffLocation: NamedLocation). The view controller calls the task method when the user selects a drop-off location.

The pick-me-up view controller still needs to know to dismiss the select drop-off location screen. To accomplish this, the DropoffLocationPickerViewModel needs to notify the PickMeUpViewModel.

Take a look at the drop-off location-picker view model:

```swift
protocol DropoffLocationDeterminedResponder {
    func dropOffUser(at location: Location)
}
```

```swift
public class DropoffLocationPickerViewModel {
    // MARK: - Properties
    // ...
    // Injected Dependency
    let dropoffLocationDeterminedResponder:
        DropoffLocationDeterminedResponder

    // ...

    // MARK: - Methods
    public init(pickupLocation: Location,
                locationRepository: LocationRepository,
                dropoffLocationDeterminedResponder:
                    DropoffLocationDeterminedResponder,
                cancelDropoffLocationSelectionResponder:
                    CancelDropoffLocationSelectionResponder) {
        // ...
    }

    // ...

    public func select(dropoffLocation: NamedLocation) {
        dropoffLocationDeterminedResponder.
            dropOffUser(at: dropoffLocation.location)
    }

    // ...
}
```

`DropoffLocationPickerViewModel` gets initialized with a `DropoffLocationDeterminedResponder`. This is actually a `PickMeUpViewModel` that conforms to the responder protocol. This allows these two view models to communicate with each other.

The drop-off-location picker view model calls `dropOffUser(at:)` on its responder when the user selects a drop-off location.

Next, look at how the `PickMeUpViewModel` responds to the new drop-off location:

```
public class PickMeUpViewModel:
  DropoffLocationDeterminedResponder,
  RideOptionDeterminedResponder,
  CancelDropoffLocationSelectionResponder {

  // ...

  func dropOffUser(at location: Location) {
    guard case let .initial(pickupLocation) = progress
      else {
        fatalError()
    }

    let waypoints = NewRideWaypoints(
      pickupLocation: pickupLocation,
      dropoffLocation: location)
    progress = .waypointsDetermined(waypoints: waypoints)
    view = .selectRideOption
    mapViewModel.dropoffLocation = location
  }

  // ...
}
```

When the user selects a new drop-off location, `PickMeUpViewModel` updates `view` to `.selectRideOption`:

```
public class PickMeUpViewController: NiblessViewController {

  // ...

  func subscribe(to publisher:
    AnyPublisher<PickMeUpView, Never>) {

    publisher
      .receive(on: DispatchQueue.main)
      .sink { [weak self] view in
        self?.present(view)
      }.store(in: &subscriptions)
  }

  func present(_ view: PickMeUpView) {
    switch view {
    case .initial:
      presentInitialState()
    case .selectDropoffLocation:
      presentDropoffLocationPicker()
    case .selectRideOption:
      dropoffLocationSelected()
    case .confirmRequest:
```

```
      presentConfirmControl()
    case .sendingRideRequest:
      presentSendingRideRequestScreen()
    case .final:
      dismissSendingRideRequestScreen()
    }
  }

  // ...

  func dropoffLocationSelected() {
    if presentedViewController is
      DropoffLocationPickerViewController {
      dismiss(animated: true)
    }
    presentRideOptionPicker()
  }

  // ...
}
```

Finally, the view controller reacts to the state change by dismissing the select drop-off location screen and showing the ride option picker.

Here's a diagram showing the entire dropoff location selection flow:

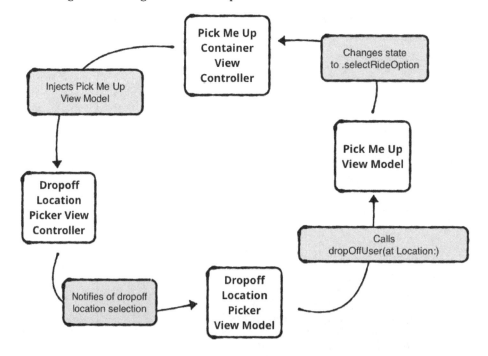

Going through the steps one by one:

1. `PickMeUpViewController` injects its `PickMeUpViewModel` into `DropoffLocationPickerViewController`. `DropoffLocationPickerViewController` creates a `DropoffLocationPickerContentRootView` with the `PickMeUpViewModel`.

2. `DropoffLocationPickerContentRootView` tells its `DropoffLocationPickerViewModel` when the user selects a new drop-off location.

3. `DropoffLocationPickerViewModel` calls `dropOffUser(at location: Location)` on its `PickMeUpViewModel`.

4. `PickMeUpViewModel` changes its state to `.selectRideOption` and `PickMeUpViewController` dismisses the screen.

Model-driven navigation decouples child view controllers from the navigation flow. Children live on their own and signal user interactions by calling task methods on their view models. The container view controller handles high-level navigation.

System-driven navigation

Koober doesn't use pure system-driven navigation anywhere in the app. So leave Koober land for a bit and take a look at a simple `UITabBarController` example.

> **Note**: The Xcode project for this example is in **TabBarExample/TabBarExample.xcodeproj**.

```
let firstViewController = UIViewController()
firstViewController.tabBarItem =
  UITabBarItem(
    title: "Red",
    image: nil,
    selectedImage: nil)
firstViewController.view.backgroundColor = .red

let secondViewController = UIViewController()
secondViewController.tabBarItem =
UITabBarItem(
  title: "Blue",
  image: nil,
  selectedImage: nil)
secondViewController.view.backgroundColor = .blue
```

```
let tabBarController = UITabBarController()
tabBarController.viewControllers =
  [firstViewController, secondViewController]

tabBarController.selectedViewController = secondViewController
```

The `UITabBarController` contains two child view controllers. The tab bar controller sets its select view controller to the second child.

The tab bar uses system-driven navigation to switch between its child view controllers. The tab bar holds on to `firstViewController` and `secondViewController` for its entire lifecycle. When `selectedViewController` changes, the tab bar handles transitions to the correct view controller.

OK, back to Koober!

Combination

The onboarding screen uses model-driven navigation from the welcome screen to the sign-in screen, and it uses system-driven navigation backwards to the welcome screen.

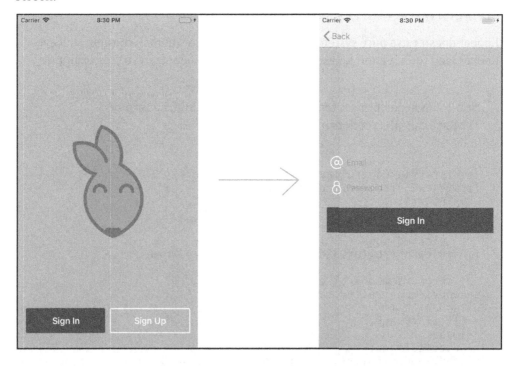

You can find the onboarding view models in **KooberKit/iOSApp/UILayer/Onboard** and the UI in **Koober_iOS/iOSApp/Onboarding**.

```swift
// NavigationAction.swift
public enum NavigationAction<ViewModelType>: Equatable
  where ViewModelType: Equatable {

  case present(view: ViewModelType)
  case presented(view: ViewModelType)
}

// OnboardingViewModel.swift
public typealias OnboardingNavigationAction =
  NavigationAction<OnboardingView>
```

`NavigationAction` tells the view whether or not it needs to be presented or whether it's finished presenting. This allows the view to update the user interface when the navigation transition completes.

```swift
public enum OnboardingView {
  case welcome
  case signin
  case signup

  // ...
}
```

`OnboardingView` has three possible states: welcome, sign in and sign up.

`OnboardingViewController` can present the welcome screen, sign-in screen or sign-up screen.

```swift
public class OnboardingViewModel:
  GoToSignUpNavigator, GoToSignInNavigator {

  // MARK: - Properties
  @Published public private(set)
    var navigationAction: OnboardingNavigationAction =
      .present(view: .welcome)

  // MARK: - Methods
  public init() {}

  func navigateToSignUp() {
    navigationAction = .present(view: .signup)
  }

  func navigateToSignIn() {
    navigationAction = .present(view: .signin)
  }
```

```
  public func uiPresented(onboardingView: OnboardingView) {
    navigationAction = .presented(view: onboardingView)
  }
}
```

`OnboardingViewModel` updates an `OnboardingNavigationAction` publisher when the view state changes. `OnboardingViewController` subscribes to this publisher to present the next screen:

```
public class OnboardingViewController:
  NiblessNavigationController {

  // MARK: - Properties
  // View Model
  let viewModel: OnboardingViewModel
  var subscriptions = Set<AnyCancellable>()

  // ...

  public override func viewDidLoad() {
    super.viewDidLoad()
    let navigationActionPublisher =
      viewModel.$navigationAction.eraseToAnyPublisher()
    subscribe(to: navigationActionPublisher)
  }

  func subscribe(to publisher:
    AnyPublisher<OnboardingNavigationAction, Never>) {

    publisher
      .receive(on: DispatchQueue.main)
      .removeDuplicates()
      .sink { [weak self] action in
        guard let strongSelf = self else { return }
        strongSelf.respond(to: action)
      }.store(in: &subscriptions)
  }

  func respond(to navigationAction:
    OnboardingNavigationAction) {

    switch navigationAction {
    case .present(let view):
      present(view: view)
    case .presented:
      break
    }
  }

  func present(view: OnboardingView) {
    switch view {
```

```
      case .welcome:
        presentWelcome()
      case .signin:
        presentSignIn()
      case .signup:
        presentSignUp()
      }
    }

    func presentWelcome() {
      pushViewController(welcomeViewController,
                         animated: false)
    }

    func presentSignIn() {
      pushViewController(signInViewController,
                         animated: true)
    }

    func presentSignUp() {
      pushViewController(signUpViewController,
                         animated: true)
    }
  }
```

`OnboardingViewController` subscribes to the `OnboardingViewModel` current `OnboardingNavigationAction` publisher. The view controller calls `present(view: OnboardingView)` to push the next view controller onto the navigation stack.

On present, sign-in view controller gets pushed onto a `UINavigationController` stack. At this point, the system takes control of navigation.

The onboarding view controller doesn't handle the navigation backwards when the user taps the Back button in the sign-in screen.

`OnboardingView` state still needs to update to `.welcome` after the sign-in screen gets dismissed. Onboarding view controller updates the state using `UINavigationControllerDelegate` methods:

```
extension OnboardingViewController:
  UINavigationControllerDelegate {

  // ...

  public func navigationController(
    _ navigationController: UINavigationController,
    didShow viewController: UIViewController,
    animated: Bool) {

    guard let shownView =
```

```
        onboardingView(associatedWith: viewController) else {
            return
    }

    viewModel.uiPresented(onboardingView: shownView)
  }
}
```

Onboarding view controller updates state anytime a view controller gets shown on the navigation stack. The `onboardingView(associatedWith: UIViewController)` method returns the view state depending on the view controller's type.

After the backwards transition back to the welcome screen, the view model view state is set back to `.welcome`.

Managing state

When you navigate between screens, there are two ways to manage state:

- Create a new view each time the application presents a new screen.

- Reuse views anytime the application presents a screen.

New views on navigation

Creating a new view each time you present a new screen makes state management easier. You guarantee the screen starts from the initial state each time it's presented.

The main app navigation that navigates from the getting-location screen to the pick-me-up screen to the waiting-for-pick-up screen is an example of creating new views on navigation.

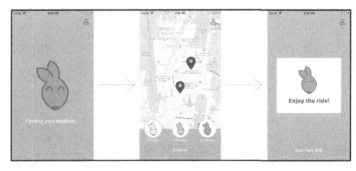

The `SignedInViewController` drives navigation between
`GettingUsersLocationViewController`, `PickMeUpViewController`, and
`WaitingForPickupViewController`.

You can find the view controller file in **Koober_iOS/iOSApp/Onboarding/SignIn**:

```
protocol SignedInViewControllerFactory {
  func makeGettingUsersLocationViewController() ->
    GettingUsersLocationViewController

  func makePickMeUpViewController(pickupLocation: Location) ->
    PickMeUpViewController

  func makeWaitingForPickupViewController() ->
    WaitingForPickupViewController
}

public class SignedInViewController: NiblessViewController {

  // ...

  // MARK: Factories
  let viewControllerFactory: SignedInViewControllerFactory

  // ...

  func present(_ view: SignedInView) {
    switch view {
    case .gettingUsersLocation:
      let viewController = viewControllerFactory.
        makeGettingUsersLocationViewController()
      transition(to: viewController)
    case .pickMeUp(let pickupLocation):
      let viewController = viewControllerFactory.
        makePickMeUpViewController(
          pickupLocation: pickupLocation)
      transition(to: viewController)
    case .waitingForPickup:
      let viewController = viewControllerFactory.
        makeWaitingForPickupViewController()
      transition(to: viewController)
    }
  }

  // ...

  func transition(to viewController: UIViewController) {
    remove(childViewController: currentChildViewController)
    addFullScreen(childViewController: viewController)
    currentChildViewController = viewController
  }
}
```

`SignedInViewController` uses a factory to create its child view controller. `SignedInViewController` calls the `present(_: SignedInView)` method each time the `SignedInView` state changes.

On state changes, `SignedInViewController` destroys and deallocates the current child. Then, it adds the next child on screen. Children are only instantiated when needed — no one holds a reference to previous child.

> **Note**: `remove(_:)` and `addFullScreen(_:)` call view controller containment methods on the child view controllers.

Reusing views on navigation

Reusing views on navigation makes state management harder. Each time you present a new screen, you need to make sure the state is reset back to the original state. The onboarding flow is an example of reusing views on navigation.

`OnboardingViewController` drives navigation from `WelcomeViewController` to `SignInViewController`. As you saw in the **Driving Navigation — Combination** section above, `OnboardingViewController` initially shows a `WelcomeViewController`. `OnboardingViewController` pushes a `SignInViewController` onto the navigation stack when the user taps the Sign In button.

You can find the View Controller file in **Koober_iOS/Onboarding**:

```swift
public class OnboardingViewController:
  NiblessNavigationController {

  // ...

  // Child View Controllers
  let welcomeViewController: WelcomeViewController
  let signInViewController: SignInViewController
  let signUpViewController: SignUpViewController

  // ...

  func presentWelcome() {
    pushViewController(welcomeViewController,
                       animated: false)
  }

  func presentSignIn() {
    pushViewController(signInViewController,
```

```
                      animated: true)
  }

  func presentSignUp() {
    pushViewController(signUpViewController,
                       animated: true)
  }
}
```

`UINavigationController` reuses views when moving backwards. `OnboardingViewController` holds a reference to the welcome view controller while displaying the sign-in view controller. When the user taps the Back button, the navigation stack doesn't create a new welcome screen.

The onboarding view controller must ensure the welcome screen is in the correct state when the navigation stack pops the sign-in screen.

Managing scopes: Onboarding to signed in

During the onboarding flow, no authenticated user exists. There's no reason to create a map, since the map needs an authenticated user to work.

When the user signs in, you switch the scope from unauthenticated to authenticated. At this point, you can destroy and deallocate all onboarding screens and create a new map screen.

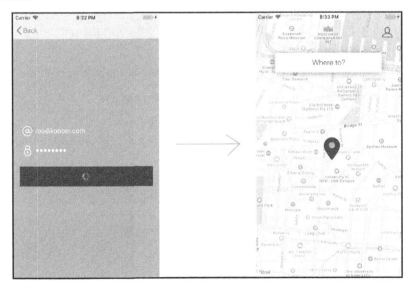

You can find the view controller files in **Koober_iOS/iOSApp** and **Koober_iOS/iOSApp/Onboarding**:

```swift
public class MainViewController: NiblessViewController {

  // MARK: - Properties
  // View Model
  let viewModel: MainViewModel

  // Child View Controllers
  let launchViewController: LaunchViewController
  var signedInViewController: SignedInViewController?
  var onboardingViewController: OnboardingViewController?

  // ...
}
```

`MainViewController` drives navigation between `OnboardingViewController` and `SignedInviewController`, moving the app from the onboarding to signed-in states.

`OnboardingViewController` contains the welcome, sign-in and sign-up screens.

`SignedInviewController` contains the map, ride-option picker, and displays the user-profile screen.

```swift
public class MainViewController: NiblessViewController {

  // ...

  public func presentOnboarding() {
    let onboardingViewController =
      makeOnboardingViewController()
    onboardingViewController.modalPresentationStyle =
      .fullScreen
    present(onboardingViewController, animated: true) {
      [weak self] in
      guard let strongSelf = self else {
        return
      }

      strongSelf.remove(childViewController:
        strongSelf.launchViewController)
      if let signedInViewController =
        strongSelf.signedInViewController {
        strongSelf.remove(childViewController:
          signedInViewController)
        strongSelf.signedInViewController = nil
      }
    }
    self.onboardingViewController = onboardingViewController
  }
```

```
  // ...
}
```

In the onboarding flow, the signed-in screen doesn't exist. That screen requires a valid user session as a dependency — during the onboarding flow, no valid user session exists.

After `MainViewController` presents a new `OnboardingViewController`, `MainViewController` removes and deallocates any previous `SignedInViewController` from the view hierarchy. This could happen on a sign out:

```
// ...
  public func presentSignedIn(userSession: UserSession) {
    remove(childViewController: launchViewController)

    let signedInViewControllerToPresent:
      SignedInViewController
    if let vc = self.signedInViewController {
      signedInViewControllerToPresent = vc
    } else {
      signedInViewControllerToPresent =
        makeSignedInViewController(userSession)
      self.signedInViewController =
        signedInViewControllerToPresent
    }

    addFullScreen(childViewController:
      signedInViewControllerToPresent)

    if onboardingViewController?.
      presentingViewController != nil {
        onboardingViewController = nil
        dismiss(animated: true)
    }
  }
}
// ...
```

When the user signs in, `MainViewController` creates a brand new `SignInViewController`. Then, `MainViewController` removes any previous `OnboardingViewController` from the view hierarchy.

After the app switches from non-authenticated to authenticated scope, only the `SignedInViewController` exists. For any UI that existed in the non-authenticated scope, the application tears it down and deallocates it.

Pros and cons of MVVM

Pros of MVVM

1. View model logic is easy to test independently from the user interface code. View models contain zero UI — only business and validation logic.

2. View and model are completely decoupled from each other. View model talks to the view and model separately.

3. MVVM helps parallelize developer workflow. One team member can build a view while another team member builds the view model and model. Parallelizing tasks gives your team's productivity a nice boost.

4. While not inherently modular, MVVM does not get in the way of designing a modular structure. You can build out modular UI components using container view and child views, as long as your view models know how to communicate with each other.

5. View models can be used across Apple platforms (iOS, tvOS, macOS, etc.) because they don't import `UIKit`. Especially if view models are granular.

Cons of MVVM

1. There is a learning curve with `Combine` (compared to MVC.) New team members need to learn `Combine` and how to properly use view models. Development time may slow down at first, until new team members get up to speed.

2. Typical implementation requires view models to collaborate. Managing memory and syncing state across your app is more difficult when using collaborating view models.

3. Business logic is not reusable from different views, since business logic is inside view specific view models.

4. It can be hard to trace and debug, because UI updates happen through binding instead of method calls.

5. View models have properties for both UI state and dependencies. This means that view models can be difficult to read, because state management is mixed with side effects and dependencies.

Key points

- The **model layer** reads and writes data to disk and tells the view model when data has changed.
- The **view model layer** contains all the view layer's state and handles user interactions. The view model listens for change in the model layer and updates its state.
- The **view layer** reacts when view model state changes and tells the view model when the user interacts with its components.
- **Repositories** are a façade for networking and persistence. View models use repositories for data access instead of performing the actions themselves.
- The view layer and model layer are completely decoupled. They each only communicate with the view model layer.

Where to go from here?

Koober is meant to be a real-world use case, and there's a ton of code in the example project we couldn't cover in one chapter. Feel free to explore the codebase on your own.

Here's a few places to look:

1. Check out how the signed-in dependency container gets created in **Koober_iOS/iOSApp/SignedIn/KooberSignedInDependencyContainer.swift**. The container creates all the screens that require an authenticated user session.

2. Before Koober shows the map, you have to fetch the user's current location. Follow the flow showing the Getting Your Location screen, before navigating to the map. Check out:

- **Koober_iOS/iOSApp/SignedIn/SignedInViewController.swift** for the navigation.

- **KooberKit/UILayer/SignedIn/GettingUsersLocation/GettingUsersLocationViewModel.swift** for the fetching location logic.

- **Koober_iOS/iOSApp/SignedIn/GettingUsersLocation/GettingUsersLocationRootView.swift** for calling the view model's task method.

3. Look into how the drop-off-location picker search works. The drop-off-location picker view controller contains a custom observable search UI controller, and it binds the search input to the drop-off-location picker view model. The view model fetches new locations using a repository, and it updates its search results state. Check out:

- **KooberKit/UILayer/SignedIn/PickMeUp/SelecDropoffLocation/DropoffLocationPickerViewModel.swift** for the view model.

- **Koober_iOS/iOSApp/SignedIn/PickMeUp/SelectDropoffLocation/DropoffLocationPickerContentViewController.swift** for the view.

Chapter 6: Architecture: Redux

By René Cacheaux & Josh Berlin

At Facebook, some years ago, a bug in the desktop web app sparked a new architecture. The app presented the unread count of messages from Messenger in several views at once, not always presenting the same amount of unread messages. This could get out of sync and report different numbers, so the app looked broken. Facebook needed a way to guarantee data consistency and, out of this problem, a new unidirectional architecture was born — Flux.

After Facebook moved to a Flux based architecture, views that showed the unread message count got data from the same container. This new architecture fixed a lot of these kinds of bugs.

Flux is a pattern, though, not a framework. In 2015, Dan Abramov and Andrew Clark created Redux as a JavaScript implementation of a Flux inspired architecture. Since then, others have created Redux implementations in languages such as Swift and Kotlin.

What is Redux?

Redux is an architecture in which all of your app's state lives in one container. The only way to change state is to create a new state based on the current state and a requested change.

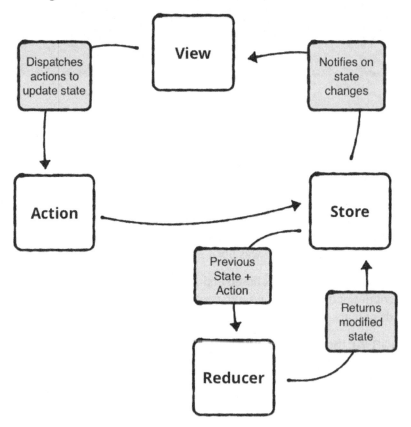

The **Store** holds all of your app's state.

An **Action** is immutable data that describes a state change.

A **Reducer** changes the app's state using the current state and an action.

Store

The Redux store contains all state that drives the app's user interface. Think of the store as a living snapshot of your app. Anytime its state changes, the user interface updates to reflect the new state.

You might think storing everything in one place is insane — that's a valid thought. Instead of creating one massive file for the state, split it up into different sub-states. Each screen cares about a part of the entire apps state, anyway. We'll talk more about keeping the store organized in the example code section of this chapter.

Types of state

A Store contains data that represents an app's user interface (UI). Here are some examples:

- **View state** determines which user elements to show, hide, enable, disable or whether a spinner is animating.

- **Navigation state** determines which view to present to the user and which views are currently presented.

- **High-level state** determines whether the user is signed in or signed out. Current user profile metadata and authentication tokens could be contained in the high-level state.

- **Data from web services** include things like responses from a REST API. The response gets parsed into models and placed in the store. In Koober, the available ride options displayed on the map live in the store.

- **Formatted strings** are strings that get transformed for display from raw model data from an API.

The store is the source of truth for your app. All views get data from the same store, so there's no chance of two views displaying different data, as was happening during Facebook's bug.

Derived values

The store doesn't contain larger files, such as images or videos. Instead, it contains file URLs pointing to media on disk.

The entire store is in memory at all times. If your app has tons of video files or images in the store instead of file references, iOS may crash your app to free up memory.

Modeling view state

In a Redux architecture, views store no state. They only listen and react to state changes. So, any state that changes how the view behaves lives in the store. Stores consist of immutable value types. When data in the store changes, views get a new, immutable state to re-render the user interface.

Sign-in screen

Onboarding displays a welcome screen where you can navigate to the sign-in or sign-up screens. The app state determines which screen is currently shown to the user. When the app state changes, the app presents a new screen to the user.

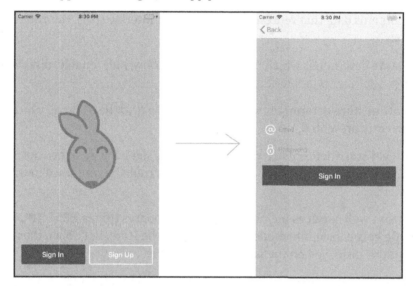

The `Onboarding` state shows the unauthenticated screens before the user logs in. The `Signed In` state shows the authenticated screens after the user logs in.

The Onboarding state contains three states:

1. Welcoming
2. Signing In
3. Signing Up

Welcoming displays the welcome screen, which has Sign In and Sign Up buttons. When you tap the Sign In button, you set the app state to `Signing In`. When you tap the Sign Up button, you set the app state to `Signing Up`.

At any moment, you can look at the state of the Redux store to determine what screen the user interface is presenting.

Loading and rendering initial state

Koober has two high-level app states:

- **Launching** loads any data that the app needs to function, like a previous user session.

- **Running** displays either the onboarding flow or the map screen.

The **Running** state has two sub-states:

- **Onboarding** displays the sign-in or sign-up screen so that the user can authenticate.

- **Signed In** displays the map and needs a valid user session.

Koober starts in the "launching" state.

Once the "launching" state reads the user session, the app transitions to the "running" state. Next, the user interface displays either the onboarding flow or the signed-in screens. The Redux store always has an initial state and never has an invalid state. Redux forces you to declare every possible state for your app.

If you don't persist data between launches, that data must have an initial default in the store. For example, Koober has ride options you can choose before requesting a ride: Wallaby, Wallaroo and Kangaroo. These values can change, so they come from the server. Before you download them, the initial state in the Redux store is an empty array. The user interface should be able to gracefully handle this empty state.

Subscription

For a view to render, it subscribes to changes in the store. Each time state changes, the view gets wholesale changes containing the entire state — there is no middle ground. This is unlike MVVM, where you manipulate one property at a time.

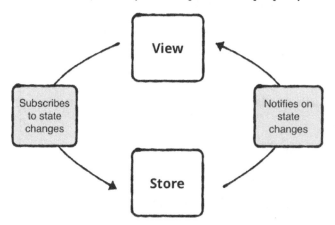

Using **Focused Observation**, the view can subscribe to pieces of state that it's interested in, avoiding updates when any app state changes occur. The view still gets the piece of state in one update.

Views need the current state from the store each time the view loads. On load, they always have an empty state. After subscribing to the store, it fires an update and the view re-renders.

There's a short delay between when the app presents the view on screen and when the subscription fires its first update. The duration is usually short enough where you don't notice the first update. But make sure all views can gracefully display an empty state.

Responding to user interactions

Actions are immutable data that describe a state change. You create actions when the user interacts with the user interface.

Dispatching an action is the only way to change state in the Redux store. No sneaky view can grab the store and make changes without the rest of the app finding out. Redux works because actions change the store, and it notifies subscribers across the app.

For example, in the Welcome screen, there are two buttons, Sign In and Sign Up.

When the Sign Up button gets tapped, you create and dispatch a Go to Sign Up action. The store updates its state, and it notifies the `OnboardingViewController`. Then, the `OnboardingViewController` pushes the sign-up screen onto the navigation stack.

Reducers describe possible state changes. Reducers are the step between dispatching an action and changing the store's state. After an action is dispatched, it travels through a reducer. The *only* place the store's state can mutate is in a reducer. Reducers are free functions that take in the current store's state along with an action describing a state. They mutate a copy of the current state based on the action, and return the new state. Reducer functions should not introduce side effects. They should not make API calls or modify objects outside of their scope.

In addition to updating state based on actions, reducers can run business logic to transform state. Date formatting logic lives in reducers to transform data for display. For example, a reducer can transform a `Date` object to a presentable `String`.

Koober contains a lot of logic in reducers. It's already enough trouble keeping view controllers small. The last thing you need is a massive reducer file.

Redux recommends to split your reducers into sub-reducers. Sub-reducers help keep your reducer logic focused and readable. Koober has sub-reducers for the onboarding flow, the sign-up screen, the sign-in screen and so on.

Threading

In Redux, it's important to run all the reducers on the same thread. It doesn't have to be the main thread, but the same serial queue.

If you run the reducers on multiple threads, the input state of the reducer could change while it's running on another thread. Redux is a synchronization point by design.

`ReSwift`, a Redux implementation of unidirectional data flow architecture in Swift, lets you run reducers on any serial queue, but defaults to the main queue. The simplest approach is to run on the main queue because the user interface and store are completely in sync. Then, there's no need to hop on main queue when observing the store.

> **Note**: In a complex app, reducers might take some time. In this case, it can be a good idea to run reducers on another serial queue that's not the main queue. Most of the time, the main queue is fine.

Performing side effects

Side effects are any non-pure functions. Any time you call a function that can return a different value given the same inputs is a side effect. Pure functions are deterministic. Given the same inputs, the function always has the same outputs.

Reducers should be pure functions, free of side effects. In Redux, you handle side effects before dispatching actions and after the store updates.

For example, apps commonly make asynchronous API calls to a server and wait for a response. In Redux, you never make these asynchronous API calls in reducer functions. Instead, create multiple actions for different stages of your network request.

Stages of a network request:

1. Network request is in progress.
2. Network request completed successfully.
3. Network request failed.

Before starting the network request, dispatch an In-progress action. The reducer updates the state in the store to indicate the network request is in-progress. The view updates its user interface to reflect the change by showing a spinner and disabling UI elements as needed.

Next, make the network request. Once the API call completes, dispatch a *Network Request Succeeded* or *Network Request Failed* action. The store updates its state, and the view updates to show a success or failed message, and enables its UI elements. You can also dispatch actions during the network requests to update percentage complete state in the store.

A network request is one example of an asynchronous operation, and any asynchronous task can follow the same process: dispatch actions before, during and after the task completes.

Rendering updates

Redux is a "reactive" architecture. The word "reactive" is thrown around a lot these days. In Redux, "reactive" means the view receives updated state via subscriptions, and it "reacts" to the updates. Views never ask the store for the current state; they only update when the store fires an update that data changed.

Diffing

Each time a view receives new state via subscription, it gets the whole state. The view needs to figure out what changed and then properly render the update.

The simple solution is to reload the entire UI, although this might look clunky. Another solution is to diff the new state with the current state of the UI and render necessary updates.

Diffing helps avoid unnecessary changes. It also allows views to animate changes, since you know exactly which user interface element changed.

`UIKit` sometimes won't render unnecessary changes. You can test this by subclassing a `UIView`, set a property to some test value, and check if the system calls draw rect or needs display.

Example: Onboarding to signed-in

Koober has two high-level app states:

- **Onboarding** displays the sign-in or sign-up screen when the user is not authenticated.
- **Signed-in** displays the map screen after the user signs in.

Koober handles the transition from onboarding to signed-in in the main view — a container view that can display the sign-in screen or the map screen.

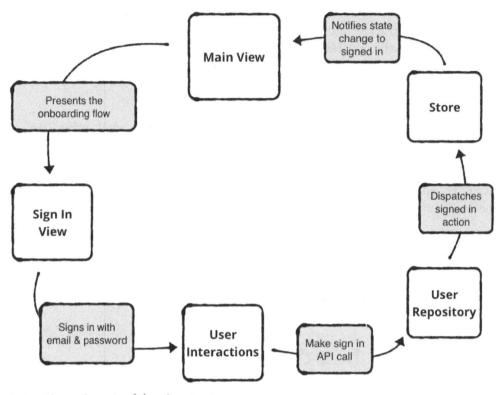

Going through each of the sign-in steps:

1. Main view initially presents the sign-in screen.

2. The user enters an email and password and then taps the Sign In button.

3. The Sign-in view tells its user interaction object to sign the user in to Koober.

4. The user interaction object asks its repository to make the sign-in API call.

5. Once the API call completes, the user interactions object dispatches a Signed-in action containing the new user session.

6. The store notifies the main view to transition to Signed-in and display the map.

Next, let's look at the Sign-in view in more detail.

Example: Signing in

The sign-in screen contains a Username / Email text field, Password text field and a Sign In button. Tapping the Sign In button signs you in using the username and password inputs.

If a sign in succeeds, an action gets dispatched containing the new user session. If sign in fails, an action gets dispatched containing the Error message to present.

The sign-in state contains four `Boolean` values and error messages:

1. Email input enabled.
2. Password input enabled.
3. Sign In button enabled.
4. Sign-in activity indicator animating.
5. A list of errors to present.

The sign-in screen dispatches actions on user interaction, which updates the sign-in state in the store. Redux broadcasts the new state and the sign-in screen reacts by updating its user interface.

The sign-in screen can dispatch four actions:

1. **Signing in** to signal a sign-in operation is in progress.
2. **Sign-in failed** to signal sign-in failed along with the error message.
3. **Finished presenting error** to signal the user has acknowledged the error.
4. **Signed in** to signal the sign-in succeeded with a valid user session.

Let's go through each in more detail.

Signing In Action is dispatched after the user enters a username and password, and taps the Sign In button.

The signing-in action gets dispatched before you make the call to the Koober API to sign in, and the reducer updates the store's state.

Then, the store notifies the view the state changed to signing in.

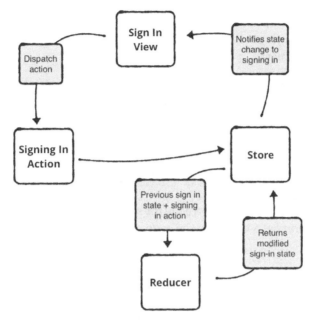

Sign-in failed action is dispatched after the Koober API returns a failed response from the sign-in call. The state change includes the error message for the view to present.

Finished presenting error action is dispatched after the view dismisses the error message. This state is important when you want to modify the user interface while the error is displayed on screen. You might also want to present a second error only after the user dismisses the first error.

Signed in action is dispatched after the Koober API returns a successful response. In this state, the sign-in screen can transition to a success state which includes the valid user session object.

After the user successfully signs in to Koober, the sign-in screen has no more responsibilities. The main view transitions the app from the unauthenticated state to the authenticated state, and shows the map screen.

Applying theory to iOS apps

If we had to guess, you're probably ready for some Kangaroo-filled code examples after all that theory! Let's dive into the code and see how Redux actually works in practice.

Redux in iOS apps

ReSwift and Katana are the two main Swift Redux implementations. Both have a strong following on GitHub and are great choices for your Redux library. Redux is a simple concept, and you could write your own Redux library. All the Redux libraries are super small by design. Either way, use of a library is recommended.

Koober uses ReSwift since it's the most established library. For more details about ReSwift, check out the GitHub repo located at https://github.com/ReSwift/ReSwift.

> **Note**: Most of the code snippets are subsets of the full files. Feel free to open **06-architecture-redux/final/KooberApp/KooberApp.xcodeproj** while reading if you'd like to follow along and check out the full source.

Building a view

Before you can hop on a Kangaroo around Sydney, you have to sign in to Koober. You sign in to the app in the sign-in screen, which contains an Email field, Password field and a Sign In button.

Tapping the Sign In button makes an authentication call to the Koober API and signs you in to the app.

View controller

The `SignInViewController` configures the `SignInRootView` and observes store state changes.

Let's take a look at the `SignInViewController` initializer:

```swift
public class SignInViewController: NiblessViewController {
  // MARK: - Properties
  // ...

  // MARK: - Methods
  init(state: AnyPublisher<SignInViewControllerState, Never>,
       userInteractions: SignInUserInteractions) {
    self.statePublisher = state
    self.userInteractions = userInteractions
    super.init()
  }

  // ...
}
```

`SignInViewController` has two initializer dependencies:

- A `Combine` publisher to subscribe to `SignInViewControllerState` changes.
- A `SignInUserInteractions` object to handle user interactions in the `SignInRootView`.

You'll notice there are no `ReSwift` dependencies in the view controller. You can abstract `ReSwift` away from view controllers so that you can change libraries or paradigms without needing to refractor view layer code. This section walks you through how to do that.

Sign-in view state

Open, **SignInViewControllerState.swift** inside **KooberKit**:

```swift
public struct SignInViewState: Equatable {

  // MARK: - Properties
  public internal(set) var emailInputEnabled = true
  public internal(set) var passwordInputEnabled = true
  public internal(set) var signInButtonEnabled = true
  public internal(set) var signInActivityIndicatorAnimating
    = false

  // MARK: - Methods
  public init() {}
}
```

The `SignInViewState` describes all states of the `SignInRootView`. The first three Boolean values determine if user interactions are possible in the root view. The `signInActivityIndicatorAnimating` value determines if the activity indicator is spinning or hidden.

```swift
public struct SignInViewControllerState: Equatable {

  // MARK: - Properties
  public internal(set) var viewState = SignInViewState()
  public internal(set) var errorsToPresent: Set<ErrorMessage>
    = []

  // MARK: - Methods
  public init() {}
}
```

The `SignInViewControllerState` encapsulates the root view state and error handling.

The view controller gets its own state because it presents errors using view controller presentation APIs.

The error messages are a collection in case there are multiple error messages to display in succession.

Sign-in user interactions

The `SignInUserInteractions` protocol describes possible user interactions in the sign-in screen:

```
public protocol SignInUserInteractions {
  func signIn(email: String, password: Secret)
  func finishedPresenting(_ errorMessage: ErrorMessage)
}
```

The user can sign in by tapping the Sign In button after entering an email and password. Once the user taps the button, the `signIn(email:password:)` method gets called.

If signing in fails, the view controller displays an error on the screen. After the user dismisses the error, or the error dismisses after a short period of time, the `finishedPresenting(_:)` method gets called.

The sign-in view controller has no clue about the underlying implementations for these methods. The view controller gets a concrete instance of `SignInUserInteractions` on initialization.

App state

`SignInViewControllerState` describes the sign-in screen in isolation. But the state is part of a larger state tree.

As you might remember from the **Example: Onboarding to signed in** section, Koober has two high-level app states.

In the **Onboarding** state, the user is unauthenticated, and Koober can present the sign-up or sign-in screen.

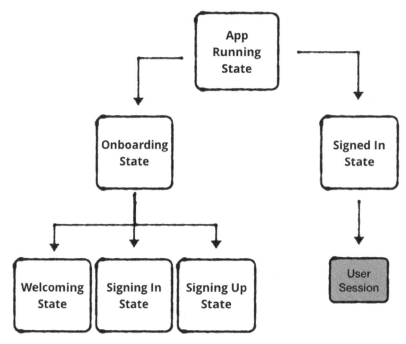

In the **Signed In** state, the user has authenticated in the sign-up or sign-in flow.

```
public enum AppRunningState: Equatable {
    case onboarding(OnboardingState)
    case signedIn(SignedInViewControllerState, UserSession)
}
```

AppRunningState describes the high level app states. Each state has its own sub-state which contains extra information.

Let's go over the OnboardingState first:

```
public enum OnboardingState: Equatable {

    case welcoming
    case signingIn(SignInViewControllerState)
    case signingUp(SignUpViewControllerState)

    // ...
}
```

The Onboarding flow has three states:

- **Welcoming** displays the welcome screen, which can navigate to the sign-up or sign-in screen.
- **Signing in** lets you sign in as an existing user. The `SignInViewControllerState` describes the possibles states isolated to the sign-in screen. These are described above in **sign-in view state**.
- **Signing up** lets you sign up as a new user. The `SignUpViewControllerState` describes the possible states isolated to the sign-up screen.

The signed-in state is the authenticated state, where you can request a Koober on the map. The important piece of the state in the `.signedIn` app running state is the `UserSession`.

```swift
public class UserSession: Codable {

  // MARK: - Properties
  public let profile: UserProfile
  public let remoteSession: RemoteUserSession

  // MARK: - Methods
  public init(profile: UserProfile,
              remoteSession: RemoteUserSession) {
    self.profile = profile
    self.remoteSession = remoteSession
  }
}
```

```swift
public struct RemoteUserSession: Codable, Equatable {

  // MARK: - Properties
  let token: AuthToken

  // MARK: - Methods
  public init(token: AuthToken) {
    self.token = token
  }
}
```

```swift
public struct UserProfile: Equatable, Codable {

  // MARK: - Properties
  public let name: String
  public let email: String
  public let mobileNumber: String
  public let avatar: URL
```

```
// MARK: - Methods
public init(name: String,
            email: String,
            mobileNumber: String,
            avatar: URL) {
  self.name = name
  self.email = email
  self.mobileNumber = mobileNumber
  self.avatar = avatar
  }
}
```

The `UserSession` object contains information about the current authenticated user, like the authentication token, name and avatar URL.

The signed-in state *always* has a valid user session — it's a dependency of the `.signedIn` state. If the user logs out, the user session gets destroyed, and the app switches back to the `.onboarding` state.

Equatable state models

To prevent duplicate calls, make your state models `Equatable`. Otherwise, multiple calls to UI methods could occur. For example, you could present a view controller over and over again — not a great user experience!

Make sure your state enums with associated values behave properly when compared. Swift 4.2 and later handles auto synthesizing `Equatable` and `Hashable` for most models.

Using Combine to observe ReSwift

Koober abstracts the `ReSwift` dependency from all user interface code, including `UIViewControllers` and `UIViews`. This makes it easier to switch the Redux implementation down the road, since none of the user interface code needs to change. Koober still gets the benefits of `ReSwift`, though. It still dispatches actions and changes state in pure reducer functions. The difference is `Combine` drives the user interface updates instead of `ReSwift` store subscriptions.

ReSwift publishers

Instead of subscribing directly to the `ReSwift` state store, view controllers in Koober subscribe to Combine publishers created from the `ReSwift` store. For this to work, a `Combine Subscription` forwards the `ReSwift` store subscriber updates to `Combine` publisher subscribers:

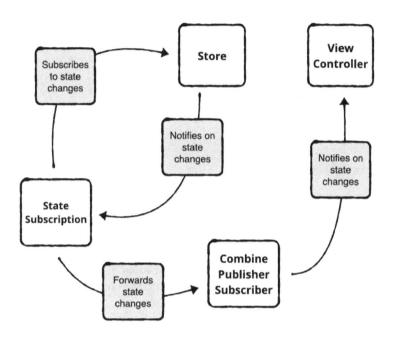

```
private final class StateSubscription
  <S: Subscriber, StateT: Any>:
  Combine.Subscription, StoreSubscriber
  where S.Input == StateT {

  var requested: Subscribers.Demand = .none
  var subscriber: S?

  let store: Store<StateT>
  var subscribed = false

  init(subscriber: S, store: Store<StateT>) {
    self.subscriber = subscriber
    self.store = store
  }
```

```
  func cancel() {
    store.unsubscribe(self)
    subscriber = nil
  }

  func request(_ demand: Subscribers.Demand) {
    requested += demand

    if !subscribed, requested > .none {
      // Subscribe to ReSwift store
      store.subscribe(self)
      subscribed = true
    }
  }

  // ReSwift calls this method on state changes
  func newState(state: StateT) {
    guard requested > .none else {
      return
    }
    requested -= .max(1)

    // Forward ReSwift update to subscriber
    _ = subscriber?.receive(state)
  }
}
```

A `StateSubscription` handles the ReSwift store subscription. After subscribing to the store, ReSwift calls `newState(state:)` when state changes and forwards it to the Combine subscriber's `receive(_:)` method.

Publishers get created in an extension on the ReSwift store:

```
extension Store where State: Equatable {

  public func publisher() -> AnyPublisher<State, Never> {
    return StatePublisher(store: self).eraseToAnyPublisher()
  }

  //...

}
```

`publisher()` creates and returns a `StatePublisher` that creates a `StateSubscription` that gets called whenever the ReSwift State changes. In Koober, publishers get injected into view controllers. View controllers subscribe to the publisher, the publisher creates a Combine subscription, the Combine subscription subscribes to the ReSwift store, and then the view controllers receive updates when the ReSwift store state changes.

Focusing the publisher

Each view only cares about a subset of the `ReSwift` store's state tree. For example, the user profile screen displays user information and knows nothing about the map. There's no point for the store to notify the profile screen when the user's location changes or more Kangaroos become available for a ride.

The profile screen only needs to re-render when user profile data changes.

The flow now looks like this:

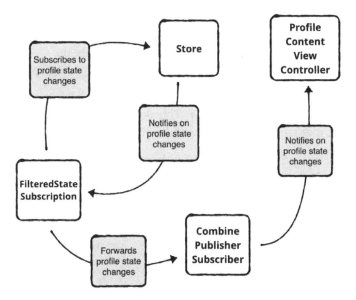

Let's follow the code path for creating the user profile screen's focused publisher:

```swift
public class
  ProfileContentViewController: NiblessViewController {

  // MARK: - Properties
  // State
  let statePublisher:
    AnyPublisher<ProfileViewControllerState, Never>
  var subscriptions = Set<AnyCancellable>()

  // User Interactions
  let userInteractions: ProfileUserInteractions

  // ...
}
```

The `ProfileContentViewController` has two dependencies:

- An `AnyPublisher` that publishes values of type `ProfileViewControllerState`, a small subset of Koober's `AppState`.

- A `ProfileUserInteractions` to handle user interactions such as signing out and closing the screen.

`ReSwift` allows you to subscribe to a subset of the `Store` using the `select()` method on *ReSwift's* `Subscription` class. When you subscribe to the Redux Store *without* using `select()`, you subscribe to the entire app's state.

For the `ProfileContentViewController`, you "select" only the `ProfileViewControllerState` from the larger `AppState` to create the publisher.

The publisher is created in the `Koober_iOS` target. Specifically, in the `KooberSignedInDependencyContainer`. This dependency container creates publishers and other view controller dependencies in the authenticated app state.

You can find the full implementation at **Koober_iOS/iOSApp/SignedIn/KooberSignedInDependencyContainer.swift**.

```swift
// ...
public func makeProfileViewControllerStatePublisher() ->
  AnyPublisher<ProfileViewControllerState, Never> {

  let statePublisher = stateStore.publisher { subscription in
    subscription.select(self.signedInGetters
                          .getProfileViewControllerState)
  }
```

```
    return statePublisher
}

// ...
```

This method passes in a custom subscription to create the publisher. The custom subscription "selects" only the `ProfileViewControllerState`, and the publisher fires only when that state changes.

Scoped state

When using enums to model app state, views might be observing state that goes out of scope. When an enum case changes, some part of the state tree goes away. For example, in the pick-me-up flow, there's an enum for the step of the ride request the user engaged in. As the user moves through the cases, anything observing an associated value in a changed case goes out of scope. In practice, you don't ever want to observe an out-of-scope state. Going out of scope means a view controller is living longer than you designed it to live for.

The ability to detect when you go out of scope helps detect bugs. Scoping is necessary because `Combine` subscriptions observe associated values in an enum case, and the `Combine` subscription has to be able to handle when that enum case is no longer set.

You could make the `Combine` publisher-subscription data type optional, but then your view controller can live across scopes. A view controller for one user could suddenly be sent data for another user after logging out and in. Handling the optional case everywhere is also a pain and makes the code less readable.

The `Combine` subscriptions in Koober observe `ScopedState`, which is either `.outOfScope` or `.inScope` with the `StateType` wrapped inside:

```
public enum ScopedState<StateType: Equatable>: Equatable {
  case outOfScope
  case inScope(StateType)
}
```

Once the state which a view controller is observing goes out of scope, the `Combine` subscription finishes - no more events will flow through it:

```swift
// ...

func newState(state: ScopedState<SelectedStateT>) {
  guard requested > .none else {
    return
  }
  requested -= .max(1)

  switch state {
  case let .inScope(inScopeState):
    _ = subscriber?.receive(inScopeState)
  case .outOfScope:
    _ = subscriber?.receive(completion: .finished)
  }
}

// ...
```

When the `ProfileViewControllerState` publisher is created by the dependency container, the publisher is set to observe the value returned from the `getProfileViewControllerState(appState:)` method:

```swift
// ...

func getProfileViewControllerState(appState: AppState)
  -> ScopedState<ProfileViewControllerState> {

  let signedInScopedState = getSignedInState(appState)
  guard case .inScope(let signedInViewControllerState) =
    signedInScopedState
  else {
      return .outOfScope
  }

  return .inScope(signedInViewControllerState
                   .profileViewControllerState)
}

// ...
```

If the `signedInViewControllerState` doesn't exist, the subscription won't fire. If the `signedInViewControllerState` exists, the subscription fires with the new `ProfileViewControllerState` value.

User session persistence

Koober persists the user session on disk between sessions. On launch, the app reads the user session from persistence. If it exists, the user is authenticated and can request rides. If it doesn't exist, the user must go through the onboarding flow.

`LaunchViewController` handles the initial app launch. Since the operation to read the user session is asynchronous, the launch screen displays until the read operation completes.

`MainViewController` handles the transitions between `LaunchViewController`, `OnboardingViewController` and `SignedInViewController`.

First, `MainViewController` presents the `LaunchViewController` which looks like this:

```
public class LaunchViewController: NiblessViewController {

  // MARK: - Properties
  // User Interactions
  let userInteractions: LaunchingUserInteractions

  // State
  let statePublisher:
    AnyPublisher<LaunchViewControllerState, Never>
  var subscriptions = Set<AnyCancellable>()

  // MARK: - Methods
  // ...
  public override func viewDidLoad() {
    super.viewDidLoad()
    observeState()
    userInteractions.launchApp()
  }
  // ...
}
```

```
public protocol LaunchingUserInteractions {
  func launchApp()
  func finishedPresenting(errorMessage: ErrorMessage)
}
```

`LaunchViewController` has a `LaunchingUserInteractions` property that performs the initial app setup in `launchApp()`. The `LaunchingUserInteractions` object also handles errors in `finishedPresenting(errorMessage:)`.

`LaunchViewController` calls `launchApp()` immediately after it loads.

ReduxLaunchingUserInteractions is the concrete implementation of
LaunchingUserInteractions:

```
public class ReduxLaunchingUserInteractions:
  LaunchingUserInteractions {

  // MARK: - Properties
  let actionDispatcher: ActionDispatcher
  let userSessionDataStore: UserSessionDataStore
  let userSessionStatePersister: UserSessionStatePersister

  // MARK: - Methods
  // ...

  public func launchApp() {
    loadUserSession()
  }

  // ...

  private func loadUserSession() {
    userSessionDataStore.readUserSession()
      .done(finishedLaunchingApp(userSession:))
      .catch { error in
        let errorMessage =
          ErrorMessage(title: "Sign In Error",
                       message: """
                         Sorry, we couldn't determine \
                         if you are already signed in.
                         Please sign in or sign up.
                         """)
        self.present(errorMessage: errorMessage)
      }
  }

  private func finishedLaunchingApp(userSession: UserSession?) {
    let authenticationState =
      AuthenticationState(userSession: userSession)
    let action =
      LaunchingActions.FinishedLaunchingApp(authenticationState:
        authenticationState)

    actionDispatcher.dispatch(action)

    userSessionStatePersister
      .startPersistingStateChanges(to: userSessionDataStore)
  }
  // ...
}
```

The user interactions object reads the persisted user session in `loadUserSession()` from the injected `UserSessionDataStore`.

If the user session is read without errors, it's passed to `finishedLaunchingApp(userSession:)`. This method dispatches a `FinishedLaunchingApp` action containing the user session if found or empty if not.

At the end of the method, the user interaction object asks the `UserSessionStatePersister` to start persisting changes to the user session. When the user signs in or signs up, the persister saves the user session to disk. When the user signs out, the persister removes the user session from the data store.

The trick is the persister can't start observing right away. The app needs to load the initial state from disk first in `ReduxLaunchingUserInteractions`.

Let's look at how the persister gets initialized:

```
public class ReduxUserSessionStatePersister:
  UserSessionStatePersister {

  // MARK: - Properties
  let authenticationStatePublisher:
    AnyPublisher<AuthenticationState?, Never>
  var subscriptions = Set<AnyCancellable>()

  // MARK: - Methods
  public init(reduxStore: Store<AppState>) {
    let runningGetters =
      AppRunningGetters(getAppRunningState:
        EntryPointGetters().getAppRunningState)

    self.authenticationStatePublisher =
      reduxStore.publisher { subscription in
        subscription
          .select(runningGetters.getAuthenticationState)
      }
      .removeDuplicates()
      .eraseToAnyPublisher()
  }

  // ...
}
```

```
public enum AuthenticationState: Equatable {

  case notSignedIn
  case signedIn(UserSession)

  init(userSession: UserSession?) {
```

```
      if let userSession = userSession {
        self = .signedIn(userSession)
      } else {
        self = .notSignedIn
      }
    }
  }
}
```

The `ReduxUserSessionStatePersister` is created with a store, and creates an `AuthenticationState?` publisher on `init` to monitor user session changes. The persister doesn't subscribe to the publisher until `startPersistingStateChanges(to:)` gets called.

The `AuthenticationState?` publisher emits the current state when subscribing and we don't want to persist what is already the current state. The subscription needs a `.dropFirst(1)` to skip the first state event:

```
// ...
public func startPersistingStateChanges(
  to userSessionDataStore: UserSessionDataStore) {

  self.authenticationStatePublisher
    .receive(on: DispatchQueue.main)
    .dropFirst(1)
    .sink { [weak self] authenticationState in
      self?.on(authenticationState: authenticationState,
               with: userSessionDataStore)
    }
    .store(in: &subscriptions)
}
// ...
```

This method subscribes to the `AuthenticationState?` publisher and updates `UserSessionDataStore` when authentication state changes.

Here's a diagram of the user session persistence flow:

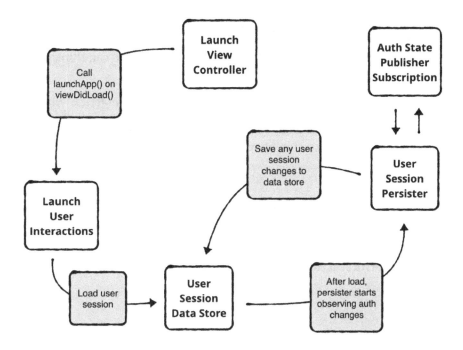

Let's review each step:

1. The launch view controller calls `launchApp()` on its user interactions object.
2. Launch user interactions loads the user session from the data store.
3. After the load completes, the user interactions object tells the persister to start saving user session changes to the data store.
4. The persister starts observing the `AuthenticationState` publisher.
5. Anytime the auth state changes, the persister saves or removes the user session from the data store.

That's it! The persister ensures the data store is always up to date so the user session is ready to load on the next launch.

Responding to user interaction

View controllers in Koober declare all possible user interactions in a user interactions protocol. The implementation of the class gets injected on initialization. Most user interactions result in a modification to the store. You can think of the user interaction objects like view models in MVVM.

The only place actions get dispatched in Koober are in user interactions objects.

Let's take a deeper look at the `SignInUserInteractions` protocol mentioned in the **Sign-in user interactions** section above:

```
public protocol SignInUserInteractions {
  func signIn(email: String, password: Secret)
  func finishedPresenting(_ errorMessage: ErrorMessage)
}
```

The implementation for the `SignInUserInteractions` is in the **ReduxSignInUserInteractions.swift** file in **KooberKit**:

```
public class ReduxSignInUserInteractions:
  SignInUserInteractions {

  // MARK: - Properties
  let actionDispatcher: ActionDispatcher
  let remoteAPI: AuthRemoteAPI

  // MARK: - Methods
  public init(actionDispatcher: ActionDispatcher,
              remoteAPI: AuthRemoteAPI) {
    self.actionDispatcher = actionDispatcher
    self.remoteAPI = remoteAPI
  }

  // ...
}
```

The user interactions object has two dependencies:

- An `ActionDispatcher` dispatches actions to the store.
- An `AuthRemoteAPI` makes the sign-in API call.

First, let's look at the `ActionDispatcher`.

The action dispatcher is a protocol that exposes the `ReSwift` store's dispatch action method:

```
protocol ActionDispatcher {
  func dispatch(_ action: Action)
}

extension Store: ActionDispatcher {}
```

Of course, you could dispatch actions directly to the store:

```
let action = SignOutAction()
store.dispatch(action)
```

This works, but you would have to inject the store into all your user interaction objects. You don't want to give them access to all the store's methods.

Instead, user interactions object dispatch actions using the dispatcher like this:

```
let action = SignOutAction()
actionDispatcher.dispatch(action)
```

Next, let's look at how the `ReduxSignInUserInteractions` signs in a user:

```
// ...
public func signIn(email: String, password: Secret) {
  indicateSigningIn()
  remoteAPI.signIn(email: email, password: password)
    .done(signedIn(to:))
    .catch(indicateErrorSigningIn)
}

private func indicateSigningIn() {
  let action = SignInActions.SigningIn()
  actionDispatcher.dispatch(action)
}

private func signedIn(to userSession: UserSession) {
  let action = SignInActions.SignedIn(
    userSession: userSession
```

```
  )
  actionDispatcher.dispatch(action)
}

private func indicateErrorSigningIn(error: Error) {
  let errorMessage = ErrorMessage(
    title: "Sign In Failed",
    message: "Could not sign in.\nPlease try again."
  )
  let action = SignInActions.SignInFailed(
    errorMessage: errorMessage
  )
  actionDispatcher.dispatch(action)
}

// ...
```

The sign-in view has three main states:

1. The sign-in request is in progress.

2. The sign-in request completed with a success.

3. The sign-in request completed with a failure.

First, the sign-in method calls `indicateSignIn()` which dispatches a `SigningIn` action. This indicates the request is in progress and the user interface can show a spinner and disable user interaction.

Next, the user interactions object signs in the user using the remote API.

If the request succeeds, the user interactions object dispatches a `SignedIn` action containing the new `UserSession` object. The app dismisses the sign-in screen and transitions to the map. If the request fails, the user interactions object dispatches a `SignInFailed` containing the error message. The user interface can display the error message, hide the spinner and enable user interaction.

Rendering updates

Actions describe a state change. Let's look at what makes up an action:

```swift
struct SignInActions {
  // Internal
  struct SigningIn: Action {}

  struct SignInFailed: Action {
    let errorMessage: ErrorMessage
  }

  struct FinishedPresentingError: Action {
    let errorMessage: ErrorMessage
  }

  // External
  struct SignedIn: Action {
    let userSession: UserSession
  }
}
```

Each action in the `SignInActions` is a `struct` that optionally contains data.

- The `SigningIn` action only describes a new app state, but doesn't need any extra data.

- The `SignedIn` action changes the app state to "Signed In" and contains a `UserSession` object.

On its own, actions can't change state in the store. They need to flow through a reducer function first. A reducer takes in the current state and an action and returns a new state.

Next, let's check out the sign-in reducer:

```swift
extension Reducers {

  static func signInReducer(
    action: Action,
    state: SignInViewControllerState?)
    -> SignInViewControllerState {

    var state = state ?? SignInViewControllerState()

    switch action {
    case _ as SignInActions.SigningIn:
      SignInLogic.indicateSigningIn(
        viewState: &state.viewState)
    // Handle other cases here.
```

```
            // ...
        default:
            break
        }

        return state
    }
}
```

```
struct SignInLogic {

    // MARK: - Methods
    static func indicateSigningIn(viewState:
        inout SignInViewState) {

        viewState.emailInputEnabled = false
        viewState.passwordInputEnabled = false
        viewState.signInButtonEnabled = false
        viewState.signInActivityIndicatorAnimating = true
    }

    // ...
}
```

The sign-in reducer takes an action and the current `SignInViewControllerState` and returns a new `SignInViewControllerState`. If no `SignInViewControllerState` is present, the reducer uses a default state.

For the `SigningIn` action, the reducer modifies variables on the `SignInViewControllerState` to disable user interaction and set the `signInActivityIndicatorAnimating` value to `true`.

Once the reducer returns, store updates its state. Then, the subscription in the sign-in view controller fires and the user interface updates.

The circle of Redux is complete! You've seen how a state change starts as an action, gets dispatched to the store and flows through a reducer to complete the update.

Next, you'll learn how views communicate with each other using the Redux store.

Communicating amongst views

In Redux, there is no direct communication between views. They observe state from the same store, so one view controller can affect another by dispatching an action. The reducer updating the store can change state another view controller is observing.

View controllers in a Redux architecture are naturally slim and focused. They fire actions and then forget about them, and may or may not care about how those actions affect the app's state.

Pick-me-up screen

The `PickMeUpViewController` contains the meat of the Koober app. It displays the map, the Where To? button and the ride-option picker.

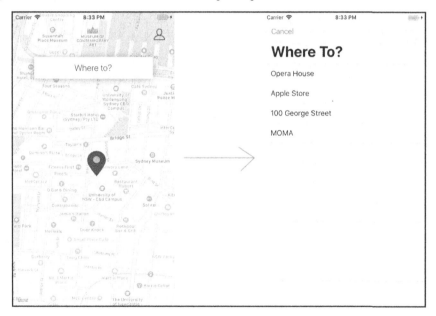

It also transitions between multiple states when you are requesting a Koober:

```
enum PickMeUpView: Equatable {
  case initial
  case selectDropoffLocation
  case selectRideOption
  case confirmRequest
  case sendingRideRequest(NewRideRequest)
  case final
}
```

For this example, let's focus on the `initial` and `selectDropoffLocation` state.

Initially, the map displays a Where To? button and a preset pick-up location. Tapping the button brings up the drop-off location-picker screen, which loads a list of possible locations to visit in a Koober. After you select a location, the picker closes, and the map displays the selected location.

Going over how the map displays the picker when you press the button:

```swift
public class PickMeUpViewController: NiblessViewController {

  // MARK: - Properties
  // Child View Controllers
  let mapViewController: PickMeUpMapViewController
  let rideOptionPickerViewController:
    RideOptionPickerViewController
  let sendingRideRequestViewController:
    SendingRideRequestViewController

  // State
  let statePublisher:
    AnyPublisher<PickMeUpViewControllerState, Never>
  var subscriptions = Set<AnyCancellable>()

  // User Interactions
  let userInteractions: PickMeUpUserInteractions

  // Factories
  let viewControllerFactory: PickMeUpViewControllerFactory

  // ...
}
```

PickMeUpViewController gets injected with a few dependencies:

- PickMeUpViewControllerState publisher fires each time the state changes.

- PickMeUpUserInteractions handles the Where To? button tap.

- PickMeUpViewControllerFactory creates a DropoffLocationPickerViewController on demand.

```swift
public struct PickMeUpViewControllerState: Equatable {

  public internal(set) var pickupLocation: Location
  public internal(set) var state: PickMeUpState
  // Other states go here.
  // ...
}
```

```swift
public enum PickMeUpState: Equatable {
  case initial
  case selectDropoffLocation(
    DropoffLocationPickerViewControllerState
  )
  // Other states go here.
  // ...
}
```

The `PickMeUpViewControllerState` has data the view controller needs to display its user interface. Each time the state updates, `PickMeUpViewController` maps the `PickMeUpState` to `PickMeUpView` state, which is easier to consume.

The `presentDropoffLocationPicker()` method creates a `DropoffLocationPickerViewController` with all its dependencies and it presents the screen modally:

```swift
// ...

func presentDropoffLocationPicker() {
  let viewController = viewControllerFactory
    .makeDropoffLocationPickerViewController()

  present(viewController, animated: true)
}
// ...
```

This method gets called when the `PickMeUpView` state changes from `initial` to `selectDropoffLocation`. The state transition starts in the pick-me-up root view.

```swift
class PickMeUpRootView: NiblessView {

  // MARK: - Properties
  let userInteractions: PickMeUpUserInteractions

  let whereToButton: UIButton = {
    let button = UIButton(type: .system)
    // ...
    return button
  }()

  // MARK: - Methods
  init(frame: CGRect = .zero,
       userInteractions: PickMeUpUserInteractions) {
    self.userInteractions = userInteractions

    super.init(frame: frame)
```

```
    addSubview(whereToButton)
    bindWhereToControl()
}

// ...

@objc
func goToDropoffLocationPicker() {
  userInteractions.goToDropoffLocationPicker()
}

// ...
}
```

`PickMeUpViewController` initializes `PickMeUpRootView` with its `PickMeUpUserInteractions` dependency.

The root view makes a call to the user interactions object when the user taps the Where To? button.

The concrete implementation of `PickMeUpUserInteractions` here is `ReduxPickMeUpUserInteractions`:

```
public class ReduxPickMeUpUserInteractions:
  PickMeUpUserInteractions {

  // MARK: - Properties
  let actionDispatcher: ActionDispatcher
  let newRideRepository: NewRideRepository

  // MARK: - Methods
  public init(actionDispatcher: ActionDispatcher,
              newRideRepository: NewRideRepository) {
    self.actionDispatcher = actionDispatcher
    self.newRideRepository = newRideRepository
  }

  public func goToDropoffLocationPicker() {
    let action = PickMeUpActions.GoToDropoffLocationPicker()
    actionDispatcher.dispatch(action)
  }

  // ...
}
```

```
struct PickMeUpActions {

  struct GoToDropoffLocationPicker: Action {}

  // ...
}
```

`goToDropoffLocationPicker()` dispatches a `GoToDropoffLocationPicker` action that tells the map to transition to the drop-off location picker.

Next, the action needs to flow through a reducer to update the store.

```
extension Reducers {

  static func pickMeUpReducer(
    action: Action,
    state: PickMeUpViewControllerState)
    -> PickMeUpViewControllerState {

    var state = state

    switch action {
    case _ as PickMeUpActions.GoToDropoffLocationPicker:
      let initialDropoffLocationViewControllerState =
        DropoffLocationPickerViewControllerState(
          pickupLocation: state.pickupLocation,
          searchResults: [],
          currentSearchID: nil,
          errorsToPresent: [])

      state.state = .selectDropoffLocation(
          initialDropoffLocationViewControllerState)
      // Other actions handled here.
      // ...
    }

    // ...

    return state
  }
}
```

The reducer handles the `GoToDropoffLocationPicker` action by creating an initial `DropoffLocationPickerViewControllerState` with the user's current pick-up location, which is already in the store. Then, it updates the store state to `.selectDropoffLocation` containing the initial location picker state.

The last step in the process is for the `PickMeUpViewController` to handle the state update:

```swift
public class PickMeUpViewController: NiblessViewController {
  // MARK: - Properties
  // ...
  // State
  let statePublisher:
    AnyPublisher<PickMeUpViewControllerState, Never>
  var subscriptions = Set<AnyCancellable>()
  // ...

  // MARK: - Methods
  // ...
  func observeState() {
    // ...
    statePublisher
      .receive(on: DispatchQueue.main)
      .map { (state: $0.state, sendingState: $0.sendingState) }
      .map (mapToView)
      .removeDuplicates()
      .sink { [weak self] view in
        self?.present(view)
      }
      .store(in: &subscriptions)
    // ...
  }

  func present(_ view: PickMeUpView) {
    switch view {
    case .initial:
      presentInitialState()
    case .selectDropoffLocation:
      presentDropoffLocationPicker()
    // Handle other view cases.
    // ...
    }
  }
  // ...
}
```

`PickMeUpViewController` observes the `PickMeUpViewControllerState` and calls `present(_:)` each time the state changes. When the state changes to `.selectDropoffLocation`, the drop-off location picker screen is presented.

Here's a diagram of the select drop-off location flow:

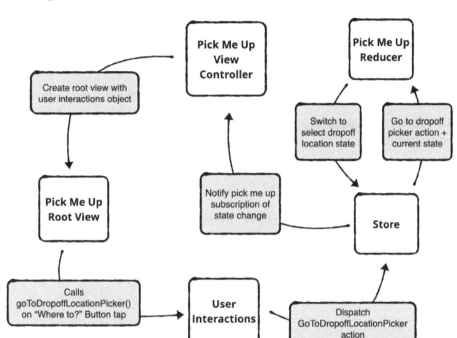

Let's review the steps one by one:

1. The pick-me-up view controller creates a root view with a user-interactions object.

2. The pick-me-up root view calls `goToDropoffLocationPicker()` on the user-interactions object when the user taps the Where To? button.

3. The user interactions dispatches a `GoToDropoffLocationPicker` to the store.

4. The store runs the action through a reducer, which switches the state to `.selectDropoffLocation`.

5. The store notifies the `Combine` subscription that the state changed.

6. The pick-me-up view controller presents the select drop-off location picker screen.

The view layer reacts to state change and the tells the user-interactions object when the user interaction happened. The view only presents or dismisses screens when the store updates its state.

Selecting a ride option

Koober has a wide variety of ride option types to choose from:

- Wallabies are tiny but cheap, and you'll get to your destination with extra cash in hand!

- Wallaroos are reliable, and they get you to your destination on time, every time.

- Kangaroos are luxurious, and you'll experience maximum hop distance on an adventurous ride.

In the previous **pick-me-up screen** example, you saw the state transition from `.initial` to `.selectDropoffLocation`. After the user selects a drop-off location, the state transitions to `.selectRideOption`:

```
public class PickMeUpViewController: NiblessViewController {

  // MARK: - Properties
  // ...

  // MARK: - Methods
  // ...
  func present(_ view: PickMeUpView) {
    switch view {
    case .initial:
      presentInitialState()
    case .selectDropoffLocation:
      presentDropoffLocationPicker()
    case .selectRideOption:
      dropoffLocationSelected()
    // Other cases handled here.
    // ...
    }
  }

  // ...

  func dropoffLocationSelected() {
    if presentedViewController is
      DropoffLocationPickerViewController {

      dismiss(animated: true)
    }

    presentRideOptionPicker()
  }

  // ...
}
```

The pick-me-up view controller transitions to the next screen in `present(_:)`. For the `.selectRideOption` state, it calls `dropoffLocationSelected()` to dismiss the drop-off location picker and to present the ride-option picker.

The logic to select a ride option lives in `RideOptionPickerViewController`:

```
public class RideOptionPickerViewController:
  NiblessViewController {

  // MARK: - Properties
  // Dependencies
  let imageCache: ImageCache

  // State
  let statePublisher:
    AnyPublisher<RideOptionPickerViewControllerState, Never>
  let pickupLocation: Location
  var selectedRideOptionID: RideOptionID?
  var subscriptions = Set<AnyCancellable>()

  // User Interactions
  let userInteractions: RideOptionPickerUserInteractions

  // ...
}
```

`RideOptionPickerViewController` gets injected with a couple dependencies:

- The `ImageCache` caches the ride option button images.

- The `RideOptionPickerViewControllerState` publisher fires when the state changes and contains data to display the ride options and errors to present.

- The `RideOptionPickerUserInteractions` handles ride-option selections.

The view controller creates its `RideOptionSegmentedControl` root view with its user interactions object:

```
class RideOptionSegmentedControl: UIControl {

  // MARK: - Properties
  let userInteractions: RideOptionPickerUserInteractions

  var viewState =
    RideOptionSegmentedControlState() {
      didSet {
        if oldValue != viewState {
          loadAndRecreateButtons(withSegments:
            viewState.segments)
        } else {
          update(withSegments: viewState.segments)
        }
      }
    }
```

```
  // ...
  // MARK: - Methods
  // ...
  // Called to create a new ride option button
  private func makeRideOptionButton(
    forSegment segment: RideOptionSegmentState)
    -> (RideOptionID, RideOptionButton) {

    let button = RideOptionButton(segment: segment)
    button.didSelectRideOption = { [weak self] id in
      self?.userInteractions.select(rideOptionID: id)
    }
    return (segment.id, button)
  }
}
```

```
public struct RideOptionSegmentedControlState: Equatable {

  // MARK: - Properties
  public var segments: [RideOptionSegmentState]

  // MARK: - Methods
  public init(segments: [RideOptionSegmentState] = []) {
    self.segments = segments
  }
}
```

```
public struct RideOptionSegmentState: Equatable {

  // MARK: - Properties
  public var id: String
  public var title: String
  public var isSelected: Bool
  public var images: ButtonRemoteImages

  // MARK: - Methods
  public init(id: String,
              title: String,
              isSelected: Bool,
              images: ButtonRemoteImages) {
    self.id = id
    self.title = title
    self.isSelected = isSelected
    self.images = images
  }

  // ...
}
```

The segmented control renders the ride options segments using the
`RideOptionSegmentedControlState`.

Each ride-option button in the segmented control is created using
`RideOptionSegmentState`, which has a ride-option ID, along with some other meta data.

The view controller state and the root view have their own states. Giving the root view a more granular state helps keep them focused on user-interface specific state.

If you'd like to read through the entire ride option segment creation process, the full code is at **Koober_iOS/iOSApp/SignedIn/PickMeUp/SelectRideOption/RideOptionSegmentedControl.swift**.

When you tap a ride option, the user-interactions object handles selecting a new ride option ID.

```
public protocol RideOptionPickerUserInteractions {

  func loadRideOptions(
    availableAt pickupLocation: Location,
    screenScale: CGFloat)
  func select(rideOptionID: RideOptionID)
  func finishedPresenting(_ errorMessage: ErrorMessage)
}
```

The implementation in the `RideOptionSegmentedControl` is a `ReduxRideOptionPickerUserInteractions`:

```
public class ReduxRideOptionPickerUserInteractions:
  RideOptionPickerUserInteractions {

  // MARK: - Properties
  let actionDispatcher: ActionDispatcher
  let rideOptionRepository: RideOptionRepository

  // MARK: - Methods
  // ...
  public func select(rideOptionID: RideOptionID) {
    let action = RideOptionPickerActions
      .RideOptionSelected(rideOptionID: rideOptionID)
    actionDispatcher.dispatch(action)
  }

  // ...
}
```

```
struct RideOptionPickerActions {

  // ...

  struct RideOptionSelected: Action {

    // MARK: - Properties
    let rideOptionID: RideOptionID
  }
  // ...
}
```

The `select(rideOptionID:)` method dispatches a `RideOptionSelected` action that contains the ride option ID. This method gets called by the segmented control each time the user taps a new ride option.

After the user interactions object dispatches the action, a reducer handles the state change:

```
extension Reducers {

  static func rideOptionPickerReducer(
    action: Action,
    state: RideOptionPickerViewControllerState?)
    -> RideOptionPickerViewControllerState {

    var state = state ??
      RideOptionPickerViewControllerState(
        segmentedControlState:
          RideOptionSegmentedControlState(segments: []),
        errorsToPresent: [])

    switch action {
    // ...
    case let action as
      RideOptionPickerActions.RideOptionSelected:

      var segments = state.segmentedControlState.segments
      for (index, segment)
        in state.segmentedControlState.segments.enumerated() {

        segments[index].isSelected =
          (segment.id == action.rideOptionID)
      }

      state.segmentedControlState.segments = segments
    // Handle other actions.
    // ...
    default:
      break
```

```
      }
      return state
    }
  }
```

The `rideOptionPickerReducer` takes in an action along with the current `RideOptionPickerViewControllerState`.

For the `RideOptionSelected` action, the reducer finds the segment matching the action's `rideOptionID`, and it sets its `isSelected` flag to `true`. Then, it updates the state's list of ride-option segments.

Next, the store notifies the subscribers of the updated state, which causes the `AnyPublisher<RideOptionPickerViewControllerState, Never>`'s subscription in the `RideOptionPickerViewController` to fire:

```
public class RideOptionPickerViewController:
  NiblessViewController {

  // MARK: - Properties
  // ...

  // MARK: - Methods
  // ...
  func observeState() {
    statePublisher
      .receive(on: DispatchQueue.main)
      .map { $0.segmentedControlState }
      .removeDuplicates()
      .sink { [weak self] segmentedControlState in
        self?.rideOptionSegmentedControl.viewState =
          segmentedControlState
      }
      .store(in: &subscriptions)
    // ...
  }
  // ...
}
```

Each time the `RideOptionPickerViewControllerState` changes, the state gets mapped to a view specific `RideOptionSegmentedControlState`, and passed to the `RideOptionSegmentedControl`.

Updating the `viewState` variable causes the segments to re-render, and the segmented control highlights the selected ride option segment.

Here's a diagram of the select ride option flow:

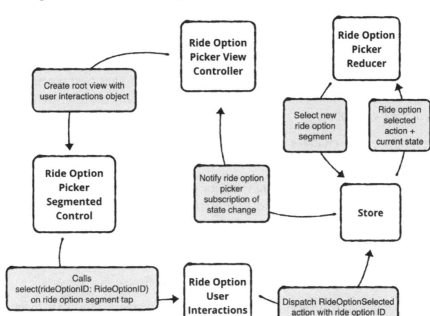

Let's review each step one by one:

1. Ride-option picker view controller creates a root view with a user interactions object.

2. Ride-option segmented control calls `select(rideOptionID:)` on the user interactions object when the user taps a ride-option segment.

3. The user-interactions object dispatches a `RideOptionSelected` action with the selected ride-option ID.

4. The store runs the action through a reducer, which updates the `isSelected` Boolean on each of the ride option segments.

5. The store notifies the `Combine` subscription that the state changed.

6. The ride option picker view controller re-renders the segmented control to show the new ride-option selection.

That's it! The ride-option segment view signals out to the store when a new ride option is selected. The view waits for the store to finish updating its state and then re-renders.

Pros and cons of Redux

Pros of Redux

1. Redux scales well as your application grows — if you follow best practices. Separate your Redux store state into sub-states and only observe partial state in your view controllers.

2. Descriptive state changes are all contained in reducers. Any developer can read through your reducer functions to understand all state changes in the app.

3. The store is the single source of truth for your entire app. If data changes in the store, the change propagates to all subscribers.

4. Data consistency across screens is good for iPad apps and other apps that display the same data in multiple places at the same time.

5. Reducers are pure functions — they are easy to test.

6. Redux architecture, overall, is easy to test. You can create a test case by putting the app in any app state you want, dispatch an action and test that the state changed correctly.

7. Redux can help with state restoration by initializing the store with persisted state.

8. It's easy to observe what's going on in your app because all the state is centralized to the store. You can easily record state changes for debugging.

9. Redux is lightweight and a relatively simple high-level concept.

10. Redux helps separate side effects from business logic.

11. Redux embraces value types. State can't change from underneath you.

Cons of Redux

1. You need to touch multiple files to add new functionality.

2. Requires a third-party library, but the library is very small.

3. Model layer knows about the view hierarchy and is sensitive to user-interface changes.

4. Redux can use more memory than other architectures since the store is always in memory.

5. You need to be careful with performance because of possible frequent deep copies of the app state struct.

6. Dispatching actions can result in infinite loops if you dispatch actions in response to state changes.

7. Data modeling is hard. Benefits of Redux depend on having a good data model.

8. It is designed to work with a declarative user interface framework like React. This can be awkward to apply to UIKit because UIKit is imperative. This isn't a blocker, just that it's not a natural fit.

9. Since the entire app state is centralized, it's possible to have reducers that depend on each other. That removes modularity and encapsulation of a model / screen / component's state. So refactoring a component's state type could cause complier issue elsewhere and this is not good. You won't run into this if you organize your reducers to only know about a module's state and no more. This is not constrained by the architecture, though, so it depends on everyone being aware.

Key points

- Redux architecture keeps all your app's state in a single **store**.
- An **action** describes a state change. The only way to change state is to dispatch an **action** to the store.
- **Reducers** are pure functions that take an action and the current state, and they return a modified state. The only place the state can change is in a reducer function.
- Convert your store subscriptions into `Combine` publishers using the publisher methods found in **ReSwiftStorePublisher.swift**. Then, you can abstract the `ReSwift` store from your view layer.
- Focus your store subscriptions on pieces of the whole state using the `select()` method so `Combine` publisher subscriptions fire only when they need to.

Where to go from here?

Koober is meant to be a production app, and there's lots more code in the sample project to explore.

Here's a few places to look:

1. Follow the path for making the new ride request in the pick-me-up screen. After selecting a ride option, and confirming the ride request, the app transitions from the `sendingRideRequest(NewRideRequest)` state to `.final` in the `PickMeUpViewController`.

   Start in **Koober_iOS/iOSApp/SignedIn/PickMeUp/PickMeUpViewController.swift** for the user interface transitions.

   Then, explore how the reducer handles the `ConfirmedNewRideRequest` and `NewRideRequestSent` actions in **KooberKit/UILayer/Features/Running/Features/SignedIn/Features/PickMeUp/Redux/PickMeUpReducer.swift**.

2. The Koober app prints out information about every dispatched action in the console.

   Check out how that's done in **KooberKit/Reusable/ReSwiftDiagnostics/ActionPrinterMiddleware.swift**. It's used to set up the store in **Koober_iOS/iOSApp/KooberAppDepedencyContainer.swift**.

Chapter 7: Architecture: Elements, Part 1

By René Cacheaux & Josh Berlin

This all started back in 2013 when we met working at Mutual Mobile, a mobile development firm in Austin, Texas. The company asked us to fly to New York and work with an iOS team at Google. It was an immediate, "Yes!" from both of us.

We weren't sure what to expect. Google didn't hire "iOS Engineers" at that time and expected their engineers to switch programming languages depending on the project. Most of the team had strong Java backgrounds and learned Objective-C specifically for this project. They seriously impressed us with their knowledge of the iOS SDK and the nuances of Objective-C. While we were able to teach them things like Core Animation, they were able to teach us about software development as a whole.

Their Java background came with an ingrained idea that every project needed dependency injection. At the time, and even today, the use of dependency injection in iOS projects is rare. Apple doesn't have a built-in framework to help manage dependencies, which doesn't help. To the Google engineers, this was absurd and they decided to use a third-party framework called **Objection** to handle dependencies in the project.

Injecting dependencies into each view controller allowed us to mock objects and write unit tests. For this project, every change request required unit tests. No exceptions. This was a departure from some of the more lax projects at Mutual Mobile. But it was a good departure. Dependency injection and unit tests changed our view on iOS development and sparked our interest in software architecture.

Back in Austin, one of the developers at Mutual Mobile started a brown bag group to watch Robert Martin — better known as Uncle Bob — videos. His videos were full of great insights about software architecture. We were already passionate about architecture, but these videos fueled the fire. Uncle Bob took ideas from multiple architectures and broke them down to their core objective: separation of concerns. He used this idea to create **clean architecture**, which divides software into multiple layers including business rules and interface adapters.

At about the same time, we started working on a brand new greenfield iOS project for a major American brand. We knew this project was going to be difficult, but we were excited to use our new-found passion for architecture to help the team succeed. The client asked us not only to build an awesome iOS app, but an SDK so other apps within the company could reuse the app's core functionality. René was the tech lead and knew architecture would be key to the project's success. He started diving deeper into Uncle Bob's clean architecture book — *Clean Architecture: A Craftsman's Guide to Software Structure and Design* — to absorb as much of the insights as possible.

The app's core feature was a chat service. We were asked to use XMPP, Extensible Messaging and Presence Protocol, but were told that we might have had to switch to a different chat protocol in 3–6 months. Our first thought was, "Are you serious?" Our next thought was the realization that, if and when we had to rewrite the chat layer, our data storage and user interface layers shouldn't need to be touched.

René decided the best way to separate the chat layer from the user interface was to create two different projects: a "Core" SDK to hold the chat code and a user interface layer, which was the actual Xcode project. This forced us to build the user interface layer in a way that isn't tied to a specific chat protocol, but gets handed immutable data objects such as a chat group or chat message. The user interface layer didn't care if they came from XMPP or MQTT, Message Queuing Telemetry Transport, or push notifications.

The clear separation allowed engineers to work on the chat layer and the user interface layer in parallel. We were able to make rapid changes to isolated layers of the project without affecting other layers. The patterns developed and used throughout the app's source code could be applied to many other iOS projects. What resulted was **Elements**.

Introducing Elements

Elements is an architecture meant to make iOS development fun and flexible. Elements organizes your codebase and makes your project easy for anyone to navigate. This organization allows you to make changes to layers of your app without affecting stability. A set of "Elements" make up the architecture. The cool thing is that you can choose which pieces to use in your own apps — there's an Element for every layer of your app, from networking to the user interface.

Elements is our take on architecture, grabbing bits and pieces from industry best practices. The theory is not completely original since it pulls from many sources based on our experience. The set of Elements was created by mixing these best practices with our ideas and has evolved over time as more architectures make their way into the iOS world.

Organization is key to well-architected project. Specific pieces of logic should be easy to find. Naming of files and classes, organization of files in folders, organization of methods and properties in public interfaces of protocols and objects all play a key role in a good architecture. A better-organized project makes for a more flexible architecture. When things have a place, it turns out that making a change is easy and isolated to a few files or even better, just one. Point is, organization is important to architecture.

There shouldn't be one and only one way to architect software. Software architecture is an artwork with some science mixed in. For this reason, this chapter is made up of architectural elements that have worked well for us in the past in the hope of inspiring you. Take what you like and change it if it makes sense. Use an Element as-is or make it it your own.

There's no such thing as one architecture to rule them all. Well-architected apps are made up of modular components. Bits and pieces made up of different structures. Elements is not a take it or leave it approach. Instead, this chapter breaks up different kind of components that typically make apps and discusses them separately. You can take bits and pieces into your own apps or come up with entirely new elements to fit your needs.

> **Note**: We feel that it's important to emphasize that most of the concepts that make up Elements are not new. Elements is a collection of existing best practices that we've found most helpful when architecting iOS apps. We've taken these practices and evolved them over time to best fit iOS development.

Elements is designed on top of some core underlying concepts. Let's take a look at these underlying concepts.

Underlying concepts of Elements

Entities allow objects to communicate

Every app has a domain. *Yelp!* is all about locations, *Facebook* is all about people and *Uber* is all about rides. Entities represent your app's domain. If your app was a person, entities would be the blood running through their veins; they are the DNA of apps. Entities are the only values that travel across architectural layers. By holding this true, you end up building extremely flexible software: Software that doesn't require you to rewrite everything every time something changes — every time a product manager comes up with a new feature, a UI designer wants to restyle a screen, a UX designer wants to change a flow or a server engineer wants to change an API.

Protocols make software flexible

Designing great protocols is key to building flexible software. They define the *what* and leave the *how* up to the implementations. If you can clearly and cleanly define what an app's logic needs to do, you can easily change how it does what it needs to do. Flexibility is the ability to effortlessly swap implementations. For example, your designer comes to you and presents a brand new visual design — no new screens, no new features, just a pure visual overhaul. If up taking such a change breaks functionality, that's a problem. Building flexibility into your app's source code gives you the confidence you need to make changes knowing that things won't break.

Encapsulation enables safe change

Let's say your team is asked to swap out the backend from an old, raggedy API to some new trendy cloud database. Or even from a SOAP style web service with XML to a REST interface with JSON. The collective response could be one of dread... "Our networking logic is scattered throughout the whole app!" Or one of excitement... "No problem, this will be easy!" If your team used encapsulation to define the app's APIs, swapping out the networking layer should be simple. Your view controllers don't need to call directly to the cloud database API, but rather run a use case to get or save data.

Encapsulation allows you to abstract all of your backend logic in remote API classes. So when your team is asked to switch to a new backend, no one will freak out.

Elements

Elements are separated into two main categories: **Core Logic** and **User Interface Logic**. Core Logic contains the app's business logic such as retrieving data from an API and caching data. User Interface Logic contains the presentation logic such as handling user input and navigation. In this section, you can read a brief description of each Element. Later in the chapter, each Element is covered in more detail.

Core Logic

Entity

Entities, also known as data-model objects, are light-weight structured data containers. They don't do anything other than store values. Entities flow throughout the app, passed between architectural layers. They're considered foundational to your app's architecture. They constitute a contract between different object interfaces. When building an object's interface, methods typically take in an entity object and perform some task. Sometimes, the method returns a new or modified entity object. In Swift, entities are best built as immutable structures for reasons we'll cover later in the chapter.

Data store

Data stores take care of the CRUD, Create, Read, Update and Delete, operations. They abstract away the underlying data storage mechanism you want to use. They can implement Core Data, NSCoder and even remote data store network logic. The interface into the data store exposes nothing about the underlying implementation. Data stores take in and pump out entity objects, another reason entities are foundational to your app.

Remote API

Remote APIs talk to the network. They can create the endpoint and handle the response. Remote APIs know if you're getting data from a cloud API like Firebase, a custom server or even a hardcoded JSON file. View controllers don't care where the data comes from. By moving these implementation details out of view controllers and into remote APIs, view controller code becomes more readable.

Remote APIs are normally used to create and update data on a remote data store, but can make any type of network call.

Use case

Use cases represent the user stories that make up your app. They have names that everyone involved in the project can understand. If you were asked to describe what your users can do with the app, you would be naming use cases. Use cases are the main unit of work. Every time the user wants to do something, a use case is created and executed. Use cases cleanly separate your app's core logic from your app's user interface logic. Think of it this way: After you build all the use cases, you should be able to build a command line interface for your app using the use cases you've defined.

Broadcaster

Broadcasters notify subscribers when something in your app happens. Multiple objects can subscribe to a single broadcaster. As an example, you could create a reusable keyboard broadcaster that subscribes to the relevant system keyboard notifications. Encapsulating this functionality removes the need for multiple objects to directly subscribe to Notification Center notifications and instead conform to the broadcaster's protocol.

User Interface Logic

Displayable entity

Displayable entity objects contain data that is presentable to a user. Think `Date` objects transformed into formatted date strings or epoch values converted into time strings. They are are created from entities, which contain only raw data. Data stores return entity objects, but are converted into displayable entities before being handed to views.

Observer

Observers are objects that receive external events. These events are input signals to view controllers. Observers know how to subscribe to events, process events and deliver processed events to view controllers. For example, a `KeyboardObserver` can process keyboard-related notifications from Notification Center when the keyboard is shown or hidden and knows which method to call on the view controller. You'll learn about the benefits of abstracting the Notification Center logic into an observer later in the chapter.

User interface

User interfaces are, well… user interfaces. These objects allow you to configure what is rendered on the screen. Each view controller's view has a user interface protocol. They expose methods such as `enableSignInButton()` or `startEditingFirstName()`. They don't however expose implementation details such as `UIKit` objects. These objects express every possible change you can make to the user interface.

Interaction responder

User interface objects are dumb. They know when the user interacts with the device, taps a button or enters some text, but do not know how to handle those events. That's where the interaction responder comes in. The user interface tells the interaction responder what to do, and the interaction responder knows how to do it. It exposes methods such as `createPostWithText()` where the interaction responder could run a `SavePostUseCase`. Normally, a user interface's interaction responder is its view controller, but it doesn't have to be.

That wraps up the introduction of Elements. In the next four sections, you'll take a deep dive into the four main elements: user interface, interaction responder, observer and use case.

> **Note**: To see examples of the other elements in action, take a look at the Elements version of Koober's Xcode project that accompanies this chapter. If you'd like to see other elements covered in a future edition of this book, let us know in the book forum.

User interface

User interface objects describe the views in your app. They allow you to configure and change what the users sees and interacts with. They usually expose methods such as `showSuccessMessage()` or `displayWidget()`. They don't however expose the guts of the interface. For example, they don't expose `UILabels`, `UIButtons` or `UITextFields`. User interface objects are meant to express what the user interface is capable of doing — the *what* instead of the *how*. The how is an implementation detail. If you do this well, you should be able to implement a completely new design by reimplementing only the user interface object.

Mechanics

This section explains how user interfaces are created and used. It's meant to briefly explain the concepts. You'll see code examples later on.

Instantiating

You create a user interface protocol for each view. Usually each view controller's root view has a single user interface protocol. Concrete instances of user interfaces are initialized with references to objects that handle user interactions. These are called **interaction responders**. This is so the user interface can wire its controls to methods that notify the interaction responder.

Providing

User interface objects are created outside and injected into their view controllers, either through the view controller's constructor or by setting a property. In most cases, the user interface object is the view controller's root view. In iOS, each view controller already has a root `UIView` set as its `view` property by default. Usually you want that view to conform to a user interface protocol. So, in the view controller's `loadView()` method, you set the injected user interface object to the `view` property.

Using

All calls to change the UI should go directly to the injected user interface object. Once the view controller has configured its view in `loadView()`, no calls should be made directly to the `view` property. The user interface protocol should expose every possible change to the view.

Injecting the user interface object into the view controller means you can mock the protocol object to write unit tests. You can verify that the correct user interface methods get called at the right times. This wouldn't work if you set your `view` to a concrete instance of a `UIView`.

Types

User interface protocol

All user interface objects implement their own protocol describing what the view is capable of doing. The protocol should not expose implementation details about how the internals operate. It shouldn't have any references to `UIKit`.

Next, check out the user interface protocol for the Sign-in view.

```
protocol SignInUserInterface {
  func render(newState: SignInViewState)
  func configureViewAfterLayout()
  func moveContentForDismissedKeyboard()
  func moveContent(forKeyboardFrame keyboardFrame: CGRect)
}
```

The protocol methods describe only what the view can do. The `render(newState: SignInViewState)` describes transitions between different states of the sign-in user interface. The `configureViewAfterLayout()` performs any extra configuration such as scrolling after the view has finished laying out its subviews.

The key takeaway here is that the user interface isn't specific to a `UIView`. Any object can conform to this protocol. You want the user interface protocol to describe every possible configuration change a caller can make on the view, without exposing implementation details. You'll see this user interface in more detail below in the example section.

One good example is a map user interface. Let's say your company is deciding between Apple Maps and Google Maps. In six months, you could completely remove Google Maps and replace them with Apple Maps.

Instead of having the view controller hold on to a concrete instance of a Google map view, `GMSMapView`, or an Apple map view, `MKMapView`, it should hold on to a `MapUserInterface` that describes everything the map can do. That way, when you decide to switch internals, the view controller doesn't need to change, only the underlying implementation of your `MapUserInterface`.

User interface view

In order to provide a user-interface object to a view controller on initialization, you have to create a concrete `UIView` object. Ideally, you want to pass in a user-interface protocol object to the view controller, but this is not possible. View controllers need a `UIView` to operate. As a compromise, you can create a `typealias` that conforms to the user-interface protocol and is also a `UIView`. Here's an example:

```
typealias SignInUserInterfaceView = SignInUserInterface & UIView
```

`SignInUserInterfaceView` is a `UIView` that conforms to the `SignInUserInterface` protocol. Passing in a `SignInUserInterfaceView` to a view controller satisfies the requirement that the view controller needs a root `UIView` and also gives the flexibility of using a user-interface protocol.

You can also mock `SignInUserInterfaceView` in tests and validate the right user-interface protocol methods are called by the view controller.

Example

In this section, you'll walk through an example so you can see how all of the user-interface pieces work in practice. The example is a simplified version of Koober's sign-in screen.

> **Note:** To ease readability, the example code in this section has been simplified from the code in the example Xcode project.

Koober's sign-in screen is implemented by `SignInViewController`. This view controller sets its root view to a `SignInUserInterfaceView`, which you saw earlier.

Since the user interface view conforms to a protocol, a dependency container should inject the concrete instance into `SignInViewController` on initialization.

The user interface object could be a real view or mock object, so you don't want the view controller to create that internally.

The view's journey starts in the `KooberOnboardingDependencyContainer`, where `SignInViewController` is initialized:

```
class KooberOnboardingDependencyContainer {
  // ...

  func makeSignInViewController() -> SignInViewController {
    // User interface element
    // 1
    let userInterface = SignInRootView()

    // Observer element
    let statePublisher =
      makeSignInViewControllerStatePublisher()
    let observer = ObserverForSignIn(state: statePublisher)

    let signInViewController =
      SignInViewController(
        userInterface: userInterface,
        signInStateObserver: observer)

    // Wire responders
    // 2
    userInterface.ixResponder = signInViewController
    observer.eventResponder = signInViewController

    return signInViewController
  }

  // ...
}
```

Here are a couple highlights from the above code:

1. The `makeSignInViewController()` creates the user-interface object, `SignInRootView` and passes it to the sign-in view controller. You'll see the view in more detail later, but it's a concrete instance of a `UIView` that conforms to `SignInUserInterface`. The view controller doesn't care about which concrete type is as long as it can call `SignInUserInterface` methods on the object.

2. The dependency container method also sets the ixResponder to the view controller. The main reason to do this here instead of in the view controller is that you pass in a SignInUserInterface and UIView object that doesn't have a property setter for the responder. The view controller can't set the responder object internally, so it has to be done at injection time on the concrete instance, SignInRootView. This responder object gets notified when the user interacts with the view. Think of it like a delegate. The view controller just needs to conform to the responder protocol and implement the responder callback methods. You'll see more about the responder in the interaction responder section.

Creating the sign-in view controller's dependencies in the container helps keep the initializer clean:

```
class SignInViewController: NiblessViewController {

  // MARK: - Properties
  let userInterface: SignInUserInterfaceView

  // ...

  // MARK: - Methods
  init(
    userInterface: SignInUserInterfaceView,
    signInStateObserver: Observer) {

    self.userInterface = userInterface
    self.signInStateObserver = signInStateObserver
    super.init()
  }

  override func loadView() {
    view = userInterface
  }

  // ...
}
```

The SignInViewController interacts with the SignInUserInterfaceView and can make calls to SignInUserInterface. Even though the view controller knows it's a UIView, it doesn't need to make calls to the UIView directly. The user interface protocol encapsulates all configuration changes to the view it needs to make.

In loadView, you set the view controller's view property to the user-interface object. Since userInterface is a UIView subclass, this call works fine.

Have a look at the `SignInUserInterface` in more detail:

```
protocol SignInUserInterface {
  func render(newState: SignInViewState)
  func configureViewAfterLayout()
  func moveContentForDismissedKeyboard()
  func moveContent(forKeyboardFrame keyboardFrame: CGRect)
}

public struct SignInViewState: Equatable {

  // MARK: - Properties
  public internal(set) var emailInputEnabled = true
  public internal(set) var passwordInputEnabled = true
  public internal(set) var signInButtonEnabled = true
  public internal(set)
    var signInActivityIndicatorAnimating = false

  // MARK: - Methods
  public init() {}
}
```

The `render(newState:)` method transitions between every possible state of the sign-in user interface. `SignInViewState` contains flags that configure the user interface:

- The `emailInputEnabled`, `passwordInputEnabled`, and `signInButtonEnabled` flags determine whether the tappable elements are enabled or disabled. The inputs are enabled by default and disabled while the sign in API call is in progress.

- The `signInActivityIndicatorAnimating` flag determines whether or not the activity spinner is shown. The spinner is shown after the user taps the sign in button which fires the sign in API call.

The `SignInViewState` is pretty simple. The key takeaway is the state struct describes every possible state of the view's user interface.

You could, of course, also accomplish this by splitting out the state into single methods like `enableEmailField()` and `disableEmailField()`.

The `configureViewAfterLayout()` method gives the user interface a chance to update its layout after the view has laid out its subviews. View controllers get notified when this layout completes in the `viewDidLayoutSubviews()` method, so they are usually the ones to call the configure method.

The other two methods, moveContentForDismissedKeyboard() and moveContent(forKeyboardFrame:) handle adjusting the layout when the keyboard is shown or hidden. These methods don't get any information about UIKit elements, just that the content needs to move with the keyboard when the methods are called.

Now, take a look at how user-interface methods are called In the SignInViewController:

```swift
class SignInViewController: NiblessViewController {
  // ...

  override func viewDidLayoutSubviews() {
    super.viewDidLayoutSubviews()
    userInterface.configureViewAfterLayout()
  }

  // ...
}

extension SignInViewController:
  ObserverForSignInEventResponder {

  func received(newViewState viewState: SignInViewState) {
    userInterface.render(newState: viewState)
  }

  func keyboardWillHide() {
    userInterface.moveContentForDismissedKeyboard()
  }

  func keyboardWillChangeFrame(keyboardEndFrame: CGRect) {
    let convertedKeyboardEndFrame = view.convert(
      keyboardEndFrame,
      from: view.window)

    userInterface.moveContent(
      forKeyboardFrame: convertedKeyboardEndFrame)
  }
}
```

Since the view controller is already configured to respond to the ObserverForSignInEventResponder, it just makes the necessary calls to the user interface on certain events. When the observer notifies the view controller that a new SignInViewState is ready, the view controller immediately calls userInterface.render(newState: viewState). The view controller just passes along the state from the observer, which removes a lot of logic from the view controller code.

Another thing to note is there's no layout code in the view controller. The user interface abstracts all of its layout away from its owner and deals with updates when its notified of a change. If you need to change the way the user interface handles keyboard updates internally, you shouldn't need to modify the view controller code.

Lastly, look at some highlights from the `SignInRootView`:

```swift
class SignInRootView: NiblessView {

  // MARK: - Properties
  let emailField: UITextField = {
    let field = UITextField()
    field.placeholder = "Email"
    // Other field configuration here...
    return field
  }()

  let passwordField: UITextField = {
    let field = UITextField()
    // field configuration here...
    return field
  }()

  let signInButton: UIButton = {
    let button = UIButton(type: .custom)
    // button configuration here...
    return button
  }()
}

extension SignInRootView: SignInUserInterface {

  ...

  func render(newState: SignInViewState) {
    emailField.isEnabled = newState.emailInputEnabled
    passwordField.isEnabled = newState.passwordInputEnabled
    signInButton.isEnabled = newState.signInButtonEnabled

    switch newState.signInActivityIndicatorAnimating {
    case true:
      signInActivityIndicator.startAnimating()
    case false:
      signInActivityIndicator.stopAnimating()
    }
  }

  func moveContentForDismissedKeyboard() {
    resetScrollViewContentInset()
  }

  func moveContent(forKeyboardFrame keyboardFrame: CGRect) {
```

```
    var insets = scrollView.contentInset
    insets.bottom = keyboardFrame.height
    scrollView.contentInset = insets
  }
}
```

The view contains all the UIKit elements needed to render the sign-in screen. The emailField and passwordField are UITextFields and signInButton is a UIButton object, all laid out by this view.

When the render(newState:) method gets called, the isEnabled fields are updated on each of the elements based on state. The activity indicator also starts or stops spinning.

The keyboard user-interface methods adjust the scroll view's content inset based on whether the keyboard is displayed or dismissed. This allows the input fields to stay visible and not hide under the keyboard.

The SignInRootView code should be pretty familiar since it's just a normal UIView. The big difference is it must conform to the SignInUserInterface and handle those methods properly. That's it for the user-interface section. Next, you'll see how the interaction responder works.

Interaction responder

The interaction responder handles user interactions. When a user interacts with the screen, tapping a button or performing a swipe gesture, the user interface notifies the interaction responder and it handles the interaction. User-interface objects only know when the user performs an interaction. They don't actually know how to handle the interaction. They're dumb objects by design.

The user interface tells the interaction responder what to do, not what happened. This removes any user interface terms from the interaction responder.

For example, the responder might expose a method that says createPost() instead of createPostButtonTapped(). If you swap out the user interface element to sign in for something other than a button, the interaction responder protocol stays the same.

Usually, a view controller is the user interface's interaction responder, but you can create a new object that handles user interactions and inject it into the view controller. Either way works. The standalone object is easier to test since you don't have to create a view controller. The view controller approach requires less code since you can just make the view controller conform to the responder protocol. Koober uses the view controller approach.

Mechanics

This section explains how interaction responders are created and used. It's meant to briefly explain the concepts. You'll see code examples further down.

Instantiating

You create an interaction-responder protocol for each user interface. Interaction responders are then provided as a reference to the user interface. Since Koober view controllers are the interaction responders, they get created in a dependency container.

Providing

User-interface objects have an interaction responder property that gets set after initialization. This is so the user interface can wire its controls to methods that notify the interaction responder on user interactions.

The view controller that conforms to the interaction responder protocol gets created with a user interface object. After the view controller is initialized, it gets set as the user interface's interaction responder.

Using

The user interface makes calls directly to its interaction responder. The view controller just needs to implement the right interaction responder methods.

Creating an interaction responder

The above diagram shows how the view controller gets initialized with a user interface and set as the interaction responder.

1. First, the dependency container creates the view controller and injects the user interface object.

2. Then, the dependency container sets the view controller as the user interface's interaction responder.

3. From then on, all user interactions are handled by the view controller, which conforms to the interaction responder protocol.

Types

Interaction responder protocol

Each view has its own interaction-responder protocol. Any interaction the user can perform on the view is described in the protocol. It doesn't expose any details about how the internals are implemented. The protocol should have no references to UIKit and nothing about what kind of user interface element triggered the user interaction.

Take a look at the sign-in view's interaction responder:

```
typealias Secret = String

protocol SignInIxResponder: AnyObject {
  func signIn(email: String, password: Secret)
}
```

The sign-in responder protocol is simple and contains a single method to sign in the user. The only user interaction a user can perform in the sign-in screen is tapping the **Sign in** button after entering an email and password.

There are two main takeaways from this protocol:

1. The responder doesn't expose any details about how the sign in was initiated, such as tapping a sign-in button or tapping the next button on the keyboard. If you redesign the user interface you shouldn't have to update the interaction responder protocol.
2. The user interface tells the interaction responder what to do, not what happened. The method isn't `signInButtonTapped()`, but rather `signIn()`, telling the responder what action to perform next. The interaction responder doesn't care about what happened. It's the user interface's responsibility to convert button taps and gestures into an actionable item for the interaction responder.

Example

In this section, you'll walk through an example so you can see how the interaction responder is used in practice. The example is from Koober's sign-in screen.

> **Note**: To ease readability, the example code in this section has been simplified from the code in the example Xcode project.

The `SignInViewController` is the interaction responder for its `SignInUserInterfaceView`, which you saw in the user interface section. When the user interacts with the `SignInUserInterfaceView`, the user interface makes a call to the interaction responder.

When the `SignInViewController` gets created in the `KooberOnboardingDependencyContainer`, it's set as the user interface's interaction responder. You saw the initialization in the user interface section, but let's go over it once more as a refresher:

```
class KooberOnboardingDependencyContainer {
  // ...

  func makeSignInViewController() -> SignInViewController {
    // User interface element
    let userInterface = SignInRootView()

    // Observer element
    let statePublisher =
      makeSignInViewControllerStatePublisher()
    let observer = ObserverForSignIn(state: statePublisher)
```

```
    // Use case element
    let signInUseCase = makeSignInUseCase()

    let signInViewController =
      SignInViewController(
        userInterface: userInterface,
        signInStateObserver: observer,
        // 1
        signInUseCase: signInUseCase)

    // Wire responders
    // 2
    userInterface.ixResponder = signInViewController
    observer.eventResponder = signInViewController

    return signInViewController
  }

  // ...
}
```

A couple highlights from this code:

1. The only interaction responder method has is to sign in the user. The sign-in use case actually performs this work. It's a dependency of the `SignInViewController`, so the interaction responder method can run the use case when the user is ready to sign in.

2. The user interface is the object that makes calls to the interaction responder. Since the sign-in view controller gets set as the user interaction responder in the dependency creation code, the view controller only has to implement the protocol methods.

   Also, since `SignInViewController` only takes in a `SignInUserInterfaceView`, which is a `SignInUserInterface` and a `UIView`, you have to set the interaction responder on the concrete instance, `SignInRootView`. Only the dependency creation code knows about the concrete type, so the dependency code needs to configure the responder.

The user interface wires its components to methods that call the interaction responder. In the `SignInRootView`, a sign in `UIButton` tap makes the call:

```swift
class SignInRootView: NiblessView, SignInUserInterface {

  // MARK: - Properties
  weak var ixResponder: SignInIxResponder?

  // ...

  override func didMoveToWindow() {
    super.didMoveToWindow()
    wireController()
    // other set up goes here ...
  }

  func wireController() {
    signInButton.addTarget(
      self,
      action: #selector(signIn),
      for: .touchUpInside)
  }

  @objc
  func signIn() {
    ixResponder?.signIn(
      email: emailField.text ?? "",
      password: passwordField.text ?? "")
  }

  // ...
}
```

The root view configures the target / action pairs as soon as it moves to the window. You could alternatively do this when the view is initialized.

The `signInButton` is configured to call the `signIn()` method whenever it's tapped. The `signIn()` method calls the interaction responder's `signIn()` method with the current email and password input. This is fairly straightforward code.

The key here is that the `UIButton` target / action can be switched to a tap gesture recognizer on another component and the interaction responder doesn't need to change.

Take a look at the interaction responder implementation:

```
extension SignInViewController: SignInIxResponder {

  func signIn(email: String, password: Secret) {
    let useCase = signInUseCase()
    useCase.start()
  }
}
```

Normally, the interaction responder methods run a use case. That's it. The bulk of the work to make API calls and change the state of the user interface is handled inside the use case.

The interaction responder implementations are only responsible for knowing which use cases to run and running them. This may seem overly simple, but you want to remove as much code from the view controller as possible. You'll get a better understanding of what happens after `start()` is called on the use case in the use case section.

That's it for the interaction responder! There's still a lot of ground to cover with the next two elements. In Part 2, you'll see how to implement Observer and Use Case elements. Before jumping into Part 2, feel free to take a break, stretch and grab a coffee or your drink of choice.

Key points

- **Elements** is an architecture meant to make iOS development fun and flexible. A set of "Elements" make up the architecture. The cool thing is you can choose which pieces to use in your own applications.

- Elements is designed on top of some core underlying concepts: entities allow objects to communicate, protocols make software flexible and encapsulation enables safe change.

- Elements are separated into two main categories: **Core Logic** and **User Interface Logic**.

- This edition of this book dives deep into the four main elements: user interface, interaction responder, observer and use case.

- **User-interface** objects describe the views in your app. They allow you to configure and change what the users sees and interacts with.

- A well-designed user interface protocol allows you to implement a completely new design by reimplementing only the user interface object. No view controller changes necessary.

- **Interaction responders** handle user interactions. When a user interacts with the screen the user interface notifies the interaction responder.

- Interaction responders allow you to safely change a view hierarchy without needing to change any view controller code. This is because interaction responders express what a user can do with a user interface as opposed to what specific view triggers what task.

Chapter 8: Architecture: Elements, Part 2

By René Cacheaux

In Chapter 7, you learned about **Elements** and how to design user interface and interaction responder elements. In this chapter, you'll take a deep dive into two more elements: **observer** and **use case**.

> **Note**: The example Koober Xcode project for this chapter is the same as Chapter 7's Xcode project. To see this chapter's material in Koober, open the Xcode project that is located in Chapter 7's project directory.

Observer

Observers are objects view controllers use to receive external events. You can think of these events as input signals to view controllers. Observers know how to:

- Subscribe to events
- Process events
- Deliver processed events to a view controller

For instance, say you're building a view controller that needs to respond to a `NotificationCenter` notification. An observer would know how to subscribe to the notification, how to pull out the relevant information from the user info dictionary and would know what view controller method to call. The view controller would then perform some work in response to the processed notification. You might be thinking, but wait, adding and removing observers from `NotificationCenter` is really easy. Why not leave this code in view controllers? Hang tight, you'll read about the benefits soon.

> **Note**: Observers allow you to decouple view controllers from event technologies such as `NotificationCenter`, target-action, etc. `Combine` also allows you to decouple view controllers from event technologies. As you read this section you might be wondering why not just use `Combine`? Using `Combine` adds boilerplate code to your view controllers making them a bit harder to read. You can use the Observer pattern alongside `Combine` to both decouple view controllers from event technologies and to make view controllers light and easy to read. Using `Combine` directly inside view controllers is also a valid approach. This decision comes down to reading preference.

Mechanics

This section explains how observers are created, used and de-allocated. If this section is a bit fuzzy, don't worry. You'll see code examples of all these concepts further down.

Instantiating

In the simplest usage, you write an observer class for every view controller that needs to observe external events. Observers are initialized with references to the systems that emit events. This is so an observer can subscribe to events when a view controller wants to start observing.

Providing

Observers are created outside view controllers; i.e., observers are provided to their respective view controller. Observers are provided to view controllers either via a view controller's initializer or by setting a view controller property. At this point, a view controller has a reference to its observer.

Observers hold references to the systems the view controller wants to observe, such as `RxSwift Observables` and `Combine Publishers`. During this phase, observers have not subscribed to any events.

During setup, observers need to be given a delegate. Observers call methods on their delegates every time they process a new event. Delegates, which are typically view controllers, are of type `EventResponder`. `EventResponder` is a protocol that you write specifically for each view controller. `EventResponder` protocols have all the methods that a view controller implements to respond to different events from different systems. For example, you might have a method for when the keyboard is dismissed.

Using

Once view controllers are ready to start observing, view controllers can call an observer's `startObserving()` method. During this method, observers subscribe to all the events that a view controller needs to observe. At this point, observers are live. They are accepting, processing and delivering events to their view controller.

View controllers can call an observer's `stopObserving()` method whenever they need to stop events from arriving. You might do this when a view controller is no longer visible but still alive in memory. If you need to start and stop observing different events at different times you can break up an observer into multiple observers. You'll see an example of this in the variation and advanced usage section.

Tearing down

In the simplest usage, observers live as long as their respective view controllers. Observer and view controller lifetimes should match. To guarantee the lifetime, make sure that a view controller is the only object holding onto an observer. Also, observers need to hold a weak reference to their event responder; i.e., view controller, to avoid retain cycles.

As a best practice, view controllers should call `stopObserving()` before being deallocated by ARC. However, you can build a nice safeguard inside observers by calling `stopObserving()` when the weak reference to an observer's event responder; i.e., view controller, `nil`s out. You can do this in a `willSet` or `didSet` property observer closure. You'll see this safeguard in the example code ahead.

Types

Observer protocol

All observers implement the `Observer` protocol.

> **Note**: If this name collides with a pre-existing type you can rename it to something similar.

View controllers should type annotate their observer property with this `Observer` protocol type as opposed to the observer's concrete class type. This is so you don't have to provide a real observer when unit testing view controllers. This is what the protocol looks like:

```
protocol Observer {
  func startObserving()
  func stopObserving()
}
```

`startObserving()` and `stopObserving()` are the only two methods that a view controller needs to call on any observer. View controllers use these methods to start observing and stop observing events.

Observer event responder protocols

When events occur, observers need to be able to call methods on their view controller to let their view controller know an event occurred and to pass any related data. In order to do this, observers hold a weak reference to their view controller.

The type of the weak reference could be the concrete view controller type; however, that gives observers access to call all visible view controller methods. Instead, you can define an `EventResponder` protocol.

You then declare conformance to this protocol by an observer's view controller. This protocol includes all the methods that an observer can call. Because observers need to hold a weak reference of this type, this protocol type can only be conformed to by class types. Here's an example:

```
protocol ObserverForSignInEventResponder: AnyObject {
    func received(newErrorMessage errorMessage: ErrorMessage)
    func received(newViewState viewState: SignInViewState)
    func keyboardWillHide()
    func keyboardWillChangeFrame(keyboardEndFrame: CGRect)
}
```

Notice how the events can come from different systems. For instance, in the example above, the first half of the methods are associated with `Combine Publisher` subscriptions and the second half of the methods are associated with `NotificationCenter` notifications. This is nice because view controllers no longer need to deal with different event technologies. This is also nice because the pattern removes subscription boilerplate code from view controllers and therefore makes view controllers much easier to read.

> **Note:** The following code examples subscribe to keyboard notifications using `NotificationCenter` APIs. Alternatively, you can subscribe to keyboard events using `Combine`. Either way, the Observer pattern does not change and that's nice because the pattern is resilient to framework choice.

Also, in the example above, notice how the keyboard event methods do not pass the info dictionary from `NotificationCenter` notifications. Observers know how to pull out the relevant information. This is really nice because related view controllers no longer need to know how to fish for data that's inside an info dictionary. Also, when unit testing, you won't have to worry about creating an info dictionary. You just need to call the view controller's event responder methods with test data. And, if later in time, events need to come from a different system — e.g., you switch from CoreData to SQLite — you won't need to change any view controllers. You'll just need to update observers.

Observer classes

Observer classes conform to the `Observer` protocol. As mentioned before, they hold a weak reference to their `EventResponder`, which is usually a view controller. Observer classes know how to subscribe to events, process events and call methods on an `EventResponder`. You implement one observer class for each view controller that needs to observe external events. Here's an example skeleton implementation:

```
class ObserverForSignIn: Observer {

  // MARK: - Properties
  weak var eventResponder: ObserverForSignInEventResponder? {
    willSet {
      if newValue == nil {
        stopObserving()
      }
    }
  }

  // MARK: - Methods
  func startObserving() {
    // Subscribe to events here.
    // ...
  }

  func stopObserving() {
    // Unsubscribe to events here.
    // ...
  }
}
```

Remember the safeguard you read about earlier? It's implemented here, in the example above. Whenever the `eventResponder` weak reference `nil`s out, the property observer calls `stopObserving()`. This makes sure the observer unsubscribes from events when the related view controller is de-allocated.

Example

In this section, you'll walk through a complete example so you can see how all the different types and objects work together. The example is from Koober's sign-in screen.

> **Note**: To ease readability, some of the example code in this section has been simplified from the code in the example Xcode project.

Koober's sign-in screen is implemented by `SignInViewController`. This view controller benefits from using an observer because it needs to observe several different events from different systems.

`SignInViewController` needs to observe the following events:

- **Sign-in view state**: A `Combine Publisher` provides the controller's `UIView` state. In order to reload the view, the controller needs to know when the view state changes. When the controller sees a new state, the controller passes the state object to its root `UIView` so the view can update itself.

- **Error messages**: The `SignInViewController` needs to be able to present a `UIAlertController` whenever an error, such as an incorrect password, occurs. The error messages come from a `Combine Publisher`.

- **Keyboard events**: The sign-in screen needs to accommodate the keyboard for short screens found on iPhones such as the iPhone SE. In order to do this, the controller needs to observe keyboard notifications from `NotificationCenter`.

By delegating event subscription to an observer, the view controller decouples itself from technologies such as `RxSwift`, `Combine` and `NotificationCenter`.

This makes the view controller's code more robust, cleaner and easier to test. Now that you're familiar with the events `SignInViewController` needs to observe, it's time to walk through the code.

The first step to building an observer for a view controller is to design an `EventResponder` protocol with all the event handling methods. The view controller should implement these methods. The view controller's observer calls into one of these methods when an event occurs. Here's the `SignInViewController`'s `EventResponder` protocol you saw earlier:

```
protocol ObserverForSignInEventResponder: AnyObject {
  func received(newErrorMessage errorMessage: ErrorMessage)
  func received(newViewState viewState: SignInViewState)
  func keyboardWillHide()
  func keyboardWillChangeFrame(keyboardEndFrame: CGRect)
}
```

This is the exact same protocol. When designing `EventResponder` protocols, avoid including any details about the event systems. For instance, the example above avoids any `Combine` types and avoids concepts from `NotificationCenter` such as user info dictionaries. The goal is to design a really clean protocol that depends on as little as possible. This is important because the point of `EventResponder` protocols is to decouple view controllers from event systems.

So that's the event responder. Once you've designed your view controller's `EventResponder` protocol, you can implement the protocol methods in the view controller similar to the following:

```
extension SignInViewController:
  ObserverForSignInEventResponder {

  func received(newErrorMessage errorMessage: ErrorMessage) {
    // ...
  }

  func received(newViewState viewState: SignInViewState) {
    // ...
  }

  func keyboardWillHide() {
    // ...
  }

  func keyboardWillChangeFrame(keyboardEndFrame: CGRect) {
    // ...
  }
}
```

Don't worry too much about how these methods are implemented. The view controller responds to these events just like any other view controller. The important point is the view controller no longer needs to know how to receive events from specific technologies and systems.

With the `EventResponder` protocol designed and with the protocol implemented in the view controller, the next step is to look at the `SignInViewController`'s observer class, `ObserverForSignIn`:

```
// 1
class ObserverForSignIn: Observer {

  // MARK: - Properties
  // 2
  weak var eventResponder: ObserverForSignInEventResponder? {
    willSet {
      if newValue == nil {
```

```
      stopObserving()
    }
  }
}

// 3
let signInState: AnyPublisher<SignInViewControllerState,
                              Never>

var errorStateSubscription: AnyCancellable?
var viewStateSubscription: AnyCancellable?

// 4
private var isObserving: Bool {
  if isObservingState && isObservingKeyboard {
    return true
  } else {
    return false
  }
}

private var isObservingState: Bool {
  if errorStateSubscription != nil
    && viewStateSubscription != nil {
      return true
  } else {
    return false
  }
}

private var isObservingKeyboard = false

// MARK: - Methods
// 5
init(signInState: AnyPublisher<SignInViewControllerState,
                               Never>) {
  self.signInState = signInState
}

// 6
func startObserving() {
  assert(self.eventResponder != nil)

  guard let _ = self.eventResponder else {
    return
  }

  if isObserving {
    return
  }

  subscribeToErrorMessages()
  subscribeToSignInViewState()
```

```
    startObservingKeyboardNotifications()
}

// 7
func stopObserving() {
  unsubscribeFromSignInViewState()
  unsubscribeFromErrorMessages()
  stopObservingNotificationCenterNotifications()
}

func subscribeToSignInViewState() {
  viewStateSubscription =
    signInState
      .receive(on: DispatchQueue.main)
      .map { $0.viewState }
      .removeDuplicates()
      .sink { [weak self] viewState in
        self?.received(newViewState: viewState)
      }
}

func received(newViewState: SignInViewState) {
  // 8
  eventResponder?.received(newViewState: newViewState)
}

func unsubscribeFromSignInViewState() {
  viewStateSubscription = nil
}

func subscribeToErrorMessages() {
  errorStateSubscription =
    signInState
      .receive(on: DispatchQueue.main)
      .map { $0.errorsToPresent.first }
      .compactMap { $0 }
      .removeDuplicates()
      .sink { [weak self] errorMessage in
        self?.received(newErrorMessage: errorMessage)
      }
}

func received(newErrorMessage errorMessage: ErrorMessage) {
  // 8
  eventResponder?.received(newErrorMessage: errorMessage)
}

func unsubscribeFromErrorMessages() {
  errorStateSubscription = nil
}

func startObservingKeyboardNotifications() {
  let notificationCenter = NotificationCenter.default
```

```swift
    notificationCenter
      .addObserver(
        self,
        selector: #selector(
          handle(keyboardWillHideNotification:)),
        name: UIResponder.keyboardWillHideNotification,
        object: nil
      )

    notificationCenter
      .addObserver(
        self,
        selector: #selector(
          handle(keyboardWillChangeFrameNotification:)),
        name: UIResponder.keyboardWillChangeFrameNotification,
        object: nil
      )

    isObservingKeyboard = true
}

@objc func handle(
  keyboardWillHideNotification notification: Notification
) {
  assert(notification.name ==
    UIResponder.keyboardWillHideNotification)

  // 8
  eventResponder?.keyboardWillHide()
}

@objc func handle(
  keyboardWillChangeFrameNotification
    notification: Notification) {

  assert(notification.name ==
    UIResponder.keyboardWillChangeFrameNotification)

  guard let userInfo = notification.userInfo else {
    return
  }
  guard let keyboardEndFrameUserInfo =
    userInfo[UIResponder.keyboardFrameEndUserInfoKey] else {
      return
  }
  guard let keyboardEndFrame =
    keyboardEndFrameUserInfo as? NSValue else {
      return
  }

  // 8
  eventResponder?
    .keyboardWillChangeFrame(
```

```
            keyboardEndFrame: keyboardEndFrame.cgRectValue)
    }

    func stopObservingNotificationCenterNotifications() {
        let notificationCenter = NotificationCenter.default
        notificationCenter.removeObserver(self)

        isObservingKeyboard = false
    }
}
```

Here are some things worth highlighting in the example above:

1. The class conforms to the `Observer` protocol you saw earlier in this chapter. Recall that this protocol allows the associated view controller to start and stop observation.

2. This is the stored property that holds a weak reference to the observer's associated view controller. The property's `willSet` closure ensures that this observer unsubscribes from event subscriptions whenever the event responder; i.e., the view controller, is de-allocated. The property is type annotated with the `ObserverForSignInEventResponder` protocol type. The protocol restricts which view controller methods the observer can call. If you feel comfortable exposing all the view controller methods you can forgo designing `EventResponder` protocols and simply use view controller concrete types in observer implementations. Though, if you need to unit test the observer, the `EventResponder` protocol is helpful because you won't have to instantiate a real view controller. You can provide a fake implementation to the observer.

3. Because view controllers should have control over when observation starts and stops, observer classes cannot subscribe to events immediately during initialization. For this reason, observer classes have to hold onto references to the systems they observe. In this case, this observer observes events coming from a `Combine Publisher`. This observer implementation has to hold onto the `Publisher` in order to subscribe and unsubscribe from the `Publisher` at later points in time. Some systems, like `NotificationCenter`, provide global default singletons for adding observers. In these cases, the observer class does not need to hold on to anything.

4. The `isObserving` computed property helps avoid accidentally subscribing to the same event stream more than once. `startObserving()` checks this value before subscribing to any events.

5. Observers should be initialized with the systems they need to observe. In this example, the observer is initialized with a `Combine Publisher`.

6. This is the `Observer` protocol's `startObserving()` method implementation. This specific implementation makes sure that the observer has a reference to the event responder; i.e., the view controller. Then, the method subscribes to two different data models from the same `Combine Publisher`. Finally, the method starts listening to two different keyboard notifications from `NotificationCenter`.

7. This is the `Observer` protocol's `stopObserving()` method implementation. In this example, the method unsubscribes from the `Combine Publisher` and removes itself as a `NotificationCenter` observer.

8. These lines of code point out where the observer is making calls to the view controller via the event responder protocol. Notice how the observer processes the data coming from both the `Combine Publisher` and processes the data coming from `NotificationCenter` *before calling the view controller*. The observer is a great place to hide away any logic that is specific to event systems, like `NotificationCenter` notification objects.

The last step in putting this pattern to practice is to add code to the view controller to **start and stop observation**.

Observers are provided to view controllers instead of view controllers instantiating their observers. This is because a view controller shouldn't need to know how to get a hold of the event system objects needed to initialize an observer.

View controllers should have an `observer` property to hold onto their observer object. View controllers can then call `startObserving()` and `stopObserving()` at appropriate points in time.

Here's how this works in `SignInViewController`:

```swift
public class SignInViewController: NiblessViewController {

    // MARK: - Properties
    // Observers
    var observer: Observer

    // User interface
    let userInterface: SignInUserInterfaceView

    // Factories
    let signInUseCaseFactory: SignInUseCaseFactory
    let makeFinishedPresentingErrorUseCase:
        FinishedPresentingErrorUseCaseFactory

    // MARK: - Methods
    init(userInterface: SignInUserInterfaceView,
```

```swift
      observer: Observer,
      signInUseCaseFactory: SignInUseCaseFactory,
      finishedPresentingErrorUseCaseFactory:
        @escaping FinishedPresentingErrorUseCaseFactory
  ) {
    self.userInterface = userInterface
    self.observer = observer
    self.signInUseCaseFactory = signInUseCaseFactory
    self.makeFinishedPresentingErrorUseCase =
      finishedPresentingErrorUseCaseFactory

    super.init()
  }

  public override func loadView() {
    view = userInterface
  }

  public override func viewWillAppear(_ animated: Bool) {
    super.viewWillAppear(animated)
    observer.startObserving()
  }

  public override func viewWillDisappear(_ animated: Bool) {
    super.viewWillDisappear(animated)
    observer.stopObserving()
  }

  // ...
}

extension SignInViewController:
  ObserverForSignInEventResponder {

  func received(newErrorMessage errorMessage: ErrorMessage) {
    // ...
  }

  func received(newViewState viewState: SignInViewState) {
    // ...
  }

  func keyboardWillHide() {
    // ...
  }

  func keyboardWillChangeFrame(keyboardEndFrame: CGRect) {
    // ...
  }
}

// ...
```

This code is fairly straightforward. All of the icky details about `Combine` and `NotificationCenter` are no longer in this view controller. Because the code is so easy to read, there's no need to walk through it step by step. The most important point is that the `SignInViewController` does not know about the observer's concrete class type. Notice how the `observer` property is type annotated with `Observer` rather than `ObserverForSignIn`. This allows you to use a fake `Observer` implementation when unit testing `SignInViewController`.

The view controller from above receives its observer via its initializer. Therefore, the observer needs to be created outside of the view controller. In Koober, observers are created in dependency containers. For this example, `ObserverForSignIn` is created and injected into `SignInViewController` in `KooberOnboardingDependencyContainer`:

```swift
public class KooberOnboardingDependencyContainer {
  // ...

  func makeSignInViewController() -> SignInViewController {
    // User interface element
    let userInterface = SignInRootView()

    // Observer element
    // 1
    let statePublisher =
      makeSignInViewControllerStatePublisher()
    let observer =
      ObserverForSignIn(signInState: statePublisher)

    // ...

    let signInViewController =
      SignInViewController(
        userInterface: userInterface,
        // 2
        observer: observer,
        // ...
      )

    // Wire responders
    userInterface.ixResponder = signInViewController
    //3
    observer.eventResponder = signInViewController

    return signInViewController
  }

  // ...
}
```

Here are the steps in `makeSignInViewController` that create and inject `ObserverForSignIn`:

1. The observer is created with a `Combine Publisher`. Subscriptions to the `Publisher` carry all the state updates needed by `SignInViewController`.

2. The observer is injected into a new `SignInViewController`. Recall that `SignInViewController` initializer's parameter for observer is type annotated with `Observer` rather than `ObserverForSignIn`.

3. Every observer needs an `eventResponder`. Event responder protocols are almost always implemented by view controllers. In this case, the `signInViewController` is set as the observer's `eventResponder`.

That's all the code needed to build, create and use observers in any codebase. This section covers the basics. There are many other ways to design observers. You'll learn about all the variations and advanced usages next.

Variations and advanced usage

There's a lot more to observers than meets the eyes. In this section, you'll explore more ways to implement observers.

Building multiple observers per view controller

Building one observer class per view controller is simple and straightforward. However, in certain situations, you might prefer to break a single observer into multiple observer classes.

Sometimes, you might need to start and stop observing different systems at different times. For example, you might want to stop observing UI related events when a view controller goes off the screen while continuing to observe non-UI related events. To do this, you'll need to build multiple observers. If you don't need to start and stop observing at different times, you still might want to build multiple observers. A single observer class might be very long. In these cases it's nice to build a separate observer for separate event systems.

To illustrate this pattern, the following code examples demonstrate how to break up the `ObserverForSignIn` from the previous section into two observers: `SignInViewControllerStateObserver` and `SignInKeyboardObserver`.

> **Note**: The example Xcode project has a different variation of the observer element. The project does not include `SignInKeyboardObserver`. However, the entire implementation for `SignInKeyboardObserver` is available below.

First, the `ObserverForSignInEventResponder` needs to be separated into these two protocols:

```swift
protocol SignInKeyboardObserverEventResponder: AnyObject {
  func keyboardWillHide()
  func keyboardWillChangeFrame(keyboardEndFrame: CGRect)
}
```

```swift
protocol SignInStateObserverEventResponder: AnyObject {
  func received(newErrorMessage errorMessage: ErrorMessage)
  func received(newViewState viewState: SignInViewState)
}
```

These protocols are nicer than the single `ObserverForSignInEventResponder` because each protocol is only responsible for a single kind of event. `SignInKeyboardObserverEventResponder` handles keyboard events and `SignInStateObserverEventResponder` handles state change events.

With the event responders figured out, the next step is to look at separate observer implementations: `SignInKeyboardObserver` and `SignInStateObserver`.

```swift
class SignInKeyboardObserver: Observer {

  // MARK: - Properties
  weak var eventResponder:
    SignInKeyboardObserverEventResponder? {
    willSet {
      if newValue == nil {
        stopObserving()
      }
    }
  }

  private var isObserving = false

  // MARK: - Methods
  func startObserving() {
    assert(self.eventResponder != nil)

    guard let _ = self.eventResponder else {
      return
    }
```

```
    if isObserving {
      return
    }

    startObservingKeyboardNotifications()
  }

  func stopObserving() {
    stopObservingNotificationCenterNotifications()
  }

  func startObservingKeyboardNotifications() {
    let notificationCenter = NotificationCenter.default

    notificationCenter
      .addObserver(
        self,
        selector: #selector(
          handle(keyboardWillHideNotification:)),
        name: UIResponder.keyboardWillHideNotification,
        object: nil)

    notificationCenter
      .addObserver(
        self,
        selector: #selector(
          handle(keyboardWillChangeFrameNotification:)),
        name: UIResponder.keyboardWillChangeFrameNotification,
        object: nil)

    isObserving = true
  }

  @objc func handle(
    keyboardWillHideNotification notification: Notification
  ) {
    assert(notification.name ==
      UIResponder.keyboardWillHideNotification)

    eventResponder?.keyboardWillHide()
  }

  @objc func handle(
    keyboardWillChangeFrameNotification
      notification: Notification
  ) {
    assert(notification.name ==
      UIResponder.keyboardWillChangeFrameNotification)

    guard let userInfo = notification.userInfo else {
      return
    }
    guard let keyboardEndFrameUserInfo =
```

```swift
      userInfo[UIResponder.keyboardFrameEndUserInfoKey] else {
        return
    }
    guard let keyboardEndFrame =
      keyboardEndFrameUserInfo as? NSValue else {
        return
    }

    eventResponder?
      .keyboardWillChangeFrame(
        keyboardEndFrame: keyboardEndFrame.cgRectValue)
  }

  func stopObservingNotificationCenterNotifications() {
    let notificationCenter = NotificationCenter.default
    notificationCenter.removeObserver(self)

    isObserving = false
  }
}
```

```swift
class SignInStateObserver: Observer {

  // MARK: - Properties
  weak var eventResponder: SignInStateObserverEventResponder? {
    willSet {
      if newValue == nil {
        stopObserving()
      }
    }
  }

  let signInState: AnyPublisher<SignInViewControllerState,
                                Never>

  var errorStateSubscription: AnyCancellable?
  var viewStateSubscription: AnyCancellable?

  private var isObserving: Bool {
    if errorStateSubscription != nil
      && viewStateSubscription != nil {
        return true
    } else {
      return false
    }
  }

  // MARK: - Methods
  init(signInState: AnyPublisher<SignInViewControllerState,
                                 Never>) {
    self.signInState = signInState
  }
```

```swift
  func startObserving() {
    assert(self.eventResponder != nil)

    guard let _ = self.eventResponder else {
      return
    }

    if isObserving {
      return
    }

    subscribeToErrorMessages()
    subscribeToSignInViewState()
  }

  func stopObserving() {
    unsubscribeFromSignInViewState()
    unsubscribeFromErrorMessages()
  }

  func subscribeToSignInViewState() {
    viewStateSubscription =
      signInState
        .receive(on: DispatchQueue.main)
        .map { $0.viewState }
        .removeDuplicates()
        .sink { [weak self] viewState in
          self?.received(newViewState: viewState)
        }
  }

  func received(newViewState: SignInViewState) {
    eventResponder?.received(newViewState: newViewState)
  }

  func unsubscribeFromSignInViewState() {
    viewStateSubscription = nil
  }

  func subscribeToErrorMessages() {
    errorStateSubscription =
      signInState
        .receive(on: DispatchQueue.main)
        .map { $0.errorsToPresent.first }
        .compactMap { $0 }
        .removeDuplicates()
        .sink { [weak self] errorMessage in
          self?.received(newErrorMessage: errorMessage)
        }
  }

  func received(newErrorMessage errorMessage: ErrorMessage) {
    eventResponder?.received(newErrorMessage: errorMessage)
```

```
    }

    func unsubscribeFromErrorMessages() {
      errorStateSubscription = nil
    }
  }
```

The implementation for these observers comes straight from `ObserverForSignIn`. Because each observer only deals with a single event system such as Combine or NotificationCenter, these observer classes are much easier to read than the single `ObserverForSignIn` from the previous section. This is a nice plus to breaking observers down into multiple classes.

Now, it's time to look at how the `SignInViewController` receives and uses the two observer instances:

```
class SignInViewController: NiblessViewController {

  // MARK: - Properties
  // 2
  var stateObserver: Observer
  var keyboardObserver: Observer

  let userInterface: SignInUserInterfaceView

  // MARK: - Methods
  // 1
  init(userInterface: SignInUserInterfaceView,
       stateObserver: Observer,
       keyboardObserver: Observer) {
    self.userInterface = userInterface
    self.stateObserver = stateObserver
    self.keyboardObserver = keyboardObserver

    super.init()
  }

  override func loadView() {
    view = userInterface
  }

  override func viewWillAppear(_ animated: Bool) {
    super.viewWillAppear(animated)
    // 3
    stateObserver.startObserving()
  }

  override func viewDidAppear(_ animated: Bool) {
    super.viewDidAppear(animated)
    // 3
```

```
    keyboardObserver.startObserving()
  }

  override func viewWillDisappear(_ animated: Bool) {
    super.viewWillDisappear(animated)
    // 4
    stateObserver.stopObserving()
    keyboardObserver.stopObserving()
  }

  // ...
}

extension SignInViewController:
  SignInStateObserverEventResponder {

  func received(newErrorMessage errorMessage: ErrorMessage) {
    // ...
  }

  func received(newViewState viewState: SignInViewState) {
    // ...
  }
}

extension SignInViewController:
  SignInKeyboardObserverEventResponder {

  func keyboardWillHide() {
    // ...
  }

  func keyboardWillChangeFrame(keyboardEndFrame: CGRect) {
    // ...
  }
}

// ...
```

This implementation of `SignInViewController` is pretty much the same as before, except, this version manages two observer instances instead of one. Here are some quick things to look at:

1. The view controller's initializer takes two observers. One for observing the keyboard and another for observing changes to the view controller and view state. Notice how, same as before, both parameters are type annotated with the `Observer` protocol instead of their concrete types.

2. The view controller needs two properties to hold each observer instance.

3. This is the main difference from the last implementation. Because the observation is built using separate observers, this view controller can now start observing state changes and keyboard events in different view controller lifecycle methods.

4. Both observers are stopped during `viewWillDisappear(_:)`.

Alright, that's most of the example.

The last thing to look at is how `KooberOnboardingDependencyContainer` injects `SignInViewController` with the two observers:

```
class KooberOnboardingDependencyContainer {
  // ...

  func makeSignInViewController() -> SignInViewController {
    // User interface element
    let userInterface = SignInRootView()

    // Observer elements
    // 1
    let statePublisher =
      makeSignInViewControllerStatePublisher()
    let stateObserver =
      SignInStateObserver(signInState: statePublisher)
    let keyboardObserver = SignInKeyboardObserver()

    // 2
    let signInViewController =
      SignInViewController(
        userInterface: userInterface,
        stateObserver: stateObserver,
        keyboardObserver: keyboardObserver)

    // Wire responders
    userInterface.ixResponder = signInViewController
    // 3
    stateObserver.eventResponder = signInViewController
    keyboardObserver.eventResponder = signInViewController

    return signInViewController
  }

  // ...
}
```

The main difference in this version of the dependency container is that the factory method needs to create, inject and wire two observers instead of one.

Some quick highlights:

1. Both observers are created.
2. The observers are injected into a new `SignInViewController`.
3. Each observer needs a reference to an event responder. `SignInViewController` conforms to both event responder protocols, therefore both observers are given the `signInViewController` as the event responder.

That's it! Breaking up a single view controller observer into single responsibility observers is a bit more work, but you get a cleaner and easier-to-read codebase. Now that you've seen these smaller single responsibility observers, you might be wondering if you could build an observer that can be reused by multiple view controllers. That's next.

Building reusable observers

What if you find yourself writing the same observer over and over again? Many of the systems that generate events in Cocoa Touch are general in nature.

The code you write to subscribe and respond to these events is virtually identical no matter what view controller you're building. For these cases, you can write a general purpose observer that you can re-use in any view controller. Observing keyboard events is a perfect example. You'll see a sample implementation of a general purpose keyboard observer next.

The first step is to design an event responder protocol that any view controller could conform to in order to respond to keyboard events. There's a problem though, Cocoa Touch doesn't have a keyboard user info data type. So how can a protocol be designed for methods such as `keyboardWillChangeFrame`?

The easiest thing to do would be to just pass along the user info dictionary to view controllers, but one of the goals of the observer pattern is to remove this kind of responsibility and complexity away from view controllers. You can accomplish this removal of responsibility by designing a custom data type to carry notification values. First, you'll explore this custom `KeyboardUserInfo` struct type:

```
struct KeyboardUserInfo {

  // MARK: - Properties
  let animationCurve: UIView.AnimationCurve
  let animationDuration: Double
  let isLocal: Bool
  let beginFrame: CGRect
```

```swift
    let endFrame: CGRect
    
    let animationCurveKey =
      UIResponder.keyboardAnimationCurveUserInfoKey
    let animationDurationKey =
      UIResponder.keyboardAnimationDurationUserInfoKey
    let isLocalKey = UIResponder.keyboardIsLocalUserInfoKey
    let frameBeginKey = UIResponder.keyboardFrameBeginUserInfoKey
    let frameEndKey = UIResponder.keyboardFrameEndUserInfoKey
    
    // MARK: - Methods
    init?(_ notification: Notification) {
      guard let userInfo = notification.userInfo else {
        return nil
      }
      
      // Animation curve.
      guard let animationCurveUserInfo =
            userInfo[animationCurveKey],
          let animationCurveRaw =
            animationCurveUserInfo as? Int,
          let animationCurve =
            UIView.AnimationCurve(rawValue: animationCurveRaw)
      else {
        return nil
      }
      self.animationCurve = animationCurve
      
      // Animation duration.
      guard let animationDurationUserInfo =
            userInfo[animationDurationKey],
          let animationDuration =
            animationDurationUserInfo as? Double
      else {
          return nil
      }
      self.animationDuration = animationDuration
      
      // Is local.
      guard let isLocalUserInfo = userInfo[isLocalKey],
          let isLocal = isLocalUserInfo as? Bool else {
        return nil
      }
      self.isLocal = isLocal
      
      // Begin frame.
      guard let beginFrameUserInfo = userInfo[frameBeginKey],
          let beginFrame = beginFrameUserInfo as? CGRect else {
        return nil
      }
      self.beginFrame = beginFrame
      
      // End frame.
```

```
      guard let endFrameUserInfo = userInfo[frameEndKey],
        let endFrame = endFrameUserInfo as? CGRect else {
          return nil
      }
      self.endFrame = endFrame
    }
  }
```

`KeyboardUserInfo` is a pure data type that's instantiated with a `Notification` object. During initialization, `KeyboardUserInfo` pulls all the values out of the notification's user info dictionary and sets those values on its own properties. Because the user info dictionary could be `nil` and because the dictionary could have a missing key-value pair, the initializer is fail-able. The reason this data type exists is to design an event responder protocol for keyboard events. What does this event provider protocol look like?

```
protocol KeyboardObserverEventResponder: AnyObject {
  func keyboardWillShow(_ userInfo: KeyboardUserInfo)
  func keyboardDidShow(_ userInfo: KeyboardUserInfo)
  func keyboardWillHide(_ userInfo: KeyboardUserInfo)
  func keyboardDidHide(_ userInfo: KeyboardUserInfo)
  func keyboardWillChangeFrame(_ userInfo: KeyboardUserInfo)
  func keyboardDidChangeFrame(_ userInfo: KeyboardUserInfo)
}
```

The protocol has a method for every kind of keyboard notification that Cocoa Touch defines. This is pretty neat, but you typically only need to write code for some of these methods. Every one of these methods is required. You wouldn't want to implement every single one of these methods in every view controller. To solve this problem, we could make this an `@objc` protocol and make the methods optional, or we can write a protocol extension with empty methods. The second option is more native to Swift. So lets look at the second option. Here's what the protocol extension looks like:

```
extension KeyboardObserverEventResponder {
  func keyboardWillShow(_ userInfo: KeyboardUserInfo) {
    // No-op.
    // This default implementation allows this protocol method
    // to be optional.
  }

  func keyboardDidShow(_ userInfo: KeyboardUserInfo) {
    // No-op.
    // This default implementation allows this protocol method
    // to be optional.
  }
```

```swift
  func keyboardWillHide(_ userInfo: KeyboardUserInfo) {
    // No-op.
    // This default implementation allows this protocol method
    // to be optional.
  }

  func keyboardDidHide(_ userInfo: KeyboardUserInfo) {
    // No-op.
    // This default implementation allows this protocol method
    // to be optional.
  }

  func keyboardWillChangeFrame(_ userInfo: KeyboardUserInfo) {
    // No-op.
    // This default implementation allows this protocol method
    // to be optional.
  }

  func keyboardDidChangeFrame(_ userInfo: KeyboardUserInfo) {
    // No-op.
    // This default implementation allows this protocol method
    // to be optional.
  }
}
```

With this extension, any object can conform to `KeyboardObserverEventResponder` without having to implement all the required methods. Awesome! That's the event responder, next is the observer implementation:

```swift
class KeyboardObserver: Observer {

  // MARK: - Properties
  weak var eventResponder: KeyboardObserverEventResponder? {
    didSet {
      if eventResponder == nil {
        stopObserving()
      }
    }
  }

  private var isObserving = false

  // MARK: - Methods
  func startObserving() {
    if isObserving == true {
      return
    }

    let notificationCenter = NotificationCenter.default

    notificationCenter.addObserver(
```

```
      self,
      selector: #selector(keyboardWillShow),
      name: UIResponder.keyboardWillShowNotification,
      object: nil
    )
    
    notificationCenter.addObserver(
      self,
      selector: #selector(keyboardDidShow),
      name: UIResponder.keyboardDidShowNotification,
      object: nil
    )
    
    notificationCenter.addObserver(
      self,
      selector: #selector(keyboardWillHide),
      name: UIResponder.keyboardWillHideNotification,
      object: nil
    )
    
    notificationCenter.addObserver(
      self,
      selector: #selector(keyboardDidHide),
      name: UIResponder.keyboardDidHideNotification,
      object: nil
    )
    
    notificationCenter.addObserver(
      self,
      selector: #selector(keyboardWillChangeFrame),
      name: UIResponder.keyboardWillChangeFrameNotification,
      object: nil
    )
    
    notificationCenter.addObserver(
      self,
      selector: #selector(keyboardDidChangeFrame),
      name: UIResponder.keyboardDidChangeFrameNotification,
      object: nil
    )
    
    isObserving = true
  }
  func stopObserving() {
    let notificationCenter = NotificationCenter.default
    notificationCenter.removeObserver(self)
    
    isObserving = false
  }
  
  @objc func keyboardWillShow(notification: Notification) {
    // 1
```

```swift
    assert(notification.name ==
      UIResponder.keyboardWillShowNotification)
    // 2
    guard let userInfo = KeyboardUserInfo(notification) else {
      assertionFailure()
      return
    }
    // 3
    eventResponder?.keyboardWillShow(userInfo)
  }

  @objc func keyboardDidShow(notification: Notification) {
    // 1
    assert(notification.name ==
      UIResponder.keyboardDidShowNotification)
    // 2
    guard let userInfo = KeyboardUserInfo(notification) else {
      assertionFailure()
      return
    }
    // 3
    eventResponder?.keyboardDidShow(userInfo)
  }

  @objc func keyboardWillHide(notification: Notification) {
    // 1
    assert(notification.name ==
      UIResponder.keyboardWillHideNotification)
    // 2
    guard let userInfo = KeyboardUserInfo(notification) else {
      assertionFailure()
      return
    }
    // 3
    eventResponder?.keyboardWillHide(userInfo)
  }

  @objc func keyboardDidHide(notification: Notification) {
    // 1
    assert(notification.name ==
      UIResponder.keyboardDidHideNotification)
    // 2
    guard let userInfo = KeyboardUserInfo(notification) else {
      assertionFailure()
      return
    }
    // 3
    eventResponder?.keyboardDidHide(userInfo)
  }

  @objc func keyboardWillChangeFrame(
    notification: Notification
  ) {
```

```
    // 1
    assert(notification.name ==
      UIResponder.keyboardWillChangeFrameNotification)
    // 2
    guard let userInfo = KeyboardUserInfo(notification) else {
      assertionFailure()
      return
    }
    // 3
    eventResponder?.keyboardWillChangeFrame(userInfo)
  }

  @objc func keyboardDidChangeFrame(
    notification: Notification
  ) {
    // 1
    assert(notification.name ==
      UIResponder.keyboardDidChangeFrameNotification)
    // 2
    guard let userInfo = KeyboardUserInfo(notification) else {
      assertionFailure()
      return
    }
    // 3
    eventResponder?.keyboardDidChangeFrame(userInfo)
  }
}
```

This observer is implemented exactly the same way as all the other observers you've seen so far. What's new here is how the observer responds to keyboard notifications in a general way. All the notification response methods follow this pattern:

1. Each response method knows how to process a particular kind of keyboard notification. So, first, the method ensures that the NotificationCenter notification passed in is of the expected kind.

2. Then, each method tries to create a KeyboardUserInfo with the notification object. Because KeyboardUserInfo's initializer is fail-able, the method needs to be able to handle initialization errors. You can handle an error in many different ways. In this example, if KeyboardUserInfo's initializer fails, the method crashes on debug builds and returns in release builds as an error here would be unlikely.

3. The event responder is called with the KeyboardUserInfo object.

You can instantiate, inject and wire this observer as you've seen in previous examples. The only difference is that this observer is not designed for a specific view controller; i.e., you can instantiate multiple instances for use by different view controllers.

> **Note**: Using this `KeyboardObserver` implementation results in a tiny bit more Objective-C method calling overhead. This is because `KeyboardObserver` subscribes to every kind of keyboard notification even if the associated view controller only implements one of the `KeyboardObserverEventResponder` methods. In most cases this is probably negligible. However, this is something to know and measure.

This reusable observer pattern works for most cases. However, in rare performance sensitive situations, you might need to implement single instance, multicast observers. You'll learn more about this in the next section.

Building multicast observers

In the case that you have a large number of view controllers on-screen, which are all listening to the same events from the same reusable observer class, your app could have a large number of observer instances all listening to the exact same notifications or events.

In rare performance sensitive environments, this could be an issue. To solve this issue, you can implement more sophisticated re-usable observers by implementing the multicast pattern.

Walking through an implementation of a multicast observer is out of scope for this book. However, you can easily find many examples of multicast objects online by searching for 'multicast delegate Swift.' The gist is that multicast observers are instantiated once. They subscribe once to notifications or events and allow for multiple event responder delegates. This is more efficient than the previous examples you've seen because all the notifications or events are only processed once by one observer as opposed to having several observer instances all subscribing and processing the same notifications or events. If you take this route, make sure to keep an eye out for memory management issues.

Composing multiple observers

Say you're working on a view controller and you've designed four different observers. You plan on calling `startObserving` and `stopObserving` on all four observers at the same time. Creating four observer properties in the view controller and calling these methods can be inconvenient.

There's got to be a better way. The good news is that the `Observer` protocol lends itself to composition nicely. Here's a sample implementation of an observer composition class:

```
class ObserverComposition: Observer {

  // MARK: - Properties
  let observers: [Observer]

  // MARK: - Methods
  init(observers: Observer...) {
    self.observers = observers
  }

  func startObserving() {
    observers.forEach {
      $0.startObserving()
    }
  }

  func stopObserving() {
    observers.forEach {
      $0.stopObserving()
    }
  }
}
```

Really simple, right? Notice how this implementation is itself an `Observer`. Also, notice how this observer does not manage any event responders. When using this pattern you need to wire the event responder to each individual observer, but not the composition. Shortly, you'll see an example of how to create a composition and how to wire the event responders.

You can use this implementation any time a view controller needs to manage a large number of observers. This pattern only works for observers that start and stop observing at the same time.

OK. What about instantiating a composition of observers? Here's an example:

```
class KooberOnboardingDependencyContainer {
  // ...

  func makeSignInViewController() -> SignInViewController {
    // User interface element
    let userInterface = SignInRootView()

    // Observer elements
    // 1
    let statePublisher =
      makeSignInViewControllerStatePublisher()
    let stateObserver =
      SignInViewControllerStateObserver(state: statePublisher)
    let keyboardObserver = KeyboardObserver()

    // 2
    let composedObservers =
      ObserverComposition(stateObserver, keyboardObserver)

    // 3
    let signInViewController =
      SignInViewController(
        userInterface: userInterface,
        observer: composedObservers
      )

    // Wire responders
    userInterface.ixResponder = signInViewController
    // 4
    stateObserver.eventResponder = signInViewController
    keyboardObserver.eventResponder = signInViewController

    return signInViewController
  }

  // ...
}
```

Walking through the code step by step:

1. The observers are created.

2. The observers are packaged into a composition.

3. The composition is injected into the view controller.

4. The individual observers are given the `signInViewController` as an event responder.

This really simplifies things for the view controller since there's now only one `Observer` to manage. The view controller has no idea the observer its given is a composition. All the view controller knows is that it, the view controller, needs to conform to multiple event responder protocols. So that's observer composition. Next is a slight twist on wiring event responders to observers.

Initializing observer with event responder

One thing you might have noticed is the event responder property on all of the observers is mutable and *not* private. If, in your code, you're following the dependency container factory method patterns shown in the examples, this isn't a huge problem because view controllers don't have access to observer's event responder properties. However, you don't have to use the dependency container pattern in order to use this `Observer` pattern.

So, if you find yourself in this situation and are worried about the event responder being changed unexpectedly, here's a different approach that you might like better:

```swift
class KeyboardObserver: Observer {

  // MARK: - Properties
  private weak var eventResponder:
    KeyboardObserverEventResponder?
  private var isObserving = false

  // MARK: - Methods
  init(eventResponder: KeyboardObserverEventResponder) {
    self.eventResponder = eventResponder
  }

  func startObserving() {
    if isObserving {
      return
    }
    // ...
    isObserving = true
  }

  func stopObserving() {
    // ...
    isObserving = false
  }

  // ...
}
```

Like all software engineering decisions, there's a tradeoff to this approach. This approach guarantees that the event responder cannot be changed by another object.

That's the benefit.

On the flip side, the view controller becomes a bit more complicated and messy. That's because you need to give the observer's initializer an event responder. The event responder, in most cases, is the view controller. It's a Catch-22 because the *view controller's* initializer wants the observer. You can't create the observer without the view controller. The only way around this is to remove the observer parameter from the view controller's initializer and to make the view controller's observer property mutable and optional:

```swift
class SignInViewController: NiblessViewController {

  // MARK: - Properties
  let userInterface: SignInUserInterfaceView
  var observer: Observer?   // < Look here.

  // MARK: - Methods
  init(userInterface: SignInUserInterfaceView) {
    self.userInterface = userInterface
    super.init()
  }

  override func loadView() {
    view = userInterface
  }

  override func viewWillAppear(_ animated: Bool) {
    super.viewWillAppear(animated)
    observer?.startObserving()
  }

  override func viewWillDisappear(_ animated: Bool) {
    super.viewWillDisappear(animated)
    observer?.stopObserving()
  }

  // ...
}
```

Because this adds a bit of complexity, I tend to prefer allowing the event responder to be mutable in observers while not allowing view controllers to know the concrete `Observer` type, so that the view controller can't change the observer's event responder. The best thing to do is to try out both variations and see which one works best for your codebase.

That wraps up all the `Observer` variations and advanced usages. You're now ready to go into your codebase and try some of these techniques out. Keep reading if you want to understand the benefits of this pattern and to learn how Josh and I ended up using this pattern.

When to use it

The `Observer` element is perfect for situations where view controllers need to update their view hierarchy in response to external events; i.e., events not emitted by the view controller's own view hierarchy. If you're taking a unidirectional approach, all of your view controllers probably need an observer to listen for view state changes.

This is true even if your view controllers are simply observing a Core Data query to update their user interfaces.

> **Note**: If you find yourself performing side effects, such as networking or persistence, in your event responder methods, consider moving the side effect triggering logic outside your content view controllers and into higher level objects such as a container view controllers or any application scoped object. Performing side effects in event responder methods is typically an indication that view controllers are performing work that they don't need to be responsible for.

Why use this element?

`Observers` help keep your view controllers small and light. They remove a lot of technology-specific boilerplate from your view controllers. This ends up making your view controllers much easier to read and reason about. Using observers, any developer can read a view controller without having to know specifics of `NotificationCenter`, `Combine`, `ReSwift` store subscriptions, etc. Anyone reading a view controller can clearly and obviously see what all external events come into the view controller by inspecting the event responder methods.

Additionally, the `Observer` element allows you to refactor where signals are coming from without having to change view controller code.

The `Observer` element helps teams parallelize work by allowing one person to work on the observation logic while the other person works on the view controller response to events.

Not only that, `Observers` make your view controllers easier to unit test. Your tests can simply make direct method calls to the event responder methods implemented by the view controller without having to go through `NotificationCenter`, `Combine`, `RxSwift`, etc.

Your tests can do this by either injecting a fake `Observer` implementation and passing calls to the view controller through the fake observer, or, by injecting a no-op `Observer` and calling view controller methods directly.

The `Observer` element is a nice and easy pattern to apply. It helps clean your code without needing to read another book or know any advanced techniques. Give it a try and let us know how it goes.

Origin

The observer element isn't a new idea. It's one of the patterns explained in the famous 1994 Gang of Four book, Design Patterns: Elements of Reusable Object-Oriented Software (https://www.oreilly.com/library/view/design-patterns-elements/0201633612/) by Erich Gamma, Richard Helm, Ralph Johnson and John Vlissides.

Josh and I started using this pattern back when Objective-C was the only iOS language and back when you had to make sure you unsubscribed your `NotificationCenter` notifications before view controllers were deallocated.

Every one of our teammates would be super nervous every time we added a new notification subscription into a view controller because we could easily crash the app if we forgot to unsubscribe.

So we thought, why not place all this logic in another class so that the view controller only needs to call unsubscribe once and so that we could easily unsubscribe all pertinent events? We also needed observers for listening to changes in our data model for rendering updates to our views. We were building a collection view for a chat app that was wired to a realtime network socket. We needed an object between the view controller and the network, to manage back pressure.

Before building an observer, we were overloading `UICollectionView` with too many animations. Building an observer helped us control when data changes were sent to the collection view.

After implementing a couple of view controller specific observers, we quickly realized all the other benefits associated with using observers. And so, it became a part of Elements early on.

So that's the `Observer` element. It can be used by itself or in conjunction with any other element. Next, you'll read all about the `UseCase` element and how use cases can also help keep view controllers stay nice and light.

Use case

Use cases are command pattern objects that know how to do a task needed by a user. Use cases know:

- What objects are needed to perform each step in a user task.
- What steps are needed to complete a user task.
- How to coordinate amongst object dependencies to complete a user task.
- How to manage asynchronous nature of I/O steps in a user task.

Use cases encapsulate all the object dependencies and all the orchestration amongst object dependencies. For example, a use case knows what objects are needed to perform networking and persistence tasks for a specific user task, such as liking a post, signing in, navigating to a screen, etc.

Mechanics

In this section you'll learn, at a high level, how to create, inject, use and de-allocate use case objects. This section is pure theory. If it's a bit fuzzy, don't worry, you'll walk through many different code examples further ahead. The theory will help you hit the ground running when reading through the code examples.

Instantiating

Use cases are created every time your app needs to perform a user task. For instance, a *Twitter* app would create a new `LikeTweetUseCase` instance every time a user taps on a tweet's Like button. Use cases are usually created and started by view controllers in response to a user's interaction with the UI. However, you can create and start a use cases in response to any system event as well; i.e., use cases aren't just for responding to UI events.

In the simplest usage, use cases can be created with four different kinds of objects:

- **Input data**: Input data is data needed to perform the user task implemented by a use case. For example, if a use case signs in users, the use case would be created with a username object and a password object. In the previous *Twitter* example, the `LikeTweetUseCase` would be created with the ID of the tweet liked by the user.

- **Side-effect subsystem objects**: These objects perform some sort of I/O such as networking or persistence. Side-effect objects allow use cases to change state in the outside world; i.e., outside the use case and outside of the object starting the use case.

- **Pure business logic objects**: Within a use case, you might need to do some pure business logic such as user input validation. These pure business logic objects perform deterministic tasks that do not change outside state.

- **Progress closures**: The pattern behind the simplest usage of use cases is an imperative, bi-directional, approach. In this usage, the object starting a use case, usually a view controller, might want to know when the use case starts, when progress is made, when the use case completes its task and/or whether the task was completed successfully. You can design use case initializers to take closures that can be called to signal use case start, progress and completion.

Providing

Because use cases are created on-demand, whenever you need to perform a user task, they cannot be injected into other objects. Say you're building a view controller for a settings screen. The view controller needs to be able to create a new use case every time a user toggles a setting. So the view controller can't be injected with a single use case instance, because the view controller might need to create more than one instance.

The solution could be as easy as letting view controllers call use case initializers to create new use case instances. There's a problem though. Use case initializers need side-effect subsystem objects that view controllers might not have.

One easy solution is to inject these side-effect subsystem objects into view controllers. That way, view controllers can pass those objects into use case initializers. This works, but in practice this solution bloats view controller initializers. If a view controller needs to be able to create upwards of three use cases, the view controller's initializer now needs to have parameters for all the different dependencies needed by all of the use cases.

In reality, the view controller doesn't depend on these objects. The **use cases** depend on these objects. Rather than inject the dependencies into a view controller you can inject view controllers with use case factories. That's next.

A **use case factory** knows how to create a type of use case. You inject a factory into any object that needs to instantiate a use case. You inject one factory for each type of use case needed to be created.

A factory can either be a closure or an object. To create a use case with a factory, you invoke the closure or a method with the input data and progress closures needed by the use case. Basically, you invoke the factory with everything except the use case's object dependencies, such as side-effect subsystem objects and pure business logic objects.

You can inject view controllers with use case factories. Then, view controllers can invoke the factory whenever they need to start a user task. This approach solves the problems with injecting view controllers with all the use cases' dependencies.

If you're using use cases and following the dependency injection pattern from Chapter 4, "Objects & Their Dependencies," you might already have all the use case factories you need. In the example section below, you'll see how to use dependency injection containers as use case factories.

Using

Use cases are super easy to use. Once you've created a use case, you just need to start it. It's similar to how you create and resume `URLSessionDataTasks`.

If you provide progress closures, use cases will call the progress closures during execution. So, if you need to for example start an activity indicator when a use case starts, you can place the activity indicator start logic inside an `onStart` closure that you provide to a use case factory.

Tearing down

This part is a bit more complicated. Ideally, use cases are created when needed and deallocated when completed. The easiest way to accomplish this is to have view controllers, or whatever objects are starting use cases, hold each use case instance in an optional stored property. When a use case finishes, the view controller can `nil` out the property.

In the code examples below, you'll notice that use cases are not held by a view controller. The use cases are created and then started. It looks like ARC should deallocate the use cases.

However, the use cases remain in memory until they finish running. The use cases remain allocated because the use case examples are held in memory by promises. The use cases are implemented using `PromiseKit` promises.

This is important because you can use whatever asynchrony technology you prefer, such as completion closures, `Combine Futures`, `RxSwift Singles`, etc., to coordinate work inside a use case. So, the technology you use might require a different approach to managing the object lifetimes of use cases.

Types

It's time to transition from theory to code. To get started, this section covers the main types you'll declare in order to build, create and use use case objects.

Use case protocol

Use cases are represented by a very simple protocol:

```
protocol UseCase {
  func start()
}
```

The protocol has a single `start` method. `start` starts all the work to be done by the use case.

You might be wondering why you would need a protocol for just a single method. The use case protocol comes in handy when writing unit tests. The protocol allows you to swap out a real use case implementation with a fake implementation while running unit tests. The protocol also allows you to hide concrete use case types from view controllers, or from any other objects needing to start use cases.

Swift Result enum

For the simplest usage, use cases report back their result. `Result` is a great way to report success or failure in a clean manner. `Result` is included starting with Swift 5:

```
// A value that represents either a success or a failure,
including an
// associated value in each case.
public enum Result<Success, Failure> where Failure : Error {

  // A success, storing a `Success` value.
  case success(Success)

  // A failure, storing a `Failure` value.
  case failure(Failure)

  // ...
}
```

Use case result type alias

Because `Result` is generic, specializing the enum in type annotations is inconvenient. Especially in closure types because the type signature becomes really long. `typealias`es, like the following one, help keep lines of code short:

```
typealias SignInUseCaseResult = Result<UserSession,
                                       ErrorMessage>
```

To follow this pattern, declare a `UseCaseResult` typealias for each use case class. The one above is used by `SignInUseCase` in the example you'll see next.

Use case classes

This is a skeleton of an example use case implementation used to sign users in to Kober:

```
// 1
class SignInUseCase: UseCase {

  // MARK: - Properties
  // 2
  // Input data
  let username: String
  let password: Secret

  // 3
  // Side-effect subsystems
  let remoteAPI: AuthRemoteAPI
```

```swift
    let dataStore: UserSessionDataStore

    // 4
    // Progress closures
    let onStart: () -> Void
    let onComplete: (SignInUseCaseResult) -> Void

    // MARK: - Methods
    // 5
    init(
      username: String,
      password: String,
      remoteAPI: AuthRemoteAPI,
      dataStore: UserSessionDataStore,
      onStart: (() -> Void)? = nil,
      onComplete: ((SignInUseCaseResult) -> Void)? = nil
    ) {
      // Input data
      self.username = username
      self.password = password

      // Side-effect subsystems
      self.remoteAPI = remoteAPI
      self.dataStore = dataStore

      // Progress closures
      self.onStart = onStart ?? {}
      self.onComplete = onComplete ?? { result in }
    }

    // 6
    func start() {
      assert(Thread.isMainThread)
      onStart()

      // Do some work and call onComplete when finished.
      // ...
    }
}
```

Here are the different parts to the implementation above:

1. Use cases are classes. They should use reference semantics because each instance represents a specific run of the use case. Also, use case classes should conform to the `UseCase` protocol.

2. These stored properties hold the input data provided in the use case's initializer.

3. These stored properties hold side-effect subsystem objects. It's a good practice to type annotate these kinds of objects using protocol types. You generally don't want to have to change a use case's implementation as a result of a side-effect object implementation change, such as a networking stack change.

4. Here are the progress closures the use case uses to report progress. In this example, the use case can run a closure when the use case starts and when the use case completes. If you have a long running use case, you can add another closure for reporting on-going progress. Notice how the `onComplete` closure uses the `SignInUseCaseResult` typealias from before.

5. The initializer has parameters for all the data and objects needed to run the use case. As described before, use case initializers are best called by use case factories. Also worth noting is the optional types on the progress closure parameters. These are optional as a convenience to the object starting the use case. Sometimes, these objects don't need to do any work in a progress closure. So it's nice not to require them.

6. This is an implementation of the `start` method from the `UseCase` protocol. You'll see the full implementation of this method soon. This code example is meant to illustrate the anatomy of a use case. Before `start` begins any work it performs a threading check and then calls the `onStart` closure. Use cases, like this one, can be required to be used from the main thread in order to simplify the threading model. Don't worry, all the work that the use case does is off the main thread. This example uses the main thread simply as a coordination queue for passing data into and out of side-effect subsystems. More on the threading model later.

Each use case should represent some piece of work that a user could explain. You should be able to design a use case for every user story in your product backlog. It's very tempting to create use cases for very small technical type of tasks.

In practice, those small technical tasks are best modeled through compose-able asynchronous methods. When you keep your use cases focused on user tasks, use cases become very easy to reason about and very easy to talk about with other people.

Use case factory type alias

In the sign-in example that you'll walk through in the next section, the `SignInViewController` needs to be able to create a use case when the user taps the **Sign in** button. `SignInViewController` creates a use case using a use case factory closure. The closure's type is too long to use inline. This use case factory `typealias` solves the closure type length problem:

```
typealias SignInUseCaseFactory =
  (
    String,
    Secret,
    @escaping () -> Void,
    @escaping (SignInUseCaseResult) -> Void
  ) -> UseCase
```

Notice how the factory closure has parameters for everything the use case needs except for side-effect subsystem object dependencies. This makes it much easier for `SignInViewController` to create a new use case because `SignInViewController` doesn't need to know how to get a reference to the side-effect subsystem object dependencies.

The only thing about this that isn't great is the fact that the closure parameters can't have labels. It's not obvious what object should go in which closure parameter. You'll see an alternative that solves this problem in the variations and advanced usage section.

> **Note:** The `UseCase` protocol is the return type in the factory signature as opposed to the concrete `SignInUseCase` class type. This is so the object that starts the `SignInUseCase` doesn't have access to anything other than the `start()` method. This lets you refactor use cases without needing to worry about breaking other code. Returning `UseCase` also lets you inject a fake implementation during unit testing, if necessary.

Example

This section uses Koober's sign-in functionality to demonstrate how use cases can be built and used. Koober's `SignInViewController` needs a use case that's capable of trying to sign a user into Koober with a username and password. In Koober, `SignInUseCase` implements the logic needed by `SignInViewController`. When a user taps the **Sign In** button on the sign-in screen, `SignInViewController` starts a `SignInUseCase`.

> **Note**: To ease readability, some of the example code in this section has been simplified from the code in the example Xcode project.

As you've seen before, to report use case completion using a `Result`, you can declare a use case result `typealias` for each use case. This helps shorten closure type signatures. Here's `SignInUseCase`'s `SignInUseCaseResult` typealias:

```
typealias SignInUseCaseResult = Result<UserSession,
                                       ErrorMessage>
```

This is the exact same `typealias` from before. And here's the complete implementation of `SignInUseCase`:

```
class SignInUseCase: UseCase {

  // MARK:    Properties
  // Input data
  let username: String
  let password: Secret

  // Side-effect subsystems
  let remoteAPI: AuthRemoteAPI
  let dataStore: UserSessionDataStore

  // Progress closures
  let onStart: () -> Void
  let onComplete: (SignInUseCaseResult) -> Void

  // MARK: - Methods
  init(
    username: String,
    password: String,
    remoteAPI: AuthRemoteAPI,
    dataStore: UserSessionDataStore,
    onStart: (() -> Void)? = nil,
    onComplete: ((SignInUseCaseResult) -> Void)? = nil
```

```swift
) {
    // Input data
    self.username = username
    self.password = password
    
    // Side-effect subsystems
    self.remoteAPI = remoteAPI
    self.dataStore = dataStore
    
    // Progress closures
    self.onStart = onStart ?? {}
    self.onComplete = onComplete ?? { result in }
}

public func start() {
    assert(Thread.isMainThread)
    onStart()
    
    // 1
    firstly {
        // 2
        self.remoteAPI.signIn(username: username,
                              password: password)
    }.then { userSession in
        // 3
        self.dataStore.save(userSession: userSession)
    }.done { userSession in
        // 4
        self.onComplete(.success(userSession))
    }.catch { error in
        // 5
        let errorMessage =
            ErrorMessage(title: "Sign In Failed",
                         message: """
                                  Could not sign in.
                                  Please try again.
                                  """)
        self.onComplete(.failure(errorMessage))
    }
  }
}
```

This implementation uses `PromiseKit` promises to coordinate asynchronous work. To coordinate work inside use cases, you can use whatever async technology you prefer. I like using promises inside use cases because promise chains are really easy to follow and because the default promise threading behavior works great for use cases.

Here's a step-by-step explanation of the promise chain above:

1. `firstly` marks the beginning of a promise chain. `firstly` is completely optional. It exists to line up the code nicely, so that the chain is easy to read. The `firstly` closure is expected to return a `Promise`.

2. Going to the cloud is the first async I/O task. In this step, Koober calls its remote API to check if the username and password provided by the user are valid credentials. If the credentials are good, the remote API responds with an auth token. The auth token gets bundled into a `UserSession` object. The `signIn` method returns a `Promise<UserSession>`. The `signIn` method is called from the main queue. The real implementation of `signIn` is expected to perform networking work asynchronously, off the main queue. If this operation fails, `signIn` returns a rejected promise and the promise chain short circuits to the `catch` closure.

3. If `signIn` completes successfully, execution returns to the main queue. The next `then` closure is run. In this step, the `UserSession` returned from the `remoteAPI` is persisted into the user session `dataStore`. Because this step also performs I/O work, the API to save the user session is asynchronous; i.e., the method returns a promise. Just like the `remoteAPI`, the `dataStore` is expected to do its work on another queue.

The promise returned by the `dataStore` carries over the `UserSession` from the `remoteAPI` so the promise chain can continue to thread the result all the way to the last promise chain step. If this step fails, the promise chain jumps to the `catch` closure.

4. If all goes well, the done closure is called. In this last step, the use case's `onComplete` closure is called with a successful `Result` carrying the `UserSession` object. This completes the promise chain execution, and therefore, completes the use case execution. At this point, the promise chain releases the reference to `self`; i.e., the use case. ARC then de-allocates this use case object.

5. If anything goes wrong, the `catch` closure is called. In this step, an error is created and the use case's `onComplete` closure is called with a failed `Result` carrying the error. This completes the promise chain execution. The use case will then be de-allocated by ARC.

> **Note**: The promise chain closures capture a strong reference to `self`; i.e., the use case object. You might be wondering if there's a retain cycle, here. The promise chain holds onto the use case. The use case is not held by any other object. The promise chain is also not held by any other object. So it's safe to capture a strong reference to `self`. This strong reference is what keeps the use case alive while the use case runs. If the reference was weak, the use case would have to be held by another object, like the view controller, in order to stay allocated.

Notice how this use case doesn't know how to do anything specific. It delegates all work to other objects. This is by design. To be effective, use cases should be lightweight objects that coordinate work amongst different abstractions. This allows you to re-use individual promise chain steps in other use cases.

Once you build several use cases in your own projects, you might be tempted to compose or chain use cases together. In theory this sounds great, but in practice it adds unnecessary complexity. Instead of trying to chain use cases together, identify the steps that need to be used in multiple use cases. Compose those steps into a single method call and then call this method from multiple use cases.

Regardless of the async technology you chose to use to coordinate work, you can follow the same threading pattern used inside `SignInUseCase`. The idea is to use a serial queue to coordinate async work. `start()` should begin by creating a serial queue. Then `start()` starts its first async task from the serial queue. The task *runs* on another queue. The result of the async task is returned back on the serial queue. Once back on the serial queue, the result from the async task is given to the next async task. So on and so forth, until all the work is finished.

`SignInUseCase` uses the main queue as its serial synchronization queue. This is OK because the coordination work is not CPU intensive. It's not likely to stall the main thread. However, you can use whatever serial queue to coordinate work inside a use case. Having a standard threading pattern, like the one used here, removes a lot of the complexity surrounding asynchrony. It also makes everyone's code much easier to reason about. This pattern might not work for every single-use case, however, it should work for the majority of use cases that are normally needed by cloud-connected mobile apps.

So that's the use case implementation. Now, it's time to walk through the code needed to create instances of this use case.

The use case factory `typealias` is the first place to look:

```
typealias SignInUseCaseFactory =
  (
    String, // username
    Secret, // password
    @escaping () -> Void, // onStart
    @escaping (SignInUseCaseResult) -> Void // onComplete
  ) -> UseCase
```

This is the exact same `typealias` you saw before. You'll need to define one of these for every use case you build. This `typealias` is completely optional. The `typealias` simply helps shorten type signatures.

Alright, it's time for the fun part. How do view controllers create instances of use cases without calling use case initializers?

Remember, the use case initializer has parameters for side-effect subsystem object dependencies that the view controller, or whatever object needs to start a use case, really shouldn't need to have. Because each instance of a use case represents one invocation of the user's task, you might need to instantiate multiple instances of the use case. For example, in the sign-in screen, say the user enters their username and password incorrectly.

When the user taps the **Sign in** button, a new `SignInUseCase` should be created. The use case fails and the error is reported to the user. The user corrects a typo and taps the **Sign in** button again. A new `SignInUseCase` should be created. For this reason, you can't simply inject a single use case object. So in order to create a use case, an object needs to be injected with a factory that the object can use to create new instances of use cases.

With that in mind, here are the relevant parts of `SignInViewController`:

```
class SignInViewController: NiblessViewController {

  // MARK: - Properties
  // 1
  let makeSignInUseCase: SignInUseCaseFactory

  let userInterface: SignInUserInterfaceView

  // MARK: - Methods
  // 2
  init(
    userInterface: SignInUserInterfaceView,
    signInUseCaseFactory: @escaping SignInUseCaseFactory
  ) {
```

```
      self.userInterface = userInterface
      self.makeSignInUseCase = signInUseCaseFactory
      super.init()
  }

  public override func loadView() {
    view = userInterface
  }

  // ...
}

extension SignInViewController: SignInIxResponder {

  // 3
  func signIn(email: String, password: Secret) {
    // 4
    let onStart = {
      // Update UI to indicate use case has started,
      // such as starting an activity indicator.
      // ...
    }
    let onComplete: (SignInUseCaseResult) -> Void = { result in
      // Process result from running use case by
      // for example, stopping activity indicator
      // and presenting error if necessary.
      // ...
    }

    // 5
    let useCase = makeSignInUseCase(email,
                                    password,
                                    onStart,
                                    onComplete)
    // 6
    useCase.start()
  }

  // ...
}
```

Here are the steps used by `SignInViewController` to create and use `SignInUseCases`:

1. This stored property holds onto the use case factory closure. This closure is injected into the view controller through the view controller's initializer. Here's where the use case factory `typealias` comes in handy. Without the `typealias` this declaration would look like: `let makeSignInUseCase: (String, Secret, @escaping () -> Void, @escaping (SignInUseCaseResult) -> Void) -> UseCase`.

2. Here's the view controller's initializer. The use case factory closure is provided to the view controller, here.

3. This is the method called by the UI when the user taps the **Sign in** button. This is where a new `SignInUseCase` needs to be created and started.

4. The first step inside `signIn` is to create the progress closures.

5. Then, the view controller uses the use case factory closure to create a new `SignInUseCase` using the username and password entered by the user along with the progress closures created in the last step.

6. Finally, the view controller starts the use case. When the use case finishes, the use case calls the `onComplete` closure created previously. The view controller can use the `onComplete` closure to know when the use case finishes and to know whether the use case run was successful or not.

This removes a ton of complexity from `SignInViewController`. If `SignInViewController` were to have more user interactions to process, the overall complexity of `SignInViewController` would be spread out to various use cases. In other words, all the complexity would be broken down into several use case objects as opposed to having moved all of the view controller's complexity into a single object, such as a view model. The great thing about use cases is that you can use them in practically any architecture pattern. For instance, you could create and start use cases inside MVVM view models.

The last thing to look at is how `KooberOnboardingDependencyContainer` injects the sign-in use case factory closure into a `SignInViewController`:

```
class KooberOnboardingDependencyContainer {
  // ...

  // 1
  func makeSignInUseCase(
    username: String,
    password: Secret,
```

```
    onStart: @escaping () -> Void,
    onComplete: @escaping (SignInUseCaseResult) -> Void
  ) -> UseCase {
    // 2
    let authRemoteAPI = self.makeAuthRemoteAPI()
    let userSessionDataStore =
      self.userSessionDataStore

    // 3
    let useCase = SignInUseCase(
      username: username,
      password: password,
      remoteAPI: authRemoteAPI,
      dataStore: userSessionDataStore,
      onStart: onStart,
      onComplete: onComplete)
    // 4
    return useCase
  }

  // 5
  func makeSignInViewController() -> SignInViewController {
    // User interface element
    let userInterface = SignInRootView()

    // Use case element
    // 6
    let signInUseCaseFactory = self.makeSignInUseCase

    // 7
    let signInViewController =
      SignInViewController(
        userInterface: userInterface,
        stateObserver: stateObserver,
        keyboardObserver: keyboardObserver,
        signInUseCaseFactory: signInUseCaseFactory)

    // Wire responders
    userInterface.ixResponder = signInViewController

    return signInViewController
  }

  // ...
}
```

There are two main pieces to this. One is the factory method that knows how to create a new `SignInUseCase` using the use case's initializer. The second piece is the `SignInViewController` factory that injects the first method as the sign-in use case factory into a new `SignInViewController`.

Here are the details, step by step:

1. This is the `SignInUseCase` factory method inside the dependency container. It accepts all the objects needed by the use case except for the side-effect subsystem objects. The side-effect subsystem objects are available inside the dependency container.

2. This is how the factory creates or gets a hold of the side-effect subsystem objects needed by the sign-in use case. The factory uses the dependency container to create a new `authRemoteAPI`. Then the factory grabs the shared `userSessionDataStore` held by the dependency container.

3. Then, the factory uses the arguments passed in alongside the side-effect subsystem objects from the dependency container in order to call the use case's initializer to instantiate a new use case.

4. Finally, the factory returns a new sign-in use case.

5. This is the `SignInViewController` factory used to create a new view controller when a user navigates to the sign-in screen.

6. This step gets a reference to the sign in use case factory method. Note that this is a reference to a method, not an object. Remember how the sign-in use case factory parameter type from `SignInViewController`'s initializer is a closure type? The closure type represented by the `SignInUseCaseFactory` typealias. Even though the parameter is a closure type, a method reference can be passed in as an argument as long as the method's signature matches the closure's signature.

7. In this step, the dependency container's sign-in use case factory method, `makeSignInUseCase`, is injected into a new `SignInViewController`. The use case factory method is injected so that the view controller can invoke this method whenever the view controller needs to create a new use case. With this approach, the view controller can create a sign-in use case *without needing to know* how to create an `authRemoteAPI` and how to get a hold of a shared `userSessionDataStore`. Cool!

OK, so that's how you design, build, create and use use cases. Now that you know the basics you can take a look at the next section to see if there's any variation of this pattern that you'd like to try.

Variations and advanced usage

You've read most of what you need to incorporate use cases into your own Xcode projects. However, there are some subtle variations that you might prefer to use. This section walks through using protocols instead of closure types for use case factories, designing unidirectional use cases and designing cancelable use cases.

Using use case factory protocols instead of closures

One of the big drawbacks with the use case factory closure type is that the parameters aren't labeled:

```
typealias SignInUseCaseFactory =
  (
    String, // username
    Secret, // password
    @escaping () -> Void, // onStart
    @escaping (SignInUseCaseResult) -> Void  // onComplete
  ) -> UseCase
```

Comments are needed to indicate what should go in each parameter. Instead of using a closure type, you can declare a use case factory protocol. This is a bit more work and adds more types to your codebase so you might not like this approach. It really comes down to preference. I like this approach because it makes it easier for someone else to create the use cases you've designed. At the factory call site, other developers may not know all the parameters needed by the closure type.

Here's what a use case factory protocol looks like:

```
protocol SignInUseCaseFactory {
  func makeSignInUseCase(
    username: String,
    password: Secret,
    onStart: @escaping () -> Void,
    onComplete: @escaping (SignInUseCaseResult) -> Void
  ) -> UseCase
}
```

The protocol is a simple single factory method protocol. The factory method signature is exactly the same as the closure's signature in the `typealias`. The only difference is that the parameters are labeled.

How does this change the view controller? Not much. Take a look:

```swift
class SignInViewController: NiblessViewController {

  // MARK: - Properties
  let signInUseCaseFactory: SignInUseCaseFactory
  let userInterface: SignInUserInterfaceView

  // MARK: - Methods
  init(
    userInterface: SignInUserInterfaceView,
    signInUseCaseFactory: SignInUseCaseFactory
  ) {
    self.userInterface = userInterface
    self.signInUseCaseFactory = signInUseCaseFactory
    super.init()
  }

  override func loadView() {
    view = userInterface
  }

  // ...
}

extension SignInViewController: SignInIxResponder {
  func signIn(email: String, password: Secret) {
    let onStart = {
      // Update UI to indicate use case has started,
      // such as starting an activity indicator.
    }
    let onComplete: (SignInUseCaseResult) -> Void = { result in
      // Process result from running use case by
      // for example, stopping activity indicator
      // and presenting error if necessary.
    }

    let useCase =
      signInUseCaseFactory.makeSignInUseCase(
        username: email,
        password: password,
        onStart: onStart,
        onComplete: onComplete
      )
    useCase.start()
  }
}

// ...
```

The only difference is that the view controller calls a method on the factory as opposed to just invoking the factory itself. Notice how in this version of the view controller, the arguments to the factory method are labeled. This is much easier to write. It's a bit more verbose to read though. That's one of the tradeoffs.

Instead of the factory closure `typealias`, this example uses a protocol. So, what object conforms to this factory protocol? Here's the dependency container:

```
class KooberOnboardingDependencyContainer {
  // ...

  func makeSignInUseCase(
    username: String,
    password: Secret,
    onStart: @escaping () -> Void,
    onComplete: @escaping (SignInUseCaseResult) -> Void
  ) -> UseCase {
    // Factory method implementation.
    // ...
  }

  // ...
}
```

If you cross reference the protocol with this code above, you'll notice that `makeSignInUseCase` matches the protocol method exactly. `KooberOnboardingDependencyContainer` already conforms to the factory protocol. Easy!

The only thing that is needed is a protocol conformance declaration:

```
extension KooberOnboardingDependencyContainer:
  SignInUseCaseFactory {}
```

With the conformance declared, the `makeSignInViewController` factory method can inject the `KooberOnboardingDependencyContainer` into a new `SignInViewController` as a `SignInUseCaseFactory`:

```
class KooberOnboardingDependencyContainer {
  // ...

  func makeSignInViewController() -> SignInViewController {
    // User interface element
    let userInterface = SignInRootView()

    let signInViewController =
      SignInViewController(
        userInterface: userInterface,
```

```
        signInUseCaseFactory: self  // < Look here.
    )
    
    // Wire responders
    userInterface.ixResponder = signInViewController
    
    return signInViewController
  }
  // ...
}
```

The main difference in this code, compared to the previous example, is that the dependency container itself is injected into the view controller as opposed to injecting the dependency container's `makeSignInUseCase` method.

Both the `typealias` and `protocol` approach do the exact same thing. Try both of them out and see what feels best.

Providing use case completion closure on start

In the main example, the sign-in use case's `onComplete` closure was provided to the use case during initialization of the use case. You might have thought that looked a bit strange.

Instead, why not provide the completion closure in the use case's `start` method?

This does look nicer:

```
class SignInViewController: NiblessViewController {
  // ...
}

extension SignInViewController: SignInIxResponder {
  func signIn(email: String, password: Secret) {
    let useCase = makeSignInUseCase(email,
                                    password,
                                    onStart,
                                    onComplete)
    useCase.start() { result in
      // Process result from running use case by
      // for example, stopping activity indicator
      // and presenting error if necessary.
      // ...
    }
  }
  
  // ...
}
```

In order to take this approach, you'll need a different `UseCase` protocol:

```
protocol UseCase {
  associatedtype Success
  associatedtype Failure: Error

  func start(
    onComplete: (Result<Success, Failure>) -> Void)
}
```

Yikes! Now, you have to deal with the infamous `associatedtype`. The associated types are needed because the `Result` type is generic. Each use case implementation can have different `Success` and `Failure` types. Because this version of the `UseCase` protocol has associated type requirements, the code below does not compile:

```
class KooberOnboardingDependencyContainer {
  // ...

  // ! Does not compile. Compiler error:
  // Protocol 'UseCase' can only be used as a generic constraint
  // because it has Self or associated type requirements
  func makeSignInUseCase(
    username: String,
    password: Secret,
    onStart: @escaping () -> Void,
    onComplete: @escaping (SignInUseCaseResult) -> Void
  ) -> UseCase { // < The problem is here, with the return type.
    // ...
  }

  // ...
}
```

It's not impossible to take this approach. You'll need to implement a type erased `AnyUseCase` to be able to type things as any kind of use case. This adds a whole lot of complexity with not a lot in return. Walking through a type erased `AnyUseCase` type is beyond the scope of this book. If you'd like to learn more, search for 'Swift associatedtype type erasure.'

Designing hybrid unidirectional-bidirectional use cases

In the main example, the `SignInUseCase` gives the `SignInViewController` the use case result via the `onComplete` closure. What if another object also needs to know the result? The `SignInViewController` could start communicating with other objects by passing the result around. However, this isn't great because object data flow becomes very hard to follow.

This approach of passing objects around can also result in inconsistent state. Because of this, it's common for iOS view controllers to listen for data changes in database(s).

If your view controllers are listening to database changes you might prefer to design your use cases like this:

```swift
typealias SignInUseCaseResult = Result<Void,
                                       ErrorMessage>
```

```swift
class SignInUseCase: UseCase {
  // MARK: - Properties
  // Input data
  let username: String
  let password: Secret

  // Side-effect subsystems
  let remoteAPI: AuthRemoteAPI
  let dataStore: UserSessionDataStore

  // Progress closures
  let onStart: () -> Void
  let onComplete: (SignInUseCaseResult) -> Void

  // MARK: - Methods
  init(
    username: String,
    password: String,
    remoteAPI: AuthRemoteAPI,
    dataStore: UserSessionDataStore,
    onStart: (() -> Void)? = nil,
    onComplete: ((SignInUseCaseResult) -> Void)? = nil
  ) {
    // Input data
    self.username = username
    self.password = password

    // Side-effect subsystems
    self.remoteAPI = remoteAPI
    self.dataStore = dataStore

    // Progress closures
    self.onStart = onStart ?? {}
    self.onComplete = onComplete ?? { result in }
  }

  func start() {
    assert(Thread.isMainThread)
    onStart()
```

```
    firstly {
      self.remoteAPI.signIn(username: username,
                            password: password)
    }.then { userSession in
      self.dataStore.save(userSession: userSession)
    }.done { userSession in
      self.onComplete(.success(())) // < Look here.
    }.catch { error in
      let errorMessage =
        ErrorMessage(title: "Sign In Failed",
                     message: """
                              Could not sign in.
                              Please try again.
                              """)
      self.onComplete(.failure(errorMessage))
    }
  }
}
```

The difference here is that the `Result` type no longer carries a value on success. The `UserSession` is saved in the `dataStore`. This implementation assumes that objects are listening to the `dataStore` to know when a user has signed in and to get access to the user's `UserSession`. This isn't purely unidirectional because the use case still returns a result to the view controller, or whatever object is starting this use case.

There's still some form of bidirectional communication. Typically, the state representing the progress of a use case is only needed by a single view controller. In most instances, having a private back and forth between a view controller and a use case works well. Or you might be going all-in on unidirectional data flow. The next two sections demonstrate unidirectional use case examples.

Designing database backed unidirectional use cases

When building apps following unidirectional data-flow patterns, you can either store your app's state in a database or in a Redux-like in-memory state store. This section demonstrates what use cases look like if you're using a database to store your app state.

Here's a unidirectional version of `SignInUseCase`:

```
class SignInUseCase: UseCase {

  // MARK: - Properties
  // Input data
  let username: String
  let password: Secret

  // Side-effect subsystems
```

```swift
  let remoteAPI: AuthRemoteAPI
  let dataStore: UserSessionDataStore
  
  // MARK: - Methods
  init(
    username: String,
    password: String,
    remoteAPI: AuthRemoteAPI,
    dataStore: UserSessionDataStore
  ) {
    // Input data
    self.username = username
    self.password = password
    
    // Side-effect subsystems
    self.remoteAPI = remoteAPI
    self.dataStore = dataStore
  }
  
  func start() {
    assert(Thread.isMainThread)
    
    firstly {
      // 1
      self.dataStore.save(signingIn: true)
    }.then { _ in
      self.remoteAPI.signIn(username: username,
                            password: password)
    }.done { userSession in
      // 2
      self.dataStore.save(userSession: userSession,
                          signingIn: false)
    }.catch { error in
      let errorMessage =
        ErrorMessage(title: "Sign In Failed",
                     message: """
                              Could not sign in.
                              Please try again.
                              """)
      // 3
      firstly {
        self.dataStore.save(signInError: errorMessage,
                            signingIn: false)
      }.catch { error in
        assertionFailure("\(error)")
      }
    }
  }
}
```

The first thing to note is that all the progress closures are gone. The use case result `typealias` is no longer needed. Unidirectional use cases are much simpler.

The other thing to note is how there's more database tasks in this use case:

1. This first step updates the state in the database to signal that the user is signing in. A view controller might be listening to the database and using the observation in order to control an activity indicator.

2. If all goes well, the user's `UserSession` is stored in the database and the signing in state is set to `false` in the database. A navigation controller could be listening for user session changes in the database and automatically take the user out of the sign-in screen and into the app when a new user session is saved.

3. If something goes wrong, the error and signing in state are saved in the database. This part is a bit odd because you have to do I/O when an error occurs and because this requires a new promise chain. If there's something wrong with the database, there's not much you can do other than crash debug builds with an `assertionFailure`. If you can recover from database errors you would place that logic in the second `catch` closure.

The drawback here is having to deal with more asynchrony than before. Another option is to use a Redux-like state store. That example is next.

Designing Redux unidirectional use cases

Use cases also work really well in apps built using the Redux architecture pattern. Here's another version of `SignInUseCase` that could be used inside Chapter 6's example project:

> **Note**: Check out Chapter 6, "Architecture: Redux," if you want to follow this example and you're not familiar with Redux.

```
class SignInUseCase: UseCase {

    // MARK: - Properties
    // Input data
    let username: String
    let password: Secret

    // Side-effect subsystems
    let remoteAPI: AuthRemoteAPI

    // Redux action dispatcher
    let actionDispatcher: ActionDispatcher

    // MARK: - Methods
```

```swift
init(
  username: String,
  password: String,
  remoteAPI: AuthRemoteAPI,
  actionDispatcher: ActionDispatcher
) {
  // Input data
  self.username = username
  self.password = password

  // Side-effect subsystems
  self.remoteAPI = remoteAPI
  self.actionDispatcher = actionDispatcher
}

func start() {
  assert(Thread.isMainThread)

  // 1
  let action = SignInActions.SigningIn()
  actionDispatcher.dispatch(action)

  firstly {
    self.remoteAPI.signIn(username: username,
                          password: password)
  }.done { userSession in
    // 2
    let action =
      SignInActions.SignedIn(userSession: userSession)
    self.actionDispatcher.dispatch(action)
  }.catch { error in
    let errorMessage =
      ErrorMessage(title: "Sign In Failed",
                   message: """
                            Could not sign in.
                            Please try again.
                            """)
    // 3
    let action =
      SignInActions.SignInFailed(errorMessage: errorMessage)
    self.actionDispatcher.dispatch(action)
  }
}
```

As in the previous unidirectional database use case example, all the progress closures are gone. The `dataStore` is also gone. In Chapter 6, "Architecture: Redux," the `dataStore` listens to the Redux store to persist the user's `UserSession`. Therefore, the `dataStore` isn't needed by the use case. And finally, there's a new dependency, the `actionDispatcher`. The `actionDispatcher` is used to dispatch Redux actions to the Redux store.

One thing you'll notice when building use cases alongside Redux is that use cases tend to dispatch several actions. For example, in the example code above:

1. An action is dispatched to signal that the app is attempting to sign in a user. The progress closures are replaced with actions that represent the progress through the use case.

2. Once the user's credentials successfully authenticate with the `remoteAPI`, an action is dispatched carrying the new `UserSession`.

3. If something goes wrong, an error action is dispatched carrying the error message.

When first applying use cases to a Redux codebase, it's tempting to design a use case for every Redux action. However, use cases are much less granular than Redux actions. Design your use cases based on the work a view controller needs to do as opposed to the state events Redux needs to update the app's state.

This use case pattern solves one of the more difficult challenges with Redux, mixing async side-effect I/O with actions. You don't have to deal with middleware. And even better, with this pattern, view controllers don't even know the app is built using Redux. All the view controller knows is what kind of use case to create and run in response to what user interaction.

That wraps up all the unidirectional variations. You might have noticed that so far, none of the use cases can be cancelled. The next section demonstrates how to build cancelable use cases you can build when you'd like your users to be able to cancel an ongoing use case.

> **Note**: The Elements version of the Koober Xcode project example that comes with this chapter uses the Redux unidirectional version of use cases. Use cases replace the `UserInteractions` objects from the Redux version of Koober.

Designing cancelable use cases

By adding some additional types, you can take what you've learn so far and add cancelation to any use case. The first type to look at is the `Cancelable` protocol:

```
protocol Cancelable {
  func cancel()
}
```

You'll need to declare this protocol yourself since it's not part of Swift. Just like the `UseCase` protocol, this protocol is very simple. It's just a single method that can be called by, for example, a view controller to cancel on-going work. The `cancel` method could have just been added to `UseCase`, but then every single use case has to be cancelable. Many use cases shouldn't cancelable. So instead of adding `cancel` to `UseCase`, you can declare the `Cancelable` protocol from above.

Next is the `CancelableUseCase` typealias:

```
typealias CancelableUseCase = Cancelable & UseCase
```

This `typealias` is a convenience for type annotating constants and variables that conform to `Cancelable` and that conform to `UseCase`. This allows a view controller to declare a use case factory, such as the one below, that returns a cancelable use case:

```
typealias SearchDropoffLocationsUseCaseFactory =
  (
    String, // query
    Location // pickupLocation
  ) -> CancelableUseCase
```

Any view controller that's injected with this factory can create, start and cancel a `SearchDropoffLocationsUseCase`.

Here's `SearchDropoffLocationsUseCase`'s implementation:

```
class SearchDropoffLocationsUseCase: CancelableUseCase {

  // MARK: - Properties
  let query: String
  let pickupLocation: Location
  let actionDispatcher: ActionDispatcher
  let remoteAPI: NewRideRemoteAPI

  // 1
  var cancelled = false
```

```swift
// MARK: - Methods
init(query: String,
     pickupLocation: Location,
     actionDispatcher: ActionDispatcher,
     remoteAPI: NewRideRemoteAPI) {
  self.query = query
  self.pickupLocation = pickupLocation
  self.actionDispatcher = actionDispatcher
  self.remoteAPI = remoteAPI
}

// 2
func cancel() {
  assert(Thread.isMainThread)
  cancelled = true
}

func start() {
  assert(Thread.isMainThread)
  // 3
  guard !cancelled else {
    return
  }

  firstly {
    remoteAPI.getLocationSearchResults(
      query: query,
      pickupLocation: pickupLocation
    )
  }.done { results in
    // 4
    guard self.cancelled == false else {
      return
    }

    let action = ReceivedSearchResultsAction(results: results)
    self.actionDispatcher.dispatch(action: action)
  }.catch { error in
    let errorMessage =
      ErrorMessage(title: "Error Searching",
                   message: """
                            Could not run location search.
                            Please try again.
                            """)
    let action =
      SignedInErrorOccuredAction(errorMessage: errorMessage)
    self.actionDispatcher.dispatch(action: action)
  }
}
}
```

Here's a walkthrough of all the additional logic added above to implement a cancelable use case:

1. The use case needs this boolean stored property to hold the cancelation state. The use case is created in the not-canceled state.

2. This implements the `cancel` method from the `Cancelable` protocol. To avoid any issues with mutating state with concurrency, this method first checks that it's running on the main thread. It then changes the state of the use case to canceled. This allows the rest of the use case to inspect and check whether the use case has been canceled.

3. One of the first things that `start` does is abort if the use case has been canceled. This would be very rare. It could happen if the use case was created but not started right after.

4. Once the networking completes, the done closure first checks to see if the use case has been canceled. If so, it exits early without dispatching any actions. This form of cancellation doesn't stop any work in progress. It abandons the processing of the result. If a use case is performing a long-lived networking task, you might want to stop the networking as soon as the use case's `cancel` method is called. You can do this by storing the promise in a property and canceling the promise chain. To learn more about canceling promises, visit `PromiseKit`'s GitHub repo.

And that's how you can incorporate cancelation into use cases. That takes care of demonstrating all the variations and advanced usages of use cases.

When to use

Most of the time, use cases are used within view controllers or view models. Use cases typically run as a response to a user's interaction with your app's UI. However, sometimes you need to do some work in response to some system event, such as a location notification. You can use use cases for these situations as well.

Why use this element?

The use case pattern is one of the most versatile patterns I've used in iOS app development. Use cases fit into nearly all architecture patterns. And, they come with a lot of benefits.

Breaking up your app's main chunks of work into use cases allows you to re-use logic in any view controller. For example, say you're building a social networking app and you're building a `LikePostUseCase` for responding to a user liking a post. If you need to add the like-post button into multiple view controllers, you can easily re-use the `LikePostUseCase` to run the logic behind the button.

In most architecture patterns, work is organized by screen rather than by use case. The logic behind any one button then gets tied to the logic for the screen that the button is in. It's much harder to re-use the button's logic when, all of the sudden, you need to add the button to another screen. This situation is very common in MVC and MVVM architecture patterns. The good news is you can incorporate use cases to both patterns. If you've ever gone through a massive app re-design you know how valuable this flexibility can be. In addition, with use cases, you can solve the massive view controller problem without moving the problem somewhere else like a massive view model.

Breaking up your app's main chunks of work into use cases also allows you to build some pretty cool functional tests. If you need to test a particular sequence of user actions, you can write an entire test suite without needing any UI objects. In the test suite you can instantiate and run a sequence of use cases. And because use cases are named after user tasks, these tests are super easy to read.

Use cases also come in handy when writing unit tests. Say you need to ensure that a piece of work is started in response to a specific notification. You can harness a unit test with a fake `UseCase` implementation that exposes a property that allows you to assert whether the `start` method was called. Then to test the behavior you can emit the notification and assert that the use case was started by whatever object is under test.

Also, the use case pattern is relatively simple. It's easy to teach and it's easy to put into practice. Incorporating use cases doesn't require you to re-architect an entire app. You end up with a simple and effective threading strategy for most common mobile app I/O tasks. Use cases also help make dependency management easier. View controllers don't need to get references to things like databases and networking objects.

When using use cases, you'll find that you won't need to change view controller code that often anymore. Usually when we are changing code, we are changing how some feature works as opposed to changing what features are in an app. For instance, if you're changing your app to use a new cloud API or a new database, you'll end up working mostly in use cases and side-effect subsystems.

Just like other elements, use cases allow you to parallelize development work amongst team members. If a view controller needs three use cases, a different developer can build each use case.

Last but not least, use cases help you communicate your work with all your team members across all disciplines. For example, you can create tasks, that everyone understands, in a backlog for each use case. I've seen this communication benefit pop up several times. Just recently, I was in a project retrospective where our product manager referenced use cases. He suggested that we could have built a first version, of whatever library we were building, by focusing on shipping one use case first. Teamwork becomes way more productive and enjoyable when everyone understands the work that's happening.

Origin

I first came across code that looked like use cases when reading Agile Principles, Patterns, and Practices in C# (https://learning.oreilly.com/library/view/agile-principles-patterns/0131857258/) by Robert C. Martin and Micah Martin. The use case pattern in Elements was inspired by the transaction pattern presented in the book's Payroll case study.

Josh and I have evolved the pattern quite a bit since we started using it five years ago as of this writing. We first used `NSOperations` to run what we called `Actions`. While this pattern worked, it was very cumbersome. For every use case you had to implement an `Action` class and a `NSOperation` subclass. We then simplified the pattern by placing all the use case logic inside each `NSOperation`.

If you'd like to see this pattern, you can watch the App Architecture (https://www.raywenderlich.com/3639-305-app-architecture) tutorial I gave at RWDevCon 2016. At the time, we were using `NSOperation` because we could chain operations together and we thought it would be handy to chain use cases together. The more we used the pattern though, the more we realized we never needed to chain use cases. `NSOperation` was just more complexity that we didn't need. So in 2017, we decided to drop `NSOperation` and model use cases using the simple `UseCase` protocol you saw here.

If you'd like to see this version of the pattern, you can watch the Advanced App Architecture (https://www.raywenderlich.com/4166-advanced-app-architecture) workshop Josh and I gave at RWDevCon 2017. In 2017 and 2018, we were learning how to build iOS apps using the Redux unidirectional pattern. We ended up evolving the pattern to its current form for use in unidirectional architectures. If you'd like to learn more about advanced unidirectional techniques using use cases you can watch my RWDevCon 2018 tutorial, Advanced Unidirectional Architecture (https://www.raywenderlich.com/5173-advanced-unidirectional-architecture).

The idea behind object-oriented use cases has been around for a while. To get a glimpse of the early thoughts, you can read Ivar Jacobson's book, Object Oriented Software Engineering: A Use Case Driven Approach (https://www.amazon.com/Object-Oriented-Software-Engineering-Approach/dp/0201544350), published in 1992.

Pros and cons of Elements

Pros of Elements

1. You can incorporate any one of the elements without needing to refactor an entire app.

2. The individual elements are simple and intuitive. They are easy to learn, teach and practice.

3. Elements are only needed to be built if needed. You won't have a bunch of boilerplate code. You won't have any empty proxy classes either. For example, if a view controller doesn't need to do any user initiated work, you don't have to build any use cases. If a view controller doesn't need to observe anything, you don't need to implement an `Observer` class.

4. You can easily distribute the development workload across your team. Different team members can build different elements in parallel.

5. Elements can be used alongside many other architecture patterns.

6. Elements helps you unit test a large portion of your codebase including view controllers, views, observers, etc. This is because every element is represented by a protocol. This allows you to use fake implementations of different Elements at runtime during unit tests.

Cons of Elements

1. Elements makes use of many different protocols. You might feel like you're working with too many protocols. This is especially true in the dependency container code. If this is the case, the protocols are all optional. Feel free to exclusively use concrete versions. Just know that you might lose some unit testing benefits.

2. Elements breaks logic down into fairly small pieces. You can end up with lots of classes. It can be difficult to navigate an Xcode project if the files aren't organized well.

3. While most of the Elements evolved from existing ideas and techniques, Elements as a whole is new and other developers might not be familiar with the patterns. As of this writing, this book is the only source of information about Elements.

Key points

- **Observers** are objects that view controllers use to receive external events. You can think of these events as input signals to view controllers.

- The Observer element is perfect for situations where view controllers need to update their view hierarchy in response to external events; i.e., events not emitted by the view controller's own view hierarchy.

- Observers help keep your view controllers small and light. They remove a lot of technology specific boilerplate from your view controllers.

- **Use cases** are command pattern objects that know how to do a task needed by a user.

- UseCases fit into nearly all architecture patterns — and they come with a lot of benefits.

- Most of the time, use cases are used within view controllers or view models. Use cases typically run as a response to a user's interaction with your app's UI.

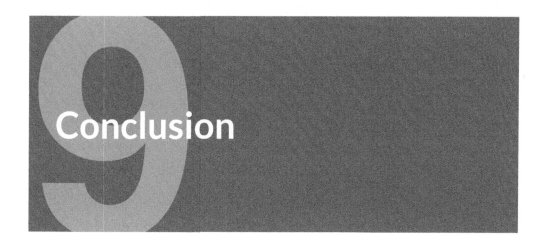

Conclusion

What a journey it's been! From exploring why architecture matters to diving deep into dependency injection, to comparing different architecture patterns, you've gotten a taste of architecting iOS apps using advanced techniques and patterns.

By putting the book concepts to practice, your codebase will become easier to work in and you'll have more fun writing code. Not only that, you'll be able to respond quickly to changing requirements.

We hope the ideas you saw in this book inspire you to explore and try out different architecture practices and maybe even inspire you to come up with some of your own!

If you're hungry for more architecture related books we recommend reading *Design Patterns by Tutorials*. Also, if you found some of the **Combine** code hard to follow, we recommend checking out *Combine Asynchronous Programming with Swift*.

If you have any questions or comments as you work through this book, please stop by our forums at https://forums.raywenderlich.com and look for the particular forum category for this book.

Thank you again for purchasing this book. Your continued support is what makes the books, tutorials, videos and other things we do at raywenderlich.com possible. We truly appreciate it!

Happy architecting!

– The *Advanced iOS App Architecture* team

Made in the USA
Las Vegas, NV
13 December 2023

82708904R00188